PAMPHILIA TO AMPHILANTHUS
IN MANUSCRIPT AND PRINT

The Other Voice in Early Modern Europe:
The Toronto Series, 59

MEDIEVAL AND RENAISSANCE
TEXTS AND STUDIES

VOLUME 523

The Other Voice in
Early Modern Europe:
The Toronto Series

SERIES EDITORS Margaret L. King *and* Albert Rabil, Jr.
SERIES EDITOR, ENGLISH TEXTS Elizabeth H. Hageman

Previous Publications in the Series

MADRE MARÍA ROSA
Journey of Five Capuchin Nuns
Edited and translated by Sarah E. Owens
Volume 1, 2009

GIOVAN BATTISTA ANDREINI
Love in the Mirror: A Bilingual Edition
Edited and translated by Jon R. Snyder
Volume 2, 2009

RAYMOND DE SABANAC AND SIMONE ZANACCHI
Two Women of the Great Schism: The Revelations of Constance de Rabastens *by Raymond de Sabanac and* Life of the Blessed Ursulina of Parma *by Simone Zanacchi*
Edited and translated by Renate Blumenfeld-Kosinski and Bruce L. Venarde
Volume 3, 2010

OLIVA SABUCO DE NANTES BARRERA
The True Medicine
Edited and translated by Gianna Pomata
Volume 4, 2010

LOUISE-GENEVIÈVE GILLOT DE SAINCTONGE
Dramatizing Dido, Circe, and Griselda
Edited and translated by Janet Levarie Smarr
Volume 5, 2010

PERNETTE DU GUILLET
Complete Poems: A Bilingual Edition
Edited by Karen Simroth James
Translated by Marta Rijn Finch
Volume 6, 2010

ANTONIA PULCI
Saints' Lives and Bible Stories for the Stage: A Bilingual Edition
Edited by Elissa B. Weaver
Translated by James Wyatt Cook
Volume 7, 2010

VALERIA MIANI
Celinda, A Tragedy: A Bilingual Edition
Edited by Valeria Finucci
Translated by Julia Kisacky
Annotated by Valeria Finucci and Julia Kisacky
Volume 8, 2010

Enchanted Eloquence: Fairy Tales by Seventeenth-Century French Women Writers
Edited and translated by Lewis C. Seifert and Domna C. Stanton
Volume 9, 2010

GOTTFRIED WILHELM LEIBNIZ, SOPHIE, ELECTRESS OF HANOVER AND QUEEN SOPHIE CHARLOTTE OF PRUSSIA
Leibniz and the Two Sophies: The Philosophical Correspondence
Edited and translated by Lloyd Strickland
Volume 10, 2011

The Other Voice in
Early Modern Europe:
The Toronto Series

SERIES EDITORS Margaret L. King *and* Albert Rabil, Jr.
SERIES EDITOR, ENGLISH TEXTS Elizabeth H. Hageman

Previous Publications in the Series

In Dialogue with the Other Voice in Sixteenth-Century Italy: Literary and Social Contexts for Women's Writing
Edited by Julie D. Campbell and Maria Galli Stampino
Volume 11, 2011

SISTER GIUSTINA NICCOLINI
The Chronicle of Le Murate
Edited and translated by Saundra Weddle
Volume 12, 2011

LIUBOV KRICHEVSKAYA
No Good without Reward: Selected Writings: A Bilingual Edition
Edited and translated by Brian James Baer
Volume 13, 2011

ELIZABETH COOKE HOBY RUSSELL
The Writings of an English Sappho
Edited by Patricia Phillippy
With translations by Jaime Goodrich
Volume 14, 2011

LUCREZIA MARINELLA
Exhortations to Women and to Others If They Please
Edited and translated by Laura Benedetti
Volume 15, 2012

MARGHERITA DATINI
Letters to Francesco Datini
Translated by Carolyn James and Antonio Pagliaro
Volume 16, 2012

DELARIVIER MANLEY AND MARY PIX
English Women Staging Islam, 1696–1707
Edited and introduced by Bernadette Andrea
Volume 17, 2012

CECILIA DEL NACIMIENTO
Journeys of a Mystic Soul in Poetry and Prose
Introduction and prose translations by Kevin Donnelly
Poetry translations by Sandra Sider
Volume 18, 2012

LADY MARGARET DOUGLAS AND OTHERS
The Devonshire Manuscript: A Women's Book of Courtly Poetry
Edited and introduced by Elizabeth Heale
Volume 19, 2012

ARCANGELA TARABOTTI
Letters Familiar and Formal
Edited and translated by Meredith K. Ray and Lynn Lara Westwater
Volume 20, 2012

PERE TORRELLAS AND JUAN DE FLORES
Three Spanish Querelle *Texts: Grisel and Mirabella, The Slander against Women, and The Defense of Ladies against Slanderers: A Bilingual Edition and Study*
Edited and translated by Emily C. Francomano
Volume 21, 2013

The Other Voice in
Early Modern Europe:
The Toronto Series

SERIES EDITORS Margaret L. King *and* Albert Rabil, Jr.
SERIES EDITOR, ENGLISH TEXTS Elizabeth H. Hageman

Previous Publications in the Series

BARBARA TORELLI BENEDETTI
Partenia, a Pastoral Play: A Bilingual Edition
Edited and translated by Lisa Sampson and Barbara Burgess-Van Aken
Volume 22, 2013

FRANÇOIS ROUSSET, JEAN LIEBAULT, JACQUES GUILLEMEAU, JACQUES DUVAL AND LOUIS DE SERRES
Pregnancy and Birth in Early Modern France: Treatises by Caring Physicians and Surgeons (1581–1625)
Edited and translated by Valerie Worth-Stylianou
Volume 23, 2013

MARY ASTELL
The Christian Religion, as Professed by a Daughter of the Church of England
Edited by Jacqueline Broad
Volume 24, 2013

SOPHIA OF HANOVER
Memoirs (1630–1680)
Edited and translated by Sean Ward
Volume 25, 2013

KATHERINE AUSTEN
Book M: A London Widow's Life Writings
Edited by Pamela S. Hammons
Volume 26, 2013

ANNE KILLIGREW
"My Rare Wit Killing Sin": Poems of a Restoration Courtier
Edited by Margaret J. M. Ezell
Volume 27, 2013

TULLIA D'ARAGONA AND OTHERS
The Poems and Letters of Tullia d'Aragona and Others: A Bilingual Edition
Edited and translated by Julia L. Hairston
Volume 28, 2014

LUISA DE CARVAJAL Y MENDOZA
The Life and Writings of Luisa de Carvajal y Mendoza
Edited and translated by Anne J. Cruz
Volume 29, 2014

Russian Women Poets of the Eighteenth and Early Nineteenth Centuries: A Bilingual Edition
Edited and translated by Amanda Ewington
Volume 30, 2014

JACQUES DU BOSC
L'Honnête Femme: The Respectable Woman in Society and the New Collection of Letters and Responses by Contemporary Women
Edited and translated by Sharon Diane Nell and Aurora Wolfgang
Volume 31, 2014

LADY HESTER PULTER
Poems, Emblems, and *The Unfortunate Florinda*
Edited by Alice Eardley
Volume 32, 2014

The Other Voice in
Early Modern Europe:
The Toronto Series

SERIES EDITORS Margaret L. King *and* Albert Rabil, Jr.
SERIES EDITOR, ENGLISH TEXTS Elizabeth H. Hageman

Previous Publications in the Series

JEANNE FLORE
Tales and Trials of Love, Concerning Venus's Punishment of Those Who Scorn True Love and Denounce Cupid's Sovereignity: A Bilingual Edition and Study
Edited and translated by Kelly Digby Peebles
Poems translated by Marta Rijn Finch
Volume 33, 2014

VERONICA GAMBARA
Complete Poems: A Bilingual Edition
Critical introduction by Molly M. Martin
Edited and translated by Molly M. Martin and Paola Ugolini
Volume 34, 2014

CATHERINE DE MÉDICIS AND OTHERS
Portraits of the Queen Mother: Polemics, Panegyrics, Letters
Translation and study by Leah L. Chang and Katherine Kong
Volume 35, 2014

FRANÇOISE PASCAL, MARIE-CATHERINE DESJARDINS, ANTOINETTE DESHOULIÈRES, AND CATHERINE DURAND
Challenges to Traditional Authority: Plays by French Women Authors, 1650–1700
Edited and translated by Perry Gethner
Volume 36, 2015

FRANCISZKA URSZULA RADZIWIŁŁOWA
Selected Drama and Verse
Edited by Patrick John Corness and Barbara Judkowiak
Translated by Patrick John Corness
Translation Editor Aldona Zwierzyńska-Coldicott
Introduction by Barbara Judkowiak
Volume 37, 2015

DIODATA MALVASIA
Writings on the Sisters of San Luca and Their Miraculous Madonna
Edited and translated by Danielle Callegari and Shannon McHugh
Volume 38, 2015

MARGARET VAN NOORT
Spiritual Writings of Sister Margaret of the Mother of God (1635–1643)
Edited by Cordula van Wyhe
Translated by Susan M. Smith
Volume 39, 2015

GIOVAN FRANCESCO STRAPAROLA
The Pleasant Nights
Edited and translated by Suzanne Magnanini
Volume 40, 2015

The Other Voice in
Early Modern Europe:
The Toronto Series

SERIES EDITORS Margaret L. King *and* Albert Rabil, Jr.
SERIES EDITOR, ENGLISH TEXTS Elizabeth H. Hageman

Previous Publications in the Series

ANGÉLIQUE DE SAINT-JEAN ARNAULD D'ANDILLY
Writings of Resistance
Edited and translated by John J. Conley, S.J.
Volume 41, 2015

FRANCESCO BARBARO
The Wealth of Wives: A Fifteenth-Century Marriage Manual
Edited and translated by Margaret L. King
Volume 42, 2015

JEANNE D'ALBRET
Letters from the Queen of Navarre with an Ample Declaration
Edited and translated by Kathleen M. Llewellyn, Emily E. Thompson, and Colette H. Winn
Volume 43, 2016

BATHSUA MAKIN AND MARY MORE WITH A REPLY TO MORE BY ROBERT WHITEHALL
Educating English Daughters: Late Seventeenth-Century Debates
Edited by Frances Teague and Margaret J. M. Ezell
Associate Editor Jessica Walker
Volume 44, 2016

ANNA STANISŁAWSKA
Orphan Girl: A Transaction, or an Account of the Entire Life of an Orphan Girl by way of Plaintful Threnodies in the Year 1685: The Aesop Episode
Verse translation, introduction, and commentary by Barry Keane
Volume 45, 2016

ALESSANDRA MACINGHI STROZZI
Letters to Her Sons, 1447–1470
Edited and translated by Judith Bryce
Volume 46, 2016

MOTHER JUANA DE LA CRUZ
Mother Juana de la Cruz, 1481–1534: Visionary Sermons
Edited by Jessica A. Boon and Ronald E. Surtz. Introductory material and notes by Jessica A. Boon. Translated by Ronald E. Surtz and Nora Weinerth
Volume 47, 2016

CLAUDINE-ALEXANDRINE GUERIN DE TENCIN
Memoirs of the Count of Comminge and The Misfortunes of Love
Edited and translated by Jonathan Walsh
Volume 48, 2016

The Other Voice in
Early Modern Europe:
The Toronto Series

SERIES EDITORS Margaret L. King *and* Albert Rabil, Jr.
SERIES EDITOR, ENGLISH TEXTS Elizabeth H. Hageman

Previous Publications in the Series

FELICIANA ENRÍQUEZ DE GUZMÁN,
ANA CARO MALLÉN, AND SOR
MARCELA DE SAN FÉLIX
Women Playwrights of Early Modern Spain
Edited by Nieves Romero-Diaz
and Lisa Vollendorf
Translated and annotated by Harley Erdman
Volume 49, 2016

ANNA TRAPNEL
Anna Trapnel's Report and Plea; or, A Narrative of Her Journey from London into Cornwall
Edited by Hilary Hinds
Volume 50, 2016

MARÍA VELA Y CUETO
Autobiography and Letters of a Spanish Nun
Edited by Susan Diane Laningham
Translated by Jane Tar
Volume 51, 2016

CHRISTINE DE PIZAN
The Book of the Mutability of Fortune
Edited and translated by Geri L. Smith
Volume 52, 2017

MARGUERITE D'AUGE,
RENÉE BURLAMACCHI,
AND JEANNE DU LAURENS
Sin and Salvation in Early Modern France: Three Women's Stories
Edited, and with an introduction by
Colette H. Winn
Translated by Nicholas Van Handel and
Colette H. Winn
Volume 53, 2017

ISABELLA D'ESTE
Selected Letters
Edited and translated by Deanna Shemek
Volume 54, 2017

IPPOLITA MARIA SFORZA
Duchess and Hostage in Renaissance Naples: Letters and Orations
Edited and translated by Diana Robin and
Lynn Lara Westwater
Volume 55, 2017

LOUISE BOURGEOIS
Midwife to the Queen of France: Diverse Observations
Translated by Stephanie O'Hara
Edited by Alison Klairmont Lingo
Volume 56, 2017

CHRISTINE DE PIZAN
Othea's Letter to Hector
Edited and translated by Renate
Blumenfeld-Kosinski and Earl Jeffrey
Richards
Volume 57, 2017

The Other Voice in
Early Modern Europe:
The Toronto Series

SERIES EDITORS Margaret L. King *and* Albert Rabil, Jr.
SERIES EDITOR, ENGLISH TEXTS Elizabeth H. Hageman

Previous Publications in the Series

MARIE-GENEVIÈVE-CHARLOTTE
THIROUX D'ARCONVILLE
*Selected Philosophical, Scientific, and
Autobiographical Writings*
Edited and translated by Julie Candler
Hayes
Volume 58, 2017

LADY MARY WROTH

Pamphilia to Amphilanthus
in Manuscript and Print

≈

Edited by
ILONA BELL

Texts by
STEVEN W. MAY and ILONA BELL

Iter Press
Toronto, Ontario

Arizona Center for Medieval and Renaissance Studies
Tempe, Arizona

2017

Iter Press
Tel: 416/978–7074   Email: iter@utoronto.ca
Fax: 416/978–1668   Web: www.itergateway.org

Arizona Center for Medieval and Renaissance Studies
Tel: 480/965–5900   Email: mrts@acmrs.org
Fax: 480/965–1681   Web: acmrs.org

© 2017 Iter, Inc. and the Arizona Board of Regents for Arizona State University.
All rights reserved.
Printed in Canada.

Library of Congress Cataloging-in-Publication Data
Names: Wroth, Mary, Lady, approximately 1586-approximately 1640, author. |
    Bell, Ilona, editor. | May, Steven W., editor.
Title: Lady Mary Wroth : Pamphilia to Amphilanthus in manuscript and print /
    edited by Ilona Bell ; texts by Steven W. May and Ilona Bell.
Description: Toronto, Ontario : Iter Press ; Tempe, Arizona :
    Arizona Center for Medieval and Renaissance Studies, 2017. | Series:
    Medieval and Renaissance texts and studies ; Volume 523 | Series: The
    other voice in Early Modern Europe: The Toronto series ; 59 | Includes
    bibliographical references and index.
Identifiers: LCCN 2017024387 (print) | LCCN 2017032304 (ebook) | ISBN
    9780866987387 (ebook) | ISBN 9780866985796 (pbk. : alk. paper)
Subjects: LCSH: Wroth, Mary, Lady, approximately 1586-approximately
    1640--Criticism, Textual.
Classification: LCC PR2399.W7 (ebook) | LCC PR2399.W7 P3 2017 (print) | DDC
    821/.3--dc23
LC record available at https://lccn.loc.gov/2017024387

Cover illustration:
Detail from a portrait of two ladies (probably) Lady Mary (Sidney) Wroth shown in the original painting with her mother Barbara Sidney, Countess of Leicester. By Marcus Gheeraerts II, 1612. Oil on Canvas. By kind permission of Viscount De L'Isle from his private collection.

Cover design:
Maureen Morin, Information Technology Services, University of Toronto Libraries

Typesetting:
Becker Associates.

Production:
Iter Press.

To my mother, Judith Magyar Isaacson, writer,
Holocaust survivor, mathematics professor, and dean of students,
whose wisdom, magnanimity, and love continue to inspire
her adoring husband, children, grandchildren,
and so many readers of her memoir, Seed of Sarah.

Contents

Acknowledgments	xv
Illustrations	xvii
Abbreviations	xix
INTRODUCTION	1
The Other Voice	1
Art and Life	1
Family, Politics, and Literary Tradition	19
The Life of Mary Sidney/Wroth	26
Wroth and Herbert: Betrothal and Marriage	33
Herbert's "Elegy" and Wroth's "Penshurst Mount"	38
"Pamphilia to Amphilanthus" in Manuscript	44
Pamphilia to Amphilanthus in Print	52
Love's Victory	53
The Countess of Montgomery's Urania	58
The Afterlife of Wroth's Sonnets	64
Editorial Principles and Practices	66
PAMPHILIA TO AMPHILANTHUS: THE MANUSCRIPT	73
PAMPHILIA TO AMPHILANTHUS: THE PRINTED TEXT	205
APPENDIX 1: Herbert's "Elegy" and Wroth's "Penshurst Mount"	267
APPENDIX 2: Table of Numbers for Manuscript and Printed Poems	275
APPENDIX 3: Copies of the 1621 Printed Text	281
Bibliography	291
Index of First Lines	301
Index	305

Acknowledgments

First and foremost, I want to thank my coeditor, Steven May, whose vast knowledge of early modern manuscript poetry, paleography, and printing practices was an incalculable boon to editing the texts of Wroth's poems, first in manuscript and then in print. I am so grateful to Steve for making time for this project amid his busy editing schedule, for helping formulate the editorial principles and practices, and for obtaining all the illustrations and permissions. I cannot imagine a more erudite and dedicated, or kind and generous, collaborator.

I am also grateful to Garth Bond for allowing us to reproduce the unexpurgated, edited texts of William Herbert's "Elegy" and Wroth's "Penshurst Mount" that appear in appendix 1.

My debts to all Wroth's previous editors and scholars are immeasurable. Preeminent among them is Josephine Roberts, whose edition introduced generations of readers to Wroth's poetry and whose research on Wroth's life and writing underlies everything that followed.

Margaret Hannay shared her extraordinary knowledge of Wroth's life and encouraged me to pursue this project from the very start. Her monumental biography, *Mary Sidney, Lady Wroth,* is a treasure trove. She is much missed. Mary Ellen Lamb's revelatory, ongoing work on William Herbert's poetry helped me imagine his side of the lyric exchange between Wroth and Herbert.

Other Voice English series editor, Elizabeth Hageman has been an extraordinarily dedicated and sage guide throughout. General editor Albert Rabil provided much appreciated guidance at the outset. Margaret English-Haskin has skillfully steered the edition through all stages of production.

I am particularly grateful to the Folger Shakespeare Library for awarding me a Short-Term Fellowship and for digitizing Wroth's autograph manuscript.

Williams College generously provided sabbatical grants and research funds. My thanks go to John Gerry for summer humanities research fellows. Samantha Barbaro, Cleo Levin, Matthew McCreary, Andrew Nguyen, Amy Nolan, and Ji Ae Rhee: Thank you, thank you, for your dedication and acumen.

Warmest gratitude to Williams College Interlibrary Loan librarian Alison O'Grady for tirelessly tracking down and obtaining the twenty-seven extant library copies of *Pamphilia to Amphilanthus.* I am grateful to the librarians who provided copies of the 1621 *Urania* listed in Appendix 3. Thanks also to Anne Shaver, who owned the twenty-eighth copy, the only copy still in private hands, and to Susanne Woods for providing copies of the poems.

xv

xvi *Acknowledgments*

Especial thanks to the superb literary biographer and critic, Rosemarie Bodenheimer and the luminous poet, Teresa Cader for making such thoughtful suggestions about the introduction.

My wonderful daughters, Kaitlin Bell Barnett and Amanda Bell, and cherished colleagues and friends, Jennifer Dowley, Darra Goldstein, Carol Ockman, Deborah Rothschild, Susan Sidlauskas, and Margaret Waller, who offered unstinting support and wise counsel as they listened to my evolving thoughts about Wroth's poetry.

The anonymous reader for the press gave the manuscript the most meticulous, insightful, and generous reading imaginable.

Finally, my beloved husband, Robert Bell, who has probably heard more about "Pamphilia to Amphilanthus" than anyone since William Herbert, cheered me on with his boundless humor and literary intelligence, even when his patience was beginning to wear a mite thin.

Illustrations

Cover Image.	Detail from a portrait of two ladies (probably) Lady Mary (Sidney) Wroth shown in the original painting with her mother Barbara Sidney, Countess of Leicester. By Marcus Gheeraerts II, 1612. Oil on Canvas. By kind permission of Viscount De L'Isle from his private collection.
Figure 1.	MS V.a.104, fol. 1r. Reproduced by permission of the Folger Shakespeare Library, Washington, DC. Formerly owned by Sir Thomas Phillipps and cited as MS 9283 in *Catalogus Librorum Manuscriptorum in Bibliotheca D. Thomae Phillipps Bart.* (1837), p. 147.
Figure 2.	MS V.a.104, fol. 29r. Reproduced by permission of the Folger Shakespeare Library, Washington, DC.
Figure 3.	*The Countesse of Mountgomeries Urania* (1621), sig. 4D1r. Reproduced by permission of the Folger Shakespeare Library, Washington, DC.
Figure 4.	MS V.a.104, fol. 9v. Reproduced by permission of the Folger Shakespeare Library, Washington, DC.
Figure 5.	Line engraving of William Herbert, Third Earl of Pembroke, by Lucas Vorsterman, early 17th century. National Portrait Gallery, London.
Figure 6.	Title page from *The Countesse of Mountgomeries Urania* (1621). Engraving by Simon van de Passe. Reproduced by permission of the Folger Shakespeare Library, Washington, DC.
Figure 7.	Double portrait of two ladies (probably) Lady Mary (Sidney) Wroth and her mother, Barbara Sidney, Countess of Leicester. By Marcus Gheeraerts II, 1612. Oil on Canvas. By kind permission of Viscount De L'Isle from his private collection.
Figure 8.	Baynard's Castle, London, from Claes Visscher's panoramic engraving of London (1616). Reproduced by permission of the Folger Shakespeare Library, Washington, DC.

Cover Image. — (no page number)
Figure 1. — 3
Figure 2. — 6
Figure 3. — 7
Figure 4. — 9
Figure 5. — 11
Figure 6. — 20
Figure 7. — 28
Figure 8. — 29

xviii *Illustrations*

Figure 9.	Loughton Hall. Essex Record Office, Chelmsford, Mint Binders Loughton 1/1. Reproduced by permission.	31
Figure 10.	The Sidney family home, Penshurst Place, depicted in 1757 by George Vertue. From Edward Hasted, *The History and Topographical Survey of the County of Kent* (Canterbury, 1778–1799). Reproduced by permission of the Folger Shakespeare Library, Washington, DC.	39
Figure 11.	The first page of *The Countesse of Mountgomeries Urania* (1621), sig. 4A1r. Reproduced by permission of the Folger Shakespeare Library, Washington, DC.	57

Abbreviations

ACE	*Ashgate Critical Essays on Women Writers in England, 1550–1700.* Vol. 4, *Mary Wroth.* Ed. Clare R. Kinney. Burlington, VT: Ashgate, 2009.
ACMRS	Arizona Center for Medieval and Renaissance Studies.
ARC	*Ashgate Research Companion to the Sidneys, 1500–1700.* Ed. Margaret P. Hannay, Mary Ellen Lamb, and Michael G. Brennan. 2 vols. Burlington, VT: Ashgate, 2015.
Briley	John Richard Briley. "A Biography of William Herbert, Third Earl of Pembroke, 1580-1630." PhD dissertation, University of Birmingham, 1961.
CRS	*Domestic Politics and Family Absence: The Correspondence (1588–1621) of Robert Sidney, First Earl of Leicester, and Barbara Gamage Sidney, Countess of Leicester.* Ed. Margaret P. Hannay, Noel J. Kinnamon, and Michael G. Brennan. The Early Modern Englishwoman, 1500–1750. Series editors Betty S. Travitsky, Anne Lake Prescott, and Patrick Cullen. Burlington, VT: Ashgate, 2005.
ELR	*English Literary Renaissance.*
F	Folger MS V.a.104.
fol.	folio.
LRW	*The Letters (1595–1608) of Rowland Whyte.* Ed. Michael G. Brennan, Noel J. Kinnamon, and Margaret P. Hannay. Philadelphia: American Philosophical Society, 2013.
MP	*Modern Philology.*
MS	Manuscript.
MSLW	Margaret P. Hannay. *Mary Sidney, Lady Wroth.* Burlington, VT: Ashgate, 2010.
ODNB	*Oxford Dictionary of National Biography: in association with the British Academy: From the Earliest Times to the Year 2000.* Ed. H. C. G. Matthew and Brian Harrison. Oxford, New York: Oxford University Press, 2004. Online edition 2008–.
OED	*Oxford English Dictionary,* 2nd ed. Ed. J. A. Simpson and E. S. C. Weiner, et al. Oxford: Oxford University Press, 1989. Online edition 2000–.
Poems	*The Poems of Lady Mary Wroth.* Ed. Josephine A. Roberts. Baton Rouge: Louisiana State University Press, 1983; Pb. 1992.
r	recto.
RMW	*Reading Mary Wroth.* Ed. Naomi J. Miller and Gary Waller. Knoxville: University of Tennessee Press, 1991.

xx *Abbreviations*

RRMW *Re-Reading Mary Wroth*. Ed. Katherine R. Larson and Naomi J. Miller with Andrew Strycharski. New York: Palgrave Macmillan, 2015.

SEL *Studies in English Literature, 1500–1900*.

sig. signature.

SJ *Sidney Journal*.

SQ *Shakespeare Quarterly*.

SS *Spenser Studies*.

TSWL *Tulsa Studies in Women's Literature*.

Urania 1 Mary Wroth. *The First Part of the Countess of Montgomery's Urania*. Ed. Josephine A. Roberts. Binghamton, NY: RETS/ MRTS, 1995.

Urania 2 Mary Wroth. *The Second Part of the Countess of Montgomery's Urania*. Ed. Josephine Roberts, completed by Suzanne Gossett and Janel Mueller. Tempe, AZ: RETS/ACMRS, 1999.

Urania Abr Mary Wroth. *The Countess of Montgomery's Urania (Abridged)*. Ed. Mary Ellen Lamb. Tempe, AZ: ACMRS, 2011.

v verso.

WW *Women's Writing: The Elizabethan to Victorian Period*.

Introduction

The Other Voice

Mary Wroth (1587–1651), author of the first collection of secular lyrics written and published by an English woman, an elaborate two-part romance, and a play, is the preeminent early modern English woman writer. Her sonnet sequence, *Pamphilia to Amphilanthus,* comprises the archetypal "other voice," a female voice speaking in a genre that in England had been the exclusive domain of male writers. Every edition influences the way we read. This edition presents both the well-known printed text of *Pamphilia to Amphilanthus,* reproduced as it appeared in 1621, and Wroth's other voice—the erotic, daring voice of a woman writing manuscript poems for herself, her lover, and her intimate friends. Wroth's imaginative scope and keen critical intelligence can be fully grasped only by reading and comparing the two sequences. Wroth's autograph manuscript, printed here for the first time, explores the joys and complications of a passionate, clandestine love affair that is still discernible, though veiled by Wroth's revisions, excisions, and reorganization, in the printed text. The two versions of "Pamphilia to Amphilanthus" illuminate the historical transition from manuscript to print, calling into question some of our most fundamental assumptions about Wroth's poetry and expanding our understanding of early modern English women. Wroth's private poetry and careful revisions complicate paradigms of early modern English women writers derived from print, and ally Wroth with women writing erotic love poetry on the continent.[1]

Art and Life

The present volume brings together for the first time in one volume two equally authorial but distinct versions of Wroth's poetry. Wroth's manuscript poetry has never appeared in print and has been readily available online only since 2012. Consequently, assumptions about her poetry have been derived from the printed text, which looks like a conventional Petrarchan tale of transcendent, unrequited love, though told from an unprecedented female point of view. The emotional core of Wroth's private manuscript poetry emerges not only from Renaissance literary tradition, but also from life as an early modern woman. The challenge and imaginative liberation of speaking and acting against dominant gender norms;

---

1. I am grateful to Anne Lake Prescott for calling my attention to the parallel between Wroth and her Continental counterparts. For connections between Wroth and Louise Labé, see Prescott's essay, "Mary Wroth, Louise Labé, and Cupid," *SJ* 15 (1997): 37–40.

2   *Introduction*

the misery of a distasteful, arranged marriage; the joys, risks, and ethics of conducting a premarital or extramarital love affair before the advent of reliable birth control; the force and vicissitudes of sexual pleasure; the happiness and fear of having and possibly losing a child in or out of wedlock: These preoccupations impel Wroth's private poetry and are still present, as a discreetly veiled subtext, in the bowdlerized, printed sequence.

Wroth's original, private lyric dialogue can still be heard in the propulsive persuasive energy that courses through her manuscript poems, urging her lover, her family, and her intimate friends to hear her point of view and come to her aid. Their responses, whether written or heard, anticipated, incorporated, or rebutted, can be gleaned from elocutionary cues embedded in her songs and sonnets. Wroth's earlier, unexpurgated songs and sonnets show her to be a greater poet—more psychologically insightful, verbally sophisticated, and boldly original—than editors and critics realized. The carefully curated, reconceptualized, printed edition of 1621 shows her to be a more self-reflexive and critically astute writer than her conventional poetic tropes might suggest. When the two extant sonnet sequences are read in light of each other, as this edition invites readers to do, the 1621 printed text becomes even more inventive and intriguing, imbued with ambiguities and obliquities that mask and diffuse the torrid, tormented love affair enacted in Wroth's manuscript poems.

To grasp the differences between the two extant versions of Wroth's poetry one needs to pay extremely close attention to details of language; to work through the multiple, sometimes contradictory meanings that make her lexicon and syntax so challenging; to peer into ellipses and tease out ambiguities; to look for elocutionary cues that signal the dramatic situation, private lyric audience, and persuasive purpose; to ponder the ways groups of poems interact with, shape, and reshape each other; and to reexamine the literary devices (abstraction, allegory, ambiguity, amphibology, apostrophe, *copia,* circumlocution, contradiction, enigma, interruption, irony, metaphor, metonymy, paradox, uncertainty, and many more) that revitalize seemingly conventional tropes.

Wroth's autograph manuscript, Folger Manuscript V.a.104, contains 117 songs and sonnets with numerous, multistage revisions. Transcribed by Wroth in her confident italic script, it is a lovely, small quarto, the perfect size to hold in one's hand. The rewritten, expurgated, and significantly reordered printed collection of 103 poems appears in a separately numbered section at the end of Wroth's romance, *The Countesse of Mountgomeries Urania,* an elegant folio published in 1621 while Wroth was still alive—the only time Wroth's poetry and romance appeared in print until the twentieth century.[2]

To be sure, there is a great deal of overlap between the manuscript and printed texts, but there are also notable differences that emerge when one looks

---

2. Mary Wroth, *The Countesse of Mountgomeries Urania* (London, 1621).

Introduction 3

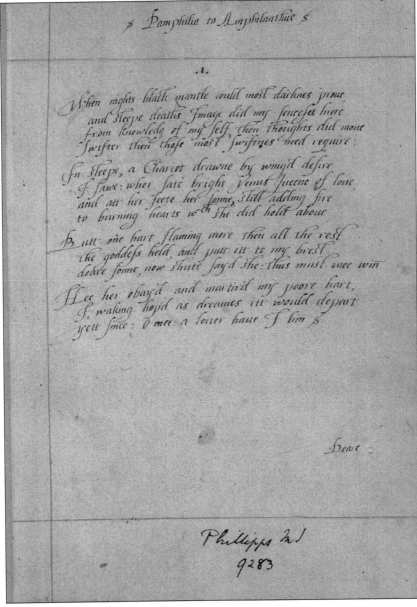

Figure 1. The first page, following the title page, of Wroth's autograph manuscript, MS V.a.104, fol. 1r. Reproduced by permission of the Folger Shakespeare Library, Washington, DC. Formerly owned by Sir Thomas Phillipps and cited as MS 9283 in *Catalogus Librorum Manuscriptorum in Bibliotheca D. Thomae Phillipps Bart.* (1837), p. 147.

4   *Introduction*

more closely. When Wroth revised a key word, or eliminated a reference to Venus, goddess of love, or removed the aubade in which Pamphilia awakens Amphilanthus after a night of lovemaking, or transposed a poem from a moment of intimacy to a period of separation and jealousy, she not only reconceived individual poems but also transformed the meaning and purpose of the collection. To avoid potential disapproval and censorship, she removed six poems including the aubade, moved nine poems to fictionalized contexts in *Urania,* added one new poem to steer readers' expectations of what is to come, and shuffled the remaining poems to veil but not entirely undo her radical challenge to literary and social convention.

Wroth's process of revision involved: 1) altering key words and phrases in her autograph manuscript collection (MS V.a.104); 2) identifying and removing poems that were too transgressive or problematic to be easily reshaped by changing key words; 3) repositioning the remaining poems (in a lost manuscript that became the basis of the printed text) in order to obscure or repurpose the unfolding drama that propelled her private poetry. All told, Wroth's alterations, cuts, and reorganization make the 1621 printed text more abstract and generalized, and more socially acceptable for an early modern woman writer.

Earlier drafts of Wroth's poems no longer exist, but she probably composed individual lyrics, or short groups of lyrics, on loose sheets or gatherings of paper, which she revised and polished before copying them neatly onto the pages that constitute Folger MS V.a.104. The highly wrought, formal structure of eight groups of six sonnets with a consistent rhyme scheme, each followed by a song (the eighth group of six sonnets has no song), culminates in the signature "Pamphilia" surrounded by four *fermesses* ($$$$), indicating that the first fifty-five poems originally constituted a separate sonnet sequence.

The following shorter groups of consecutively numbered or unnumbered songs or sonnets suggest that MS V.a.104 is a composite collection of poems and groups of poems written at different times.[3] The current binding is not original, so it is difficult to know how or when Wroth assembled the separately numbered groups of poems and then either recopied them or bound them together into MS V.a.104 before rethinking and reconceiving the entire collection to suit a wider public audience.

Wroth's manuscript collection, cited here as "Pamphilia to Amphilanthus" to distinguish it from the printed text, appears first because it was written first,

---

3. For more detailed descriptions of the material make-up of the Folger manuscript, see Gavin Alexander, "Constant Works: A Framework for Reading Mary Wroth," *SJ* 14 (1996–1997), 5–32, Heather Dubrow, "'And Thus Leave Off': Reevaluating Mary Wroth's Folger Manuscript, V.a.104," *TSWL* 22 (2003): 273–91, and Margaret P. Hannay, "The 'Ending End' of Lady Mary Wroth's Manuscript of Poems," *SJ* 31 (2013): 1–22. The paratextual signifiers discussed in these essays have as yet to be applied to a close reading of the poems themselves.

because it deserves to be read as Wroth transcribed and then revised it—free, insofar as possible, from modern assumptions about Wroth and other early modern women writers derived from print—and finally, because Wroth's revisions, deletions, and reorganization cast her later printed sequence in a fascinating new light. The 1621 printed version of *Pamphilia to Amphilanthus,* differentiated here by the italicized title, also appears in its entirety because it is important in its own right, as the rich scholarly tradition it has inspired demonstrates. This edition corrects manifest printer's errors but otherwise leaves the printed text intact so that readers who have come to love and admire the 1621 sequence can see it afresh, without the distinctive spelling and punctuation that Josephine Roberts's 1983 edition imported from the manuscript.

Wroth was lauded as a writer both during her lifetime and soon after her death, as we shall see in more detail later, but her writing was then all but lost to English literary history for over three centuries, until Gary F. Waller published his path-breaking 1977 edition of *Pamphilia to Amphilanthus.*[4] The 1621 sequence has appeared in print several times since then, most importantly in Roberts's 1983 collection, *The Poems of Lady Mary Wroth,* which has remained the authoritative text of Wroth's poetry for over three decades.[5] This edition is profoundly indebted to Roberts's pioneering scholarship and textual acumen. Like Waller, Roberts reproduced the 1621 selection and order of poems, because preserving the author's "final intentions" was the standard goal of editions from the 1970s and 1980s—an editorial tradition that goes back to the nineteenth century and that is still the benchmark for most scholarly editions.

At the time Wroth wrote her songs and sonnets, spelling and punctuation had not yet been codified. Writers customarily deployed their own distinctive spelling and punctuation, which typesetters altered and to some extent regularized for print. Roberts imported spelling, punctuation, and some, but not all, of the variants from Wroth's autograph manuscript on the grounds that they reflected Wroth's own scribal habits; however, Wroth would not have expected or wanted her poems to appear in public clothed in such intimate garb.

Roberts's edition is a hybrid, neither manuscript nor print, but an amalgamation of both. Roberts's editorial choices made sense at the time, but they elided vital differences between manuscript and print.[6] Despite her vast knowledge of

4. Waller, ed. *Pamphilia to Amphilanthus.* (Salzburg: Inst. für Anglistik & Amerikanistik, University of Salzburg, 1977).

5. Roberts, *Poems,* quoted here and throughout from the 1992 paperback edition, which adds the corrections Wroth made on the Kohler copy of the 1621 *Pamphilia to Amphilanthus* to the list of variants.

6. For information about printing practices, characteristic features of manuscript writing, and early modern writers' and readers' relation to manuscript and print, see Mark Bland, *A Guide to Early Printed Books and Manuscripts* (Malden, MA: Wiley-Blackwell, 2010), and Adrian Johns, *The Nature of the Book: Print and Knowledge in the Making* (Chicago: University of Chicago Press, 1998).

6 *Introduction*

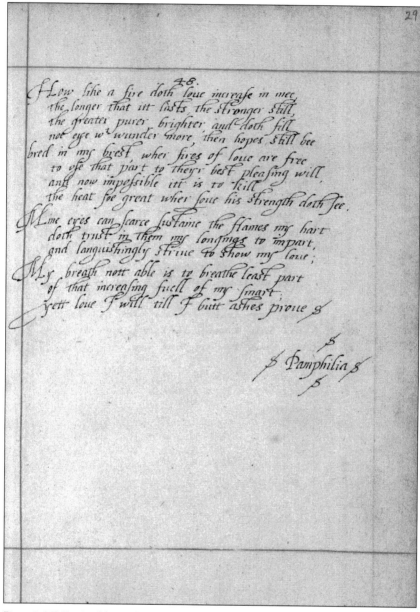

Figure 2. MS V.a.104, fol. 29r, showing the signature Pamphilia and four fermesses that mark the end of the first group of poems. Reproduced by permission of the Folger Shakespeare Library, Washington, DC.

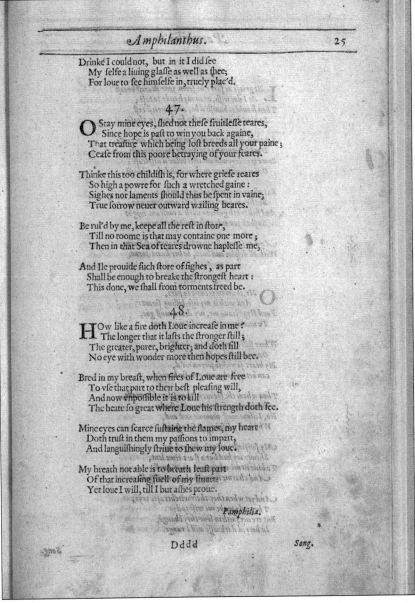

Figure 3. *The Countesse of Mountgomeries Urania* (1621), sig. 4D1r, showing the signature Pamphilia but no fermesses. Reproduced by permission of the Folger Shakespeare Library, Washington, DC.

8   *Introduction*

Wroth's life and writing, Roberts failed to recognize the significant, substantive differences between the Folger manuscript and the 1621 printed text. Anyone interested in Wroth's complete corpus could have found the complete list of Folger poems in Roberts's introduction, as well as the nine poems Wroth transposed to *Urania* and the six unprinted poems that Roberts placed in separate sections at the back.[7] Nonetheless, to reconstitute Wroth's manuscript sequence from Roberts's edition requires one to flip back and forth or to painstakingly cut and paste poems from three separate sections, and then write in Wroth's revisions from the list of variants. As far as I know, no one examined the excised poems or Wroth's original sequence and revisions closely enough to grasp their significance, which is understandable since Roberts claimed that Wroth's revisions did little more than alter accidentals of spelling and punctuation and change a few words to regularize the meter and correct the grammar.

The Folger Shakespeare Library digitized Manuscript V.a.104 in 2008; in 2012, *Mary Wroth's Poetry: An Electronic Edition,* edited by Paul Salzman, went online. Salzman's La Trobe University website includes a facsimile of each Folger poem along with a transcription of both the manuscript and printed poem.[8] His original spelling transcriptions enable scholars to compare the manuscript and printed version of a given poem, while his modernized texts make the poems more easily legible.[9]

Roberts's printed edition and Salzman's electronic edition are both enormously valuable, each in their own right, but neither one conveys the profound, fundamental differences between the two versions of Wroth's poetry. Salzman's transcriptions do not reproduce all of Wroth's multistage revisions, which can be decoded only by studying Wroth's handwriting, magnifying digital images of the manuscript, and meticulously scrutinizing one correction after another. Moreover, Salzman's decision to reproduce the manuscript sequence but not the

7. In *Poems,* 64, Roberts lists the order of the Folger poems, using the consecutive numbers she added to the 1621 printed poems and the *Urania* poems. The excised poems appear on pages 143–45. The nine poems moved from the Folger Manuscript to *Urania* appear amid the fifty-four poems from the 1621 *Urania* on pages 146–95.

8. The Folger images are available at http://luna.folger.edu/luna/servlet. The magnification makes it possible to decode Wroth's otherwise indecipherable deletions and revisions. Paul Salzman, *Mary Wroth's Poetry: An Electronic Edition,* is available at http://wroth.latrobe.edu.au/. Salzman explores the advantages of online publication in "Me and My Shadow: Editing Wroth for the Digital Age," in *Re-Reading Mary Wroth,* ed. Katherine R. Larson and Naomi J. Miller, with Andrew Strycharski (Basingstoke, UK: Palgrave Macmillan, 2015), 183–92, as does Rebecca L. Fall in "*Pamphilia* Unbound: Digital Re-Visions of Mary Wroth's Folger Manuscript, V.a.104," *RRMW,* 193–207.

9. For a detailed account and thoughtful assessment of Salzman's edition, see Clare R. Kinney, "Mary Wroth's Poetry: An Electronic Edition, ed. Paul Salzman," *Spenser Review* 44.1.9 (2014), which is available at: http://www.english.cam.ac.uk/spenseronline/review/volume-44/441/digital-projects/mary-wroths-poetry-an-electronic-edition-ed-paul-salzman/.

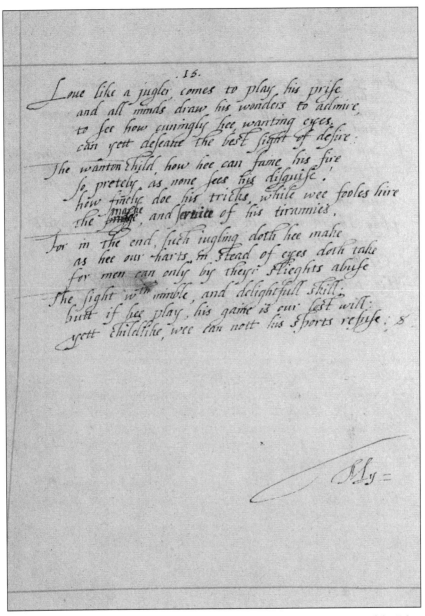

Figure 4. MS V.a.104, fol. 9v, showing Wroth's revisions. Reproduced by permission of the Folger Shakespeare Library, Washington, DC.

10 *Introduction*

printed sequence mirrors Roberts's decision to reproduce the printed sequence but not the manuscript. Neither edition enables readers to see how Wroth's reorganization altered the meaning.

The goal of this edition is twofold: 1) to provide both sequences in their entirety as Wroth prepared them to be read, first in her manuscript collection and then in print; and 2) to enable readers to see how Wroth transformed her private collection of poems into a work suitable for public consumption. To that end, the manuscript text provided here reproduces the corrections and revisions Wroth wrote onto her autograph manuscript, including numerous places not included in Roberts's or Salzman's variants where she overwrote individual letters to change a word. Wroth's important but confusing original numbers appear between bracketed sequential numbers for both sequences so that readers can find, read, compare, and cite poems in their two different contexts. Glosses for old spellings and outmoded meanings appear in the right-hand margin of the manuscript sequence; more elaborate annotations appear in footnotes. Readers of the printed text can use the sequential numbers to consult glosses and annotations in the manuscript text. To help readers analyze Wroth's revisions, substantive variants appear in footnotes below both sequences.

This edition also includes the private manuscript versions of William Herbert's "Elegy" and Mary Sidney (Wroth)'s "Penshurst Mount" (in appendix 1) because they comprise an urtext, a precipitating crisis that reverberates throughout Wroth's oeuvre.[10] The dialogic poetics of secrecy described in "Elegy" and deployed in "Penshurst Mount" offers a validation and methodology for reading "Pamphilia to Amphilanthus" as one side of a covert lyric exchange between Mary Sidney/Wroth[11] and her first cousin William Herbert, third Earl of Pembroke.

Although we do not know when their love affair began, their intimacy is indisputable because family documents record the birth of their two children, Will and Catherine, in the 1620s. It is often assumed that Wroth wrote *Pamphilia to Amphilanthus* after the death of her husband in 1614, which has also been

---

10. I am grateful to Garth Bond for permission to use the texts of "Elegy" and "Penshurst Mount" that he edited for "Amphilanthus to Pamphilia: William Herbert, Mary Wroth, and Penshurst Mount," *SJ* 31 (2013): 51–80. The texts of the poems appear in Appendix 1.

11. Deciding how to refer to early modern women can be difficult, since their names changed when they married. Throughout this edition, the form Sidney/Wroth designates Wroth's life or writing both before and after marriage. Mary Sidney (Wroth) refers to Wroth before her marriage and distinguishes her from her grandmother and aunt, whose maiden names were also Mary Sidney. Since maiden names were not used as middle names, Mary Sidney Wroth would be an anachronism; therefore, Mary (Sidney) Wroth, or simply Wroth, refers to her more generally. Except when it seems important, the present volume omits titles such as Lady and Sir and uses names instead; the exceptions are Mary (Sidney) Herbert, Countess of Pembroke, who is called "the countess" to distinguish her from her niece, Mary (Sidney) Wroth, and her son, William Herbert, who is called Herbert even after he became the third Earl of Pembroke.

Figure 5. Line engraving of William Herbert, Third Earl of Pembroke, by Lucas Vorsterman, early 17th century. National Portrait Gallery, London.

used as a *terminus a quo* for her love affair with Herbert. As a result, Wroth's poetry has been seen as belated—as conventional Petrarchan poetry repurposed to express a female point of view over a decade after the sonnet craze initiated by *Astrophil and Stella* (1591) had run its course.[12] Yet as we shall see, the specter

12. As Waller explains in *The Sidney Family Romance: Mary Wroth, William Herbert, and the Early Modern Construction of Gender* (Detroit: Wayne State University Press, 1993), 191, "The date is important: even in the time it was written, it was a culturally marginal work. 1621 is some thirty years after the main vogue of sonneteering in England.... Not only are her poems among the last recog-

12 Introduction

of an impending marriage that haunts "Penshurst Mount" and the beginning of "Pamphilia to Amphilanthus" suggests that Wroth began to write her private love poetry shortly before her arranged marriage to Robert Wroth in September 1604, five years before English Renaissance sonneteering reached its zenith with the publication of Shakespeare's sonnets in 1609.

By entitling her poems "Pamphilia to Amphilanthus" (as compared to Sidney's *Astrophil and Stella*), Wroth announces that Pamphilia's poems are addressed *to* Amphilanthus and hints that her own poems were primarily written to and for her long-term lover, Amphilanthus's real-life counterpart, William Herbert. Josephine Roberts long ago noticed that the last poem in *Pamphilia to Amphilanthus* puns on "will," connecting Amphilanthus to Wroth's beloved cousin Will. Recently, Mary Ellen Lamb has shown that Herbert's poems also pun on worth/Wroth. Wroth herself uses both puns in "Pamphilia to Amphilanthus" and *Urania* to signal that she and Herbert were writing and responding to each other in encoded poetry.[13]

Wroth's intricately interconnected poems, published romance, play, and romance continuation, probably written in that order beginning in 1604 and ending in the 1620s, elucidate the ways in which her writing interweaves art and life. Wroth's romance occupies the fabulous, hazy borderlands where real people and events metamorphose into richly multivalent, creative fiction. Pamphilia, the poet/lover of Amphilanthus and Wroth's avatar or alter ego, is both the protagonist of her romance and the speaker of her sonnet sequence, although the connection is less evident to readers today because Josephine Roberts's modern edition of *Urania* part I omits *Pamphilia to Amphilanthus*, which appeared at the end of the 1621 romance. *The Second Part of the Countess of Montgomery's Urania*, also known as the manuscript continuation because it remained unpublished until 1999, reveals more intimate aspects of Pamphilia's relationship with Amphilanthus, including a private marriage contract and a child born out of wedlock. Wroth's play *Love's Victory*, which was not published until the twentieth century, dramatizes the varieties of love experienced or written about by two generations

---

nizably Petrarchan poetry in English, but they are doubly 'belated,' to use Harold Bloom's term, in relation to her own family."

13. Roberts, "The Biographical Problem of *Pamphilia to Amphilanthus*," *Tulsa Studies in Women's Literature* 1 (1982): 49; Lamb, "'Can you suspect a change in me?': Poems by Mary Wroth and William Herbert, Third Earl of Pembroke," *RRMW*, 55–56. Gary Waller, *The Sidney Family Romance*, noticed, 199–201, that Wroth uses both puns. Hence, "if these poems were circulated among Wroth's family and close friends, the autobiographical level would surely have been recognized." Although his book juxtaposed Herbert's and Wroth's lives and writing, Waller's mistaken belief that "none of Wroth's poems seem to be 'answer poems' like those Pembroke wrote with Rudyerd" calls into question his conclusion that "the connections between the two cousins' poems are generic rather than specific" (194).

of Sidneys, most notably Mary Wroth herself and her lover, William Herbert, who probably acted the leading roles when the play was staged for family and friends.[14]

When Wroth wrote *Urania* and "Pamphilia to Amphilanthus," modern distinctions between fiction and nonfiction did not exist.[15] Autobiography as we understand it was not yet a recognized genre, though autobiographical elements peek out—from prefatory letters in printed works; prose narratives; pastoral personae that had encoded the writer's thoughts and feelings since antiquity; and, most importantly for our purposes, love poetry where the porous boundary between poet and personae, life and art, was negotiated by name puns, allegory, and ellipses.[16] Like *Urania,* "Pamphilia to Amphilanthus" is quasi-autobiographical, though not in quite the same way, since lyrics do not set out to narrate or recount a story. Rather, English sonnets in general and Wroth's in particular are artfully dramatized moments in time, written or performed as events unfold.[17]

Like the most renowned English Renaissance sonnet sequences, Wroth's "Pamphilia to Amphilanthus" began as a series of private poems, written for herself, her lover, and her close family and friends, whose responses are woven into the fabric of the poetry. The contingent nature of Wroth's private lyric dialogue would have been equally true for her most celebrated predecessors and contemporaries. "Astrophil and Stella," written by Wroth's uncle Sir Philip Sidney in 1580, circulated privately in manuscript and was published only posthumously, in an authorized edition edited by Philip's sister Mary, after it appeared in a 1591 pirated edition. Sidney invited his private lyric audience to connect Astrophil with himself and Stella with Penelope Rich by alluding to the pheon or arrowhead that graced the Sidney family coat of arms and by punning on rich/Rich. Edmund Spenser's sonnet sequence, "Amoretti," was originally written to and for Elizabeth Boyle. After she accepted his marriage proposal, Spenser wrote a sonnet addressed to three Elizabeths: his fiancée, his mother, and his queen. "Amoretti" was printed along with his "Epithalamion," or marriage song, in 1595, a year after his marriage. The carefully guarded manuscripts of John Donne's "Songs and Sonnets," which were probably written around the turn of the century, began to circulate more freely in the 1610s but remained unpublished until 1633, two years after his death. Donne's puns on "more" allude to his clandestine courtship of

---

14. See Findlay, "Lady Mary Wroth: *Love's Victory,*" ARC, 2:216.

15. See Judith H. Anderson's important study, *Biographical Truth: The Representation of Historical Persons in Tudor-Stuart Writing* (New Haven: Yale University Press, 1984).

16. As Elizabeth Heale writes in *Autobiography and Authorship in Renaissance Verse: Chronicles of the Self* (Basingstoke, UK: Palgrave Macmillan, 2003), 9, "the self-evident artfulness of verse, its foregrounded artifice … offered genres in which autobiographical and authorial selves could appear as safely figurative and rhetorical."

17. See, for example, Jennifer Lee Carrell, "A Pack of Lies in a Looking Glass: Lady Mary Wroth's *Urania* and the Magic Mirror of Romance," *SEL* 34 (1994): 80.

14   *Introduction*

Anne More, which culminated in their elopement in December 1601, Donne's imprisonment, and a court battle that legalized the marriage the following spring. Shakespeare's *Sonnets,* printed in 1609 in an authorized or unauthorized edition (scholars disagree), contains puns on "will" that are at once an expression of intention, a circumlocution for sexual desire, an allusion to Will Shakespeare's own first name, and probably also an allusion to the name of the young man (Will Herbert?) to whom many of the sonnets were originally addressed.[18]

Autograph texts of English Renaissance sonnet sequences are extremely rare. There are none for Donne's "Songs and Sonnets," or Sidney's, Spenser's, or Shakespeare's sonnet sequences. There is a surviving holograph manuscript of poems by Wroth's father, Robert Sidney, but his poems were not published until the twentieth century.[19] Unlike her father's manuscript poems, or Sidney's, Spenser's, and Shakespeare's printed poems, Wroth's lyrics exist both in her own handwriting and in books printed during her lifetime, including one rare copy of the 1621 printed text with Wroth's own handwritten corrections.[20] The remarkable survival of Wroth's poetry in *both* an autograph manuscript with distinct, separately numbered groups of poems written at different times, containing incisive multistage revisions designed to conceal the most intimate aspects of her private poetry, *and* a revised, reorganized, renumbered, corrected printed text makes "Pamphilia to Amphilanthus" an incomparable case study for this vital, transitional moment when most lyric poems were still originally written for a private lyric audience but when the advent of affordable, widely circulated printed books encouraged writers to think about how their work would be understood by an unknown reading public with continually changing attitudes and social mores.

When Roberts published *The Poems of Lady Mary Wroth* in 1983, manuscript poetry had not yet become a major field of scholarship.[21] Renaissance lit-

---

18. The connection, first made by Jonathan Gibson in "Cherchez la femme: Mary Wroth and Shakespeare's *Sonnets,*" *Times Literary Supplement* (August 13, 2004): 12–13, is developed by Penny McCarthy, "Autumn 1604: Documentation and Literary Coincidence," in *Mary Wroth and Shakespeare,* ed. Paul Salzman and Marion Wynne-Davies (London: Routledge, 2015), 37–46.

19. *The Poems of Robert Sidney,* ed. P. J. Croft (Oxford: Oxford University Press, 1984).

20. This "unique copy" was owned by Charlotte Kohler, who identified the corrections as Wroth's handwriting. It was reproduced, with Kohler's permission, in *Mary Wroth,* selected and introduced by Josephine A. Roberts, in *The Early Modern Englishwoman: A Facsimile Library of Essential Works, Part 1, Printed Writings, 1500–1640,* vol. 10, ed. Betty Travitsky and Patrick Cullen (Aldershot, UK: Scolar Press; Burlington, VT: Ashgate, 1996). Kohler gave the book to Josephine Roberts, and after her death, Roberts's husband, James Gaines, presented it to the University of Pennsylvania where it is today.

21. For some illuminating studies that explore the importance of manuscript circulation, see Arthur F. Marotti, *John Donne, Coterie Poet* (Madison: University of Wisconsin Press, 1986) and *Manuscript, Print, and the English Renaissance Lyric* (Ithaca: Cornell University Press, 1995); Steven W. May, *The Elizabethan Courtier Poets: The Poems and their Contexts* (Columbia: University of Missouri Press,

erary criticism focused on the self-analysis, self-exploration, and self-fashioning of the male poet and speaker, which reduced the sonnet lady to a shadowy reflection of male desire.[22] While praising Wroth for creating a female speaker and inverting traditional gender roles, Roberts incorporated the dominant critical methodology of the time by emphasizing the speaker, disembodying the beloved, and discounting their interactive dialogue. Roberts noticed that the last poem in the 1621 sequence contains a possible pun on Will/will, but she did not explore the implications of Wroth's hints that the poems were written to and for Will Herbert. Roberts's extensive biographical research yielded a detailed introduction to Wroth's life and work in *The Poems of Mary Wroth* as well as an essay entitled "The Biographical Problem of *Pamphilia to Amphilanthus*." Nonetheless, Roberts believed that *Pamphilia to Amphilanthus* "adhere[d] so closely to the well-defined Petrarchan mode" that, she declared, "the rhetoric of wooing, or courtship is largely absent."[23] Thus, even as Roberts was discovering invaluable information about Wroth's life—information that she and subsequent scholars deployed to explore the sophisticated layering of life and art in *Urania* and *Love's Victory*—she deterred critics from analyzing Pamphilia's lyric dialogue with Amphilanthus, or its analogue, Mary Wroth's private lyric dialogue with William Herbert.

Roberts's influential account of *Pamphilia to Amphilanthus* became the basis for subsequent interpretations, which emphasized Pamphilia's isolation, long-suffering constancy, and spiritual transcendence. Elaine V. Beilin reiterated and further instantiated Roberts's claims that Wroth's sonnets barely mention Amphilanthus, that the language of courtship is absent, and that "the reality at the core of Pamphilia's language is divine love."[24] *Reading Mary Wroth,* the important first essay collection devoted entirely to Wroth, included a seminal essay by Jeff Masten which argued that Wroth's poems "make little attempt to engage outside interlocutors" but instead "speak an almost inscrutable private language." Masten further diminished Amphilanthus's importance when he contended that Wroth

---

1991); H. R. Woudhuysen, *Sir Philip Sidney and the Circulation of Manuscripts, 1558–1640* (Oxford: Clarendon Press, 1996); Germaine Warkentin, "Robert Sidney's 'Darcke Offerings': The Making of a Late Tudor Manuscript Canzoniere," *SS* XII (1998): 37–74; Margaret J. M. Ezell, *Social Authorship and the Advent of Print* (Baltimore: Johns Hopkins University Press, 1999); and Heidi Brayman Hackel, *Reading Material in Early Modern England: Print, Gender, and Literacy* (Cambridge: Cambridge University Press, 2005).

22. For an account of the ways in which this dominant critical trend discounted the women in Renaissance love poetry, see Ilona Bell, "The Role of the Lady in Donne's *Songs and Sonets,*" *SEL* 23 (1983): 113–29, and *Elizabethan Women and the Poetry of Courtship* (Cambridge: Cambridge University Press, 1998).

23. *Poems,* 59, 48.

24. Beilin, *Redeeming Eve: Women Writers of the English Renaissance* (Princeton: Princeton University Press, 1987), 241.

16 *Introduction*

rejected Petrarchism's public voice, withdrawing into "a relentlessly private ... interiorized space" and choosing not to circulate her poems.[25]

The feminist desire to celebrate Wroth as the writer, subject, and primary audience of her own poetic creations made Amphilanthus expendable. As Mary B. Moore wrote, Wroth "depicts a female sense of self through the labyrinth—presenting a self that is isolated, enclosed, difficult, and complex" and rendering her beloved an even more spectral "gap" than is usual in Petrarchan poetry. Naomi J. Miller added that images of birth, miscarriage, and female friendship strengthen Wroth's female point of view, but Miller also reiterated Roberts's view that "Wroth makes the love experience itself, not the beloved—the locus of value and the stimulus to poetry." Wendy Wall thought that Petrarchism's absent, distant lover enabled Wroth to represent a private self. Natasha Distiller added a postmodern turn that broadened the gap between Wroth's female need not to be seen and Petrarchism's male desire for publicity and fame.[26] Ideology provided an explanation. As Ann Rosalind Jones wrote, Petrarchism offered "an ideologically safe mode for women (no proximity meant no threat to chastity)." Clare R. Kinney summarized what most critics saw as a "given[,] that the male body is not, officially, culturally imaginable as an object of female desire."[27]

While some critics and editors disparaged Wroth's poems as overly conventional Petrarchan poetry, closer scrutiny yielded greater regard. Barbara Kiefer Lewalski reiterated many of Roberts's premises but gave Wroth more credit for her revolutionary and "transgressive" use of "conventional genres to explore women's rather than men's consciousness and fantasies." Unlike Waller, Lewalski noted that Wroth and Herbert exchanged poems, but she nonetheless believed that "Wroth's sequence displaces and silences the male beloved even more completely than is usually the case with the Petrarchan lady." Heather Dubrow extended Lewalski's praise of Wroth's poetic achievement by arguing that *Pamphilia to Amphilanthus*, though festooned with conventional Petrarchan language, is not subservient to Petrarch or Petrarchism but is closer to Shakespeare's brilliantly creative sonnets.

---

25. Masten, "'Shall I turne blabb?': Circulation, Gender, and Subjectivity in Mary Wroth's Sonnets," *RMW*, 67, 69.

26. Moore, "The Labyrinth as Style in *Pamphilia to Amphilanthus*," *SEL* 38 (1998): 62, 66; Wall, *The Imprint of Gender: Authorship and Publication in the English Renaissance* (Ithaca: Cornell University Press, 1993), 330–38; Miller, "Rewriting Lyric Fictions: The Role of the Lady in Lady Mary Wroth's *Pamphilia to Amphilanthus*," in *Renaissance Englishwoman in Print: Counterbalancing the Canon*, ed. Anne M. Haselkorn and Betty S. Travitsky (Amherst: University of Massachusetts Press, 1990), 303; Distiller, *Desire and Gender in the Sonnet Tradition* (Basingstoke, UK: Palgrave Macmillan, 2008).

27. Jones, *The Currency of Eros: Women's Love Lyric in Europe, 1540–1620* (Bloomington: Indiana University Press, 1990); Kinney, "Mary Wroth's Guilty 'Secrett Art': The Poetics of Jealousy in *Pamphilia to Amphilanthus*," in *Write or Be Written: Early Modern Women Poets and Cultural Constraints*, ed. Barbara Smith and Ursula Appelt (Burlington, VT: Ashgate, 2001), 69.

Yet Dubrow also concluded, echoing earlier views by Roberts, Beilin, Lewalski, and many others, that *Pamphilia to Amphilianthus* focuses "on the mind of the lover rather than the relationships between lovers" because "Wroth is writing about spiritual love and the heightened spiritual peace it brings."[28]

Masten's essay proved almost as influential as Roberts's introduction, but his claim that Wroth removed her poetry from circulation was widely contested. Daniel Juan Gil maintained that *Pamphilia to Amphilanthus* actively engages a public readership, while Nona Fienberg thought Wroth was writing for an audience of Renaissance women. Michael G. Brennan, Margaret Hannay, and Paul Salzman provided concrete evidence that Wroth's poems did circulate, winning dedications, accolades, and fame that made Wroth known as a writer as early as 1612.[29] Meanwhile, as the focus of feminist theory evolved from the silencing and victimization of women to a growing focus on female subjectivity and agency, the premise that the personal is political, and that writing, gender, and the political unconscious are intricately intertwined, led a number of scholars to argue that, far from withdrawing into solitude and isolation, Wroth's poems comment on and critique contemporary political debates. Where Masten saw a rejection of male public discourse, later critics interpreted Wroth's rewriting of Petrarchan convention as a boldly political act. Most notably, Rosalind Smith applied the political readings of *Urania* to *Pamphilia to Amphilanthus*: "Wroth is positioning her sequence both in a wide political and religious frame, and a Protestant literary tradition integrating both Sidneian and radical Spenserian agendas."[30]

More recently, a few critics have cautiously begun to discern a latent eroticism in Wroth's poetry. Focusing on "a crowne of sonnets," Mary Moore noted Wroth's "transgressive expression of erotic desire," even though, like Beilin, Dubrow, and numerous others, Moore thought Wroth's "fictional privacy" transformed her erotic yearning into spiritual love, making "the object of desire …

---

28. Lewalski, *Writing Women in Jacobean England* (Cambridge: Harvard University Press, 1993), 244, 256, 253; Dubrow, *Echoes of Desire: English Petrarchism and Its Counterdiscourses* (Ithaca: Cornell University Press, 1995), 133. The emphasis on divine love remains central in Angela Bullard, "Love Melancholy and Creative Inspiration in Mary Wroth's *Pamphilia to Amphilanthus*," *SJ* 33 (2015): 81–102.

29. Gil, "The Currency of the Beloved and the Authority of Lady Mary Wroth," *Modern Language Studies* 29 (1999): 73–92; Fienberg, "Mary Wroth and the Invention of Female Poetic Subjectivity," *RMW*, 175–90; Brennan, "Creating Female Authorship in the Early Seventeenth Century: Ben Jonson and Lady Mary Wroth," in *Women's Writing and the Circulation of Ideas: Manuscript Publication in England, 1550–1800*, ed. George L. Justice and Nathan Tinker (Cambridge: Cambridge University Press, 2002), 73–93; Hannay, *MSLW*, 232; Salzman, *Reading Early Modern Women's Writing* (Oxford: Oxford University Press, 2006), 60–89.

30. Rosalind Smith, "Lady Mary Wroth's *Pamphilia to Amphilanthus*: The Politics of Withdrawal," *ELR* 30 (2000): 408–31.

18 *Introduction*

the ideal of love itself, rather than a human beloved." Susan Lauffer O'Hara went further, contending that Wroth's poetry enacts "the throes of orgasmic ecstasy," balanced by a "sadomasochistic obsession" and "loss of control." Paul Hecht described the "physical bliss of love consummated," leading to "rage at her seduction, and the destructive ignition of her sexual passion." For James M. Bromley, gender theory offered a fresh approach to Wroth's portrayal of sexuality: Wroth's failure to make her private erotic fantasies public entailed "an effacement of heteroerotic desire" that enables today's readers to question the very notion of heteronormativity. Finally, in "Re-Imagining Mary Wroth through Fiction," Naomi Miller explained that recent criticism "deeply influenced [her] representation of Wroth, both as a passionately sensual woman who concealed her passion in her poetry, and as a committed and successful musician."[31]

As this overview attests, there is an impressive body of literary criticism devoted to the 1621 printed version of *Pamphilia to Amphilanthus* that praises Wroth's female speaker even as it effaces the male beloved. What we need now is a thorough reevaluation of Wroth's oeuvre that examines her private manuscript poetry and explores the ways in which it alters and expands our understanding of her printed poetry and her other writing. When the 1621 printed sequence is read alongside Wroth's autograph manuscript, as this edition encourages readers to do, Wroth's poetry looks more innovative, more erotic, and more shrewdly multivalent—qualities that are further reinforced by reading Wroth's poems with her play, *Love's Victory,* and her romance, *The Countess of Montgomery's Urania,* parts 1 and 2.

The outpouring of love poetry in the last two decades of the sixteenth century and the first decade of the seventeenth produced some of the greatest collections of poetry in the English language. The layering of private and public voices in which art shapes life even as life shapes art yielded some of the most highly wrought, tensile, and multifaceted lyrics in the history of English literature, and Wroth's sonnets and songs occupy a notable position among them. "Pamphilia to Amphilanthus" pushes against the bounds of propriety, pressuring, stretching, challenging literary and social conventions more boldly than printed poems by Wroth or other early modern women writers of her generation were yet able to do, which is why it is imperative that our assumptions about early modern women and their writing incorporate not only the public voices of their printed books but also the veiled intimations of their private manuscripts.

---

31. Moore, "The Labyrinth," 190; O'Hara, *The Theatricality of Mary Wroth's* Pamphilia to Amphilanthus: *Unmasking Conventions in Context* (Selinsgrove, PA: Susquehanna University Press, 2011), 56, 59; Hecht, "Distortion, Aggression, and Sex in Mary Wroth's Sonnets," *SEL* 53 (2013): 103, 106; James M. Bromley, *Intimacy and Sexuality in the Age of Shakespeare* (Cambridge: Cambridge University Press, 2011), 159; Miller, "Re-Imagining Mary Wroth through Fiction," *SJ* 32 (2014): 40.

The remaining sections of this introduction situate "Pamphilia to Amphilanthus" in the context of her family's contributions to Elizabethan and Jacobean culture and governance, her life, her relationship to William Herbert, and her other writing. Of course, we must not allow history or biography to delimit Wroth's poems. Nonetheless, the forces that interanimate Wroth's life and writing show that her poetry was shaped both by her personal experiences and by the historical, political, and literary moment in which she lived, when most poetry was still written for private circulation even though it might end up in print. Wroth was a master of concealment, and her old antagonist, Time, has erased a lot of what her original private lyric audience would have known without being told. Still, the intimate, unfolding lyric dialogue that is simultaneously enacted and veiled by her manuscript poems, and even more adroitly occluded by her printed poetry, shows just how intrepid and pioneering she was, in art as in life.

Family, Politics, and Literary Tradition

The title page of Wroth's romance proudly displays her illustrious family heritage: "The Countesse of Mountgomeries Urania. Written by the right honorable the Lady Mary Wroath. Daughter to the right noble Robert Earle of Leicester. And neece to the ever famous, and renowned Sr Phillips Sidney knight. And to ye most exele^{n}t Lady Mary Countesse of Pembroke late deceased."

Wroth's impressive family credentials were a smart marketing strategy, but they were much more than that. The Sidney and Herbert literary mantle authorized the publication of Wroth's poetry and prose even as it gave her the means and wherewithal to become a writer.

Thanks to her privileged background, Mary Sidney (Wroth) had access to a superior private education, a library full of great literature, and a network of influential writers and powerful statesmen.[32] The family's literary, social, and political preeminence gave her great expectations, exquisite literary taste, and powerful male and female mentors and advocates, which enabled her to surmount social mores that sought to subordinate and constrain early modern women.

Mary's uncle, Sir Philip Sidney, died in October 1586 from a wound incurred at the Battle of Zutphen—a year and a day before Mary Sidney (Wroth) was born. Following his death, Sidney was celebrated as a soldier, a courtier, and above all, a writer. His fame lived on: "Our Sidney and our perfect man," William

---

32. The extent of early modern women's literacy has been widely debated. David Cressy, *Literacy and the Social Order: Reading and Writing in Tudor and Stuart England* (Cambridge: Cambridge University Press, 1980), offered a low number. Margaret Spufford, *Small Books and Pleasant Histories: Popular Fiction and Its Readership in Seventeenth-Century England* (Athens: University of Georgia Press, 1982), and Nigel Wheale, *Writing and Society: Literacy, Print and Politics in Britain 1590–1660* (London: Routledge, 1999), argue for a higher number.

20 *Introduction*

Figure 6. Title page from *The Countesse of Mountgomeries Urania* (1621). Engraving by Simon van de Passe. Reproduced by permission of the Folger Shakespeare Library, Washington, DC.

Butler Yeats wrote four centuries later.[33] As the nephew of the queen's favorite, Robert Dudley, Philip Sidney had great expectations. Although his political ambitions were never fulfilled, he lived long enough to leave his mark on English literary tradition. His writing played a vital role in his niece Mary's imagination and self-fashioning: The fictitious personae in the title of her sonnet sequence, *Pamphilia to Amphilanthus*, imitate her uncle's influential sonnet sequence, *Astrophil and Stella*, while the title of her romance, *The Countess of Montgomery's Urania*, echoes the title of his romance, *The Countess of Pembroke's Arcadia*, which includes a character named Urania.[34]

Mary Sidney (Wroth) was named not only after her grandmother but, even more immediately, after her aunt and godmother, Mary (Sidney) Herbert, Countess of Pembroke, whose manuscript and printed works prepared the way for Wroth's own literary career.[35] The Countess of Pembroke's writings, mentorship, and patronage constituted an immense source of inspiration and strength for her niece.[36] The countess was unusually close to her beloved brother Philip Sidney. The title of his romance, *The Countess of Pembroke's Arcadia*, announces what the dedicatory epistle explains: "You desired me to doe it, and your desire, to my heart is an absolute commaundement,"[37] Philip and Mary collaborated on a metrically inventive translation of the psalms, which she completed with great creativity and skill after his death. The posthumous, pirated printing of Philip Sidney's *Arcadia* and "Astrophil and Stella" prompted the countess to edit—with the help of her assistant Hugh Sanford, who will play a key role in our story—and publish authorized versions of both works.

33. "In Memory of Major Robert Gregory," *The Collected Poems of W. B. Yeats* (New York: Macmillan, 1903, repr. 1968).

34. For an invaluable account of Wroth's literary debt to Sidney, see Gavin Alexander, *Writing after Sidney: The Literary Response to Sir Philip Sidney, 1586–1640* (Oxford: Oxford University Press, 2006), chapter 9, "Mary Wroth: The Constant Art," 283–331. Christopher Warley, *Sonnet Sequences and Social Distinction in Renaissance England* (Cambridge: Cambridge University Press, 2005), 177, sums up Wroth's widely discussed debts to her uncle thus: "Wroth's patrimony makes possible—in a way simply not available to any other contemporary sonneteer—her appropriation of the noble ideals associated with Astrophil."

35. For additional information about the countess, see Margaret Hannay's biography, *Philip's Phoenix: Mary Sidney, Countess of Pembroke* (Oxford: Oxford University Press, 1990).

36. On Wroth's close bond to her aunt, see Margaret P. Hannay, "'Your Vertuous and learned Aunt': The Countess of Pembroke as a Mentor to Mary Wroth," *RMW*, 15–34.

37. "To my Deare Ladie and Sister, the Countesse of Pembroke," in *The Countesse of Pembrokes Arcadia. Written by Sir Philip Sidney Knight* (London, 1593). For an account of the countess's literary achievements, see Margaret P. Hannay, "The Countess of Pembroke's Agency in Print and Scribal Culture," in Justice and Tinker, 17–49.

22 *Introduction*

The countess had access to the great library at Wilton House, the Herbert country estate in Wiltshire, which included a valuable collection of Italian literature.[38] She translated Petrarch's *Triumph of Death,* which inspired the Petrarchan dream vision that begins Wroth's sonnet sequence. The countess's learning, taste, and patronage helped shape several literary careers, most notably Samuel Daniel's, who apparently tutored her eldest son, William Herbert, who became Wroth's lover and most important lyric interlocutor.

Wroth emulated, and even in some ways exceeded, her uncle's and aunt's exquisite poetic craftsmanship. Wroth's own intricate metrical experimentation was indebted both to the Sidney psalter and to "Astrophil and Stella."[39] Like her uncle, Wroth wrote both English, or Shakespearean sonnets with three quatrains and a couplet (ababcdcdefefgg), and Italian, or Petrarchan sonnets with a set rhyme scheme in the octave (abbaabba) and a variety of sestets, though she surpassed Sidney by using all possible rhyming combinations and fashioning intricately interconnected groups of poems linked by carefully constructed formal patterns of songs and sonnets. Wroth's relationship to her uncle Philip's romance is far too multifarious to do justice to here, but one fact stands out: Her heroine and alter ego Pamphilia is represented as a poet/lover who inherits her uncle's kingdom.

In addition to emulating her aunt's and uncle's artistry, Wroth adapted numerous dramatic situations and generic conventions from Sidney's "Astrophil and Stella," including the lyric pursuit of a passionate, extramarital love affair; the dramatic immediacy of thoughts and feelings evolving and suddenly shifting course as the poem unfolds; the dialogic imperative of private manuscript poetry that invites an answering response; the deployment and playful critique of Petrarchan literary traditions; the self-reflective invocation of classical myths (Sidney allied himself with Cupid, Wroth with Venus); a fanciful delight in a wide variety of rhetorical figures; personae, name puns, and allegorical tales that hint at, even as they veil, links between art and life; the competing tugs of passion, reason, and propriety; intense, anguished nighttime reveries about an absent, desired beloved.

Wroth also absorbed her family's love of drama. The Sidneys were actively involved with the theater, as playwrights, amateur actors, and patrons for three generations.[40] The Countess of Pembroke played an influential role in the development of English Renaissance drama by publishing *Antonius,* her translation of Robert Garnier's closet drama, in 1592; by extending her patronage to a circle of promising writers; and by encouraging her protégé Samuel Daniel to write English drama modeled on classical principles. Wroth's play, *Love's Victory,* follows in the dramatic tradition modeled and advocated by her aunt.

38. See Joseph L. Black's splendid essay, "The Sidneys and Their Books," *ARC,* 2:4.

39. Salzman, "Lady Mary Wroth's Poetry," *ARC,* 2:253.

40. See Arthur Kinney's illuminating study, "The Sidneys and Public Entertainments," *ARC,* 1:241–59.

Introduction 23

Mary's father, Robert, who was Philip's and Mary's younger brother, shared the family's literary and political aspirations.[41] As a young man, Robert traveled in Italy, where he apparently acquired some twenty volumes of Italian poetry and poetics preserved in the Sidney family library at Penshurst, replicating many of the holdings in his sister's library at Wilton. As a result, Mary had ready access to the classics of Renaissance literary tradition. She also read at least some of the manuscript poems written by her father, which remained unpublished until 1984. Wroth's "a crowne of Sonetts dedicated to Love" (MS 82–MS 95[42]), a formal tour de force and one of the most widely discussed parts of her sequence, was inspired by her father's unfinished corona. Wroth's fourteen interlocking sonnets repeat the last line of one sonnet (sometimes with a slight variation) in the first line of the following poem, coming full circle when the fourteenth line of the fourteenth sonnet reprises the first line of the first sonnet.

Mary Sidney's marriage to Henry Herbert, the second Earl of Pembroke, cemented the powerful multigenerational bond between the Sidneys and the Herberts.[43] Robert Sidney hoped his political prospects would improve when his nephew, William Herbert, was invited to court in July 1599 by his godmother, Queen Elizabeth. At first, Rowland Whyte, Robert Sidney's estate manager and trusted advisor, wrote that Herbert "was much blamed for his cold and weak manner of pursuing her Majesty's favor," but before long Whyte reported that Herbert had mastered the art of courtship and "was much bound to her Majesty for her gracious favor."[44]

Upon the death of his father on January 19, 1601, William Herbert became the third Earl of Pembroke and one of the wealthiest men in England. Herbert's prospects plummeted when Mary Fitton, Queen Elizabeth's maid of honor, was revealed to be carrying his child in January, 1601. Herbert admitted his paternity but refused to marry Fitton, despite pressure from the queen. When he remained adamant, he was sent to the Fleet prison in March, 1601, released a month later, and placed under house arrest. William Herbert's intimacy with his cousin Mary

---

41. For additional information, see Millicent V. Hay, *The Life of Robert Sidney, Earl of Leicester (1563–1626)* (Washington, DC: Folger Books, 1984).

42. MS 82–MS 95 are the consecutive numbers added to Wroth's manuscript poems in this edition; PRINT 82–85 refers to consecutive numbers added to Wroth's printed poems. For more information on the numbers used in this edition, as well as Wroth's own numbers, see "Editorial Principles and Practices," the final section of this introduction.

43. Michael G. Brennan and Noel J. Kinnamon, *A Sidney Chronology, 1554–1654* (Basingstoke, UK: Palgrave Macmillan, 2003), summarize the main Sidney family events. For a valuable account of family connections, see Michael G. Brennan, "Family Networks: The Sidneys, Dudleys, and Herberts," *ARC*, 1:3–19. I am grateful to Brennan for sharing this essay with me while the volume was in production.

44. *LRW*, 331, 350. *LRW* provides carefully edited, annotated texts of Whyte's letters.

24 *Introduction*

Sidney (Wroth) probably blossomed during this period, since the Herberts and the Sidneys visited each other even more frequently than usual while he was living at home, exiled from court.

Queen Elizabeth died in March 1603, and Herbert seized the opportunity to seek the favor of her successor, James VI of Scotland, who became James I of England. That year William Herbert, along with his brother, Philip, and his sister Anne, joined the aristocratic entourage that went to escort the new king and queen to London. The Herbert and Sidney family fortunes soared at the Jacobean court. Robert Sidney was appointed Queen Anne's Lord Chamberlain in May 1603. William and his younger brother, Philip, were made Gentlemen of the king's Privy Chamber. When the plague hit London, the new king sought refuge outside the city. The royal entourage visited the Herberts at Wilton on three separate occasions: in August, October, and again in December, 1603, when Shakespeare's company, the King's Men, performed a play. King James became so close to William's younger brother, Philip, that the king joined the intimate group that paid the traditional visit to the bridal chamber the morning after Philip's marriage to Susan de Vere. In May 1605, Philip Herbert was made Baron of Shurland and Earl of Montgomery, and Mary's father, Robert Sidney, became Viscount Lisle.

Thanks to the family's close relationships with King James and Queen Anne, the Herbert and Sidney cousins won coveted roles in several court masques—multimedia, dramatic extravaganzas acted by members of the court and high society.[45] Most importantly for our story, Mary Wroth danced the role of Baryte in Ben Jonson's *Masque of Blackness* in January 1605 and sat among the royal spectators at the *Masque of Beauty* in 1608. These heady theatrical experiences, along with her aunt's translation of the closet drama *Antonius*, inspired Wroth's own play, *Love's Victory*, with its masque-like interludes, written to be performed by and for family and friends. A manuscript of *Love's Victory* was acquired for performance at an amateur theatrical venue in the 1620s.[46]

Back at the Jacobean court, the Herberts and the Sidneys continued to thrive. In 1612 the king appointed Philip Herbert as Keeper of Elsings, a former royal palace that was serendipitously close to the Wroths' home at Durance in Enfield. As a result, "Lady Wroth's dearest friends became her near neighbors," Margaret Hannay observes.[47] Thus the title of Wroth's romance, *The Countess of Montgomery's Urania*, is not only an allusion to her uncle Philip's romance, *The Countess of Pembroke's Arcadia*, but also a tribute to the time Wroth and her sister-in-law, the Countess of Montgomery, spent together—and probably also an acknowledgment of the interactive process of writing and reading romance.

---

45. For additional information about the family's involvement in court masques, see Hannay, *MSLW*, 124–30.

46. T. N. S. Lennam, "Sir Edward Dering's Collection of Playbooks, 1619–1624," *SQ* 16 (1965): 145–53.

47. *MSLW*, 138.

Introduction 25

Meanwhile William Herbert's influence at King James's court and Robert Sidney's influence at Queen Anne's court continued to grow. Herbert became an active member of the Privy Council and parliament and was appointed Lord Chamberlain to King James in 1615. Mary's father, Robert Sidney, was often at court fulfilling his duties as Queen Anne's Lord Chamberlain. In July 1618 Sidney was created Earl of Leicester, Queen Anne's final gesture on his behalf. When she died the following March, Robert Sidney was responsible for arranging the royal funeral. Among the twenty-one court ladies who processed behind the queen's coffin were his sister, Mary Herbert, dowager Countess of Pembroke, his wife, Barbara Sidney, Countess of Leicester, and his daughter, Lady Mary Wroth.

When King James died in March 1625, William Herbert arranged the royal funeral and processed directly in front of the coffin. Robert Sidney's responsibilities at court came to an end with Queen Anne's death, but Herbert's political influence outlasted the Jacobean regime. At King Charles's coronation the following February, William Herbert carried the crown and his brother, Philip, carried the spurs. In 1626 William was appointed Lord Steward of King Charles's household, and Philip inherited the role of Lord Chamberlain.

William Herbert was not only one of the wealthiest and most powerful courtiers of his era, but he was also its most prominent literary patron.[48] He was appointed Chancellor of Oxford University in 1617, and gave one hundred pounds to the new Bodleian Library, to which he later donated his significant collection of Greek manuscripts. William Herbert is the leading contender for Mr. W. H., "the onlie begetter" of Shakespeare's sonnets.[49] The first folio of Shakespeare's plays was dedicated to William Herbert and his brother, Philip. And most salient for our story, William Herbert wrote occasional poems, many, it seems, addressed to his cousin Mary Wroth.[50]

Whether through her own role in Jonson's court masques, or her father's duties as Queen Anne's Lord Chamberlain, or Herbert's role as King James's Lord Chamberlain, or Herbert's patronage, Mary Wroth developed a friendship with

---

48. See Brian O'Farrell, *Shakespeare's Patron: William Herbert, Third Earl of Pembroke, 1580–1630: Politics, Patronage, and Power* (London: Continuum, 2011), and Michael G. Brennan, *Literary Patronage in the English Renaissance: The Pembroke Family* (London: Routledge, 1988).

49. Katherine Duncan-Jones' introduction to *Shakespeare's Sonnets* (Nashville, TN: Thomas Nelson, 1997), 53–69, makes a strong case for identifying William Herbert as W. H., "the onlie begetter of these insuing sonnets."

50. The posthumous first edition, *Poems Written by the Right Honorable William Earl of Pembroke* (London, 1660), has deterred scholars from working on Herbert's poetry because the editor, John Donne the Younger, included numerous poems not written by Herbert. A sorely needed modern edition is in the works, edited by Mary Ellen Lamb with Steven W. May and Garth Bond, for the Renaissance English Text Society. Lamb's essay, "The Poetry of William Herbert, Third Earl of Pembroke," *ARC*, 2:269–79, explains the textual challenges.

26 *Introduction*

Ben Jonson. When Jonson published his collected *Works* in 1616, he included two epigrams addressed to Lady Mary Wroth (103 and 105) along with fulsome tributes to her husband in "To Sir Robert Wroth" and her parents in "To Penshurst." Intriguingly, Jonson hinted at Wroth's intimacy with Herbert by grouping epigrams and dedicatory epistles addressed to each of them.[51] Jonson's preferred poetic mode was the epigram, but he demonstrated his regard for Wroth's poetry by writing her a sonnet. Jonson did not include the sonnet in his 1616 *Works*, probably because it praised Wroth not only as a poet but also as a lover: "Since I exscribe your Sonnets, am become / A better lover, and much better Poet." Wroth apparently showed Jonson her poems in manuscript since he specifically thanked her for the opportunity to transcribe them. Jonson's good friend William Drummond of Hawthornden wrote an ode and a sonnet praising Wroth's poetry. Drummond had never met Wroth, and was probably introduced to her poetry by Jonson, who may also have shown or mentioned Wroth's poems to other members of his literary coterie, though there is no evidence that he did so.

Beginning in 1611, Wroth was praised in print by several writers in the Sidney circle, including George Chapman, Joshua Sylvester, John Davies of Hereford, George Wither, and William Gamage.[52] Although they may not have read her poems, they celebrated her as the heir to her uncle Philip's literary fame. They were also clearly hoping that Wroth would continue the family tradition of literary patronage, because the dedications came to an end in 1614 when her husband died, leaving his widow with sizeable debts. The publication of *Urania* in 1621 precipitated a new round of tributes to Wroth's literary accomplishments and Sidney family heritage. In 1622 Henry Peacham described Wroth as the "inheritrix of the Divine Wit of her Immortall Uncle," and in 1624 Thomas Heywood referred to her as "the ingenious Ladie, the late composer of our extant Urania."[53]

The Life of Mary Sidney/Wroth

Even as a girl, Mary would have been conscious of her privileged position as a Sidney. On one memorable occasion, the twelve-year-old "Mistress Mary ... danced before the Queen two galliards with one Mr. Palmer, the admirablest dancer of this time. Both were much commended by her Majesty."[54]

51. Michael G. Brennan makes this point very convincingly in "'A SYDNEY though un-named': Ben Jonson's Influence in the Manuscript and Print Circulation of Mary Wroth's Writings," *SJ* 17 (1999): 31–52.

52. Roberts, *Poems*, 17–22, and Salzman, *Reading*, 84–89, contain additional information.

53. Peacham, *The Compleat Gentleman* (London 1622), 16; Heywood, *Gynaikeion* (London, 1622), 398.

54. *LRW*, 21.

Mary's parents were married in 1584. Her mother, Barbara Gamage, was the sole heir of a wealthy Welsh family that had close ties to Elizabeth's court. Robert Sidney was able to make this extremely advantageous match thanks to the support of his father, Henry Sidney, and even more importantly, his brother-in-law, Henry Herbert, second Earl of Pembroke. Mary was born on October 18, 1587, the first of eleven children, six of whom lived to adulthood.[55]

Herbert family records were destroyed in the great London fire of 1666, but Mary was almost certainly born at Baynard's Castle, the Herbert family's London mansion, and christened in the Great Hall there.

The castle was so large that Robert Sidney's family had its own apartment. Upon the death of his older brother, Philip, a year before her birth, Mary's father had inherited Penshurst Place, the Sidney family estate in Kent, which is still occupied by the family today. Mary spent most of her childhood at Penshurst, with frequent visits to her aunt and cousins at Wilton and Baynard's Castle.

Mary was two years old when her father succeeded his deceased brother, Philip, as Governor of Flushing, an important port five miles from the southern coast of the Netherlands—a position Robert held until England finally returned Flushing to the Dutch three decades later. His responsibilities kept him away from home for much of Mary's childhood. His absence produced a paper trail of incalculable value to Wroth scholars. Thanks in large measure to the letters Robert wrote to his wife, Barbara, and the letters he received from his estate manager and close friend, Rowland Whyte, there is "more documentation about [Mary Wroth] than for almost any early modern writer," as Margaret P. Hannay observes in *Mary Sidney, Lady Wroth,* the wonderfully capacious and only full-length biography of Wroth to date.[56]

Robert Sidney's letters to Rowland Whyte have not survived, but Whyte's letters contain detailed accounts of estate business, court politics, Sidney's professional aspirations, and family life. Even as a young girl of seven Mary showed a great affinity for reading and writing. "Mistress Mary and Mistress Kate do much profit in their book," Whyte reported in September 1595. Around the time of her eighth birthday, Mary sent her father a missive that delighted him: "I thank Malkin for her letter and am exceeding glad to see she writes so well." Indeed, Robert was so pleased with his daughter's writing ability that he promised to give her "a new gown for her letter." Later that month Whyte singled out Mary as "very

---

55. *Poems,* 6. Roberts's path-breaking accounts of Wroth's life in *Poems,* 3–40, and "The Biographical Problem of *Pamphilia to Amphilanthus*" provide the basis for subsequent studies of Wroth's life and works. Mary Ellen Lamb, "Wroth, Lady Mary (1587–1651)," *ODNB,* summarizes what is known about Wroth's life and its connection to her writing; Lamb's introduction to *Urania Abr* contains a fine short biography that explains the links between Wroth's life and works.

56. *MSLW,* xi. In "Sleuthing in the Archives: The Life of Lady Mary Wroth," *RRMW,* 19–33, Hannay describes her most important discoveries and corrects previous misprisions.

Figure 7. Double portrait of two ladies (probably) Barbara Sidney, Countess of Leicester, and her daughter, Lady Mary (Sidney) Wroth. By Marcus Gheeraerts II, 1612. Oil on Canvas. By kind permission of Viscount De L'Isle from his private collection.

Figure 8. Map of London with Baynard's Castle. From Claes Visscher's panoramic engraving of London (1616). Reproduced by permission of the Folger Shakespeare Library, Washington, DC.

30   *Introduction*

forward in her learning, writing, and other exercises she is put to, as dancing and the virginals."[57]

Whyte assured Sidney that the children were "well taught, and brought up in learning and qualities fit for their birth and condition."[58] Although Robert wanted to send the older children away to be educated, as was customary in their social milieu, Barbara was eager to keep them with her. Young Mall or Malkin, as her father liked to call his cherished oldest daughter, accompanied her mother and siblings to visit her father in Flushing on at least three occasions. Her father hated being so far away from family and friends and often sought the queen's permission to return. In 1596–97 he lobbied unsuccessfully to obtain a position closer to home.[59]

As Mary approached adolescence, Rowland Whyte urged her father to find his older daughters a husband. Robert Sidney dragged his feet for reasons that remain uncertain, although it is clear that raising money for his daughters' dowries placed a tremendous burden upon him. A marriage between Mary Sidney and Robert Wroth was broached in 1601, but negotiations were allowed to lapse.[60] Then, in July 1604 Robert Sidney began to "hastily" raise money for her dowry. The wedding took place on September 27, 1604. The marriage got off to a rocky start, as we shall see more fully below.

The bridegroom, Sir Robert Wroth, had been knighted a year earlier, in May 1603, shortly after James's accession to the throne. Robert Wroth seems not to have shared his wife's literary interests, since only one book, a treatise on mad dogs, was dedicated to him. He was an avid hunter who preferred the country to court or city. When his father died in 1606, Wroth inherited the family estate in Enfield known as Durance and Loughton Hall.

Wroth was appointed to his father's position as Riding Forester, which gave him responsibility for leading the king and his entourage on hunting expeditions in Essex forest. In "To Sir Robert Wroth," Ben Jonson lauds Wroth as the king's host and hunting companion: "oft roused for thy master's sport / Who, for it, makes thy house his court." Despite the epigram's encomiastic tone, Jonson privately told a friend, "My lady Wroth is unworthily married on a jealous husband."[61]

---

57. *LRW*, 46; *RS*, 76; *LRW*, 67.

58. Lamb, "Wroth, Lady Mary," *ODNB*.

59. *MSLW*, 29; *LRW*, 19.

60. Hannay, *MSLW*, 84, offers several possible explanations for why "Sidney was not eager to arrange Mall's marriage and had to be repeatedly prompted by Whyte." The earlier negotiations with Wroth, discussed in *MSLW*, 99, remain somewhat murky.

61. *Ben Jonson*, ed. C. H. Herford, Percy Simpson, and E. M. Simpson, 14 vols. (Oxford: Clarendon Press, 1925), 1:142.

Figure 9. Essex Record Office, Chelmsford, Mint Binders Loughton 1/1. Reproduced by permission.

The Wroths' only child, James, named after his godfather, King James, was born in February 1614, a decade after his parents' marriage. As John Chamberlain observed, "Sir Robert Wroths lady after long longing hath brought him a sonne."[62] Despite the differences that marred the beginning of their marriage, the couple had reached a peaceful accord by the time their son was born. Robert Wroth's will, dated March 2, 1614, the day before his son's christening, named Robert Sidney and William Herbert as overseers of his estate and thanked his "deere and loving wife" for her "sincere love, loyaltie, virtuous conversation, and behaviour towards me."[63] The affection sounds genuine, though the tribute prefaced his apology that she "deserved a farre better recompense, yf the satisfying of my debts and supporting my house would have permitted the same." Along with "her books and furniture of her studdye and closett," Wroth bequeathed his wife £23,000 of debts, much of which had been incurred by his father while serving at Elizabeth's court.[64]

On March 14, 1614, only five weeks after the birth of his son, Robert Wroth died from "a gangrene *in pudendis*."[65] His death may have been caused by tes-

---

62. *Letters of John Chamberlain*, ed. Norman E. McClure, 2 vols. (Philadelphia: American Philosophical Society, 1939), 1:512.

63. Quoted in *Poems*, 23.

64. *MSLW*, 137, 140, 169–71. Waller, *Sidney Family Romance*, 120.

65. *Letters of John Chamberlain*, 1:510.

32 *Introduction*

ticular cancer, as Hannay suggests,[66] but it was more likely just what the phrase declares: a virulent gangrenous infection of the genitals that quickly becomes fatal. Mary Wroth repaid half of her husband's debts during the first year after his death. But then, little James died on July 5, 1616—a heavy blow to his mother, who lost her only child after less than a year and a half. Deprived of the income from her husband's estate, which passed to his uncle John Wroth, Mary Wroth spent the rest of her life valiantly striving to repay the remaining debts. From 1623 to 1631 she received an annual protection from her creditors under the king's Privy Seal.[67]

Scholars have sometimes assumed that Wroth lived in poverty and seclusion after her husband's and son's deaths; however, that is a misconception, as Hannay's biography demonstrates. Wroth continued to live comfortably at Loughton Hall, the luxurious home she and her husband had renovated and furnished. She entertained family and friends at Loughton and visited them in the nearby countryside and in London. She maintained a study at Baynard's Castle, Herbert's London mansion, where she may have written some of *Urania,* since a letter to her from George Manners, seventh Earl of Rutland, refers to "a Manuscrip" of *Urania* "you shewed me in your study att Banerds Castell."[68] After her husband's death, Wroth was courted by Henry de Vere, the eighteenth Earl of Oxford, but nothing came of it.

William Herbert married Mary Talbot in December 1604, three months after his cousin Mary married Robert Wroth. As the Earl of Clarendon later remarked, Herbert "paid much too dear for his wife's fortune by taking her person into the bargain."[69] Herbert's wife did not have an easy time adjusting to her husband and his family, it seems, because Roland Whyte's letters strove valiantly to reassure her father that all was well.

The Herberts, Sidneys, and Wroths were often together. During the summers they visited each other at Penshurst, Loughton, and Wilton, but Herbert's wife was rarely present. In the winters, Mary Wroth and her father often stayed at Baynard's Castle.[70] In 1620 Mary rented a house in London, though it is not clear what prompted her to do so after staying at Baynard's Castle for so many years. The Herberts' only child was born in 1620 but died shortly afterward. Herbert's wife lived another thirty years without providing a legitimate heir to the Pembroke title and estates.

---

66. *MSLW,* 172.

67. Hannay, "Sleuthing," *RRMW,* 29.

68. The letter is printed in *Poems,* 244–45.

69. *MSLW,* 97.

70. In "'Can you suspect,'" *RRMW,* 54–55, Lamb lists the times that Wroth and Herbert are known to have been together.

How intimate were William Herbert and Mary Wroth during these years? How and when did the family, and especially his wife, learn of their love affair? There are hints but no hard evidence. As we have already noted, Ben Jonson seems to have known about their intimacy when he published his collected *Works* in 1616. Wroth's own writings imply that her relationship with Herbert continued to heat up and cool down over the years. One thing is clear: Wroth and Herbert had two "natural," or out of wedlock, children in the spring of 1624, three years after the publication of *Urania* and *Pamphilia to Amphilanthus*. Wroth's husband had been dead for a decade. Herbert's wife was still alive.

Herbert's cousin, Lord Herbert of Cherbury, celebrated the occasion by writing "A merry Rime sent to Lady Mary Wroth / upon the Birth of my L[ord] of Pembroke's / Child. Born in the Spring." That summer there were whisperings of a widow "said to be learned and in print"—almost certainly Wroth—who had given birth to twins. Wroth's close friend Judith Fox left bequests to both children. The richest source of information is a family history, *Herbertorum Prosapia*, written by a cousin, Sir Thomas Herbert, which records William Herbert's "two natural Children by the Lady Mary Wroth.... William who was a Captain under Sr. Hen Herbert, Colonel under Grave Maurice, and died unmarried and Catherine the wife of Mr. Lovel near Oxford." Wroth and the children were not ostracized as is sometimes assumed. Instead, as Hannay's biography demonstrates, the children were accepted and supported by the family and called by their father's name. Katherine's marriage and Will's career both benefited from the Sidney/Herbert kinship networks.[71]

Less is known about Mary Wroth's later years, but she continued to live comfortably, spending most of her time at Loughton Hall. William Herbert died on April 10, 1630. Mary Wroth lived another two decades until her death in late March 1651.

Wroth and Herbert: Betrothal and Marriage

So much has been discovered about Mary Wroth's life and works over the last three decades that Margaret Hannay's magisterial biography comprises some 350 pages. Comparatively little has been written about William Herbert.[72] Their relationship raises important, unanswered questions that have provoked considerable

---

71. For more information about the two children, see *MSLW*, 152, 279–80, 283.

72. The fullest account of Herbert's life is still John Richard Briley's PhD dissertation, "A Biography of William Herbert, Third Earl of Pembroke, 1580–1650" (University of Birmingham, 1961). For a full-length modern biography, see O'Farrell, *Shakespeare's Patron*. Waller, *Sidney Family Romance*, chapter 2, "'A Free Man': The Gendering of William Herbert, Earl of Pembroke," 53–92, explores Herbert's life "in the patriarchal system ... his gender assignments—upbringing, marital arrangements, careers at court, family responsibilities, economic independence" (53).

34 *Introduction*

speculation. When did their love affair begin, and why did they each marry some-one else in such quick succession in the fall of 1604? Why would Herbert have married for financial gain after inheriting one of the richest estates in England? Why would Barbara and Robert Sidney have arranged a marriage for their be-loved eldest daughter Mary when she was passionately in love with her cousin?[73] And why did Mary assent when love and marriage were so important to her? We may never find definitive, incontrovertible answers to these questions, but it is worth pausing to scrutinize the period leading up to Mary Sidney's marriage to Robert Wroth on September 27, 1604 and William Herbert's marriage to Mary Talbot on November 4, 1604, only three months later, because their marriage negotiations have not been fully examined in light of each other and because their intricately intertwined nuptials had profound ramifications for all Wroth's writing, especially "Pamphilia to Amphilanthus," the heart of the present edition. One must, of course, proceed with extreme caution when drawing connections between a writer's life and art. Nonetheless, when read in tandem, Wroth's and Herbert's respective marriages can help us understand, or at least imagine what Wroth's writing alludes to but does not fully explain, even as her writing can help us reconstruct what might have occurred in the gaps left by the surviving docu-mentary evidence.

Biographers and editors have often wondered whether Mary Sidney and William Herbert made a clandestine marriage contract before their respective marriages to someone else in 1604, because in the manuscript continuation of *Urania* their fictional alter egos, Pamphilia and Amphilanthus, make a private marriage contract before five witnesses. Although not a church ceremony, it was, Wroth writes, as "perfect"—"as absolute beefore God and as fast a t[y]ing, for such a contract can nott bee broken by any lawe whatsoever."[74] Like Wroth and Herbert, Pamphilia and Amphilanthus are first cousins, but marriage between first cousins was not prohibited. A duly witnessed private marriage contract would have been legally binding and would have taken precedence over a subse-quent betrothal to someone else. Furthermore, a *per verba de praesenti* marriage contract, that is, a betrothal made in the present tense, and then consummated, constituted a common-law marriage.[75]

The Sidney family was definitely not Herbert's equal in wealth or rank. Robert Sidney's star continued to rise when he became Queen Anne's Lord Chamberlain and Earl of Leicester, but that was later. At the time of his daughter Mary's marriage, he could not have provided a dowry to match what the wealthy

---

73. As Hannay observes, *MSLW*, 101, "it is difficult to figure out why such a loving father should have been so blind to the desires of his daughter, who was desperately in love with her cousin Pembroke."

74. *Urania*, 2:45.

75. See Bell, *Elizabethan Women*, 33–52, and Rebecca Probert, *Marriage Law and Practice in the Long Eighteenth Century* (Cambridge: Cambridge University Press, 2009), 34.

Introduction 35

and powerful Earl of Shrewsbury offered to induce Herbert to marry his eldest daughter, Mary Talbot. Nonetheless, several of Herbert's family members made marriages for love rather than social or financial gain.[76] His father was dead, his mother loved and admired her niece, and Herbert had inherited one of the country's most valuable estates. He was certainly wealthy enough and independent enough to marry whomever he pleased.

When his younger brother, Philip, privately betrothed himself to the woman he loved and then overcame her family's objections thanks to King James's intervention, William Herbert wrote to Shrewsbury that his brother's betrothal was "as joyful unto me as any thing that ever fell out since my birth," which is rather odd considering that William's own marriage to Shrewsbury's daughter was imminent.[77] If a marriage for love seemed so wonderful to Herbert, why did he agree to a purely pragmatic match that had little or no chance of making him happy?

Herbert's marriage negotiations, as recorded in letters exchanged by his future father-in-law, Gilbert Talbot, seventh Earl of Shrewsbury, and Shrewsbury's representative at court, Thomas Edmondes, provide the first clues. A marriage between William Herbert and Mary Talbot had been broached in 1602, but negotiations came to naught because Herbert was not interested. Then, in September 1603 negotiations were reopened at the behest of Herbert's steward, Hugh Sanford. From the outset, Herbert insisted on complete secrecy until the marriage had been "absolutelie concluded or cleane broken of[f]."[78] Above all, Herbert was anxious to conceal the matter from his uncle, Robert Sidney. In November Shrewsbury was informed that Herbert had still not told Sidney but had finally agreed to do so, even though Sidney was expected to raise objections. Why was Herbert so concerned about Sidney's reaction and so sure he would protest? Had Sidney been led to believe that Herbert would marry Sidney's own daughter Mary? Sanford provided assurances that Herbert would proceed regardless of Sidney's reaction, but his uncle's opposition seems to have given Herbert pause because negotiations came to a halt shortly thereafter. It was not until six months later that Herbert renewed negotiations, writing some notes summarizing his position, which finally enabled the two parties to reach an agreement on or about July 7.[79]

William Herbert's betrothal to Mary Talbot was the precipitating factor that prompted Robert Sidney to arrange a marriage for his daughter and Robert Wroth. On July 14, only one week after Herbert finally settled with Shrewsbury, Robert Sidney wrote the first in a series of letters to his wife, Barbara, recounting

76. See Josephine A. Roberts, "'The Knott Never to Bee Untide': The Controversy Regarding Marriage in Mary Wroth's *Urania*," *RMW*, 123–26.

77. *Illustrations of British History in the Reign of James I*, ed. Edmund Lodge, 3 vols. (London: John Chidley, 1838), 1:100-01.

78. Briley, 447.

79. Briley, 450–51.

36 *Introduction*

his efforts "hastily" to arrange their daughter's marriage to Robert Wroth.[80] Herbert had visited Sidney in the interim and offered to try to raise £1,000 to move Sidney's negotiations with Wroth along. Herbert's offer is generally seen as evidence of close family ties, but it was probably also his way of making amends for reneging on his promise to marry Sidney's daughter Mary.

After informing Barbara that Robert Wroth was on his way to Penshurst, Sidney's letter continues, "My Lord of Pembroke took notice of me of your letter to Sanford." Herbert's steward, Hugh Sanford, who had been instrumental in promoting Herbert's marriage to Mary Talbot, had apparently told Barbara something that Sanford and Herbert had agreed not to tell Robert, for the letter continues, even more mysteriously, "I believe Mr Sanford will be at Penshurst tomorrow for so he told me, and I think it be to talk with you about it, but to me he hath not said one word of it." What exactly does "it" refer to, and why has Sanford "not said one word of it" to Robert Sidney? Early modern women were often involved in marriage negotiations, as Hannay remarks, but Sidney's puzzlement suggests that there was more to Sanford's calculated silence.

Sanford must have told Barbara something that made her tell her husband the marriage must take place as soon as possible, for Sidney is at pains to assure her that he was doing his best: If the money for the dowry "cannot be had now, then must the marriage be put off till Michaelmas term" (September).[81] Sidney twice expresses concern that Barbara was not well, though he does not say, or perhaps does not know, what was troubling her. At any event, the pressure to expedite matters was definitely not coming from the Wroths, because Sidney's next letter to Barbara, written only two days later, reports that "both the father and son think the marriage cannot well be till about the beginning of Michaelmas term." As Sidney indicates but does not explain, it was Sanford who created the sense of urgency: "I have perused Mr Sanford's letter and do send it back to you again, and my judgment of it is that there will be some difficulty in procuring the money hastily.... I do not doubt of Mr Sanford since he writes so directly." Given Sanford's longstanding relationship with the Countess of Pembroke and William Herbert, one cannot help but wonder why Sidney felt it was necessary to reassure Barbara and himself that Sanford could be trusted. Sidney was expecting to see Sanford soon, but he nonetheless wrote a brief addendum, dated the same day, urging his wife to "write a letter of thanks to Mr Sanford and let him know that he shall hear shortly from you again"[82]—a further indication that Sidney was not fully privy to what Sanford was confidentially telling Barbara.

On September 27, 1604, shortly before her eighteenth birthday, Mary Sidney married Robert Wroth at Penshurst. There are no letters describing the event,

---

80. The letters are printed in *CRS*, 115–23.

81. *CRS*, 115.

82. *CRS*, 116, 117.

since the family had come together for the ceremony. Two weeks later Robert was back in London, writing to Barbara, who was still not well and worried about something. Sidney writes that he was "trouble[d]" by the "word of grief" appended to her last letter: "I do not understand, neither cannot conceive except it be touching that which you told me somewhat of, the morning which I came away. If it be so, I must confess it a great misfortune unto us all: and yet I see no reason why we may not have hope of amendment of it."[83] Why did Barbara wait until after their daughter was safely married to tell her husband what was worrying her? Probably, she didn't want to upset him since Mall, as he liked to call his oldest daughter, had always been such a favorite. And Barbara wouldn't have wanted to burden him with information that would have complicated his negotiations with the Wroths.

Whatever "it" was, it was probably connected to what Barbara learned from Sanford that they kept from Robert, because even at this juncture Barbara has only belatedly told him "somewhat" of "it," and only after the wedding, on the morning of his departure. Sidney goes on to warn Barbara that if the reason for her "grief" is what she confided to him before he left, then it must "be very secret kept and that by no circumstance be discovered." Once again, Sidney does not provide even the slightest hint about what "it" is, but he clearly thought that it would be "a great misfortune" to the entire family were it to be discovered.[84]

The very next day Sidney wrote Barbara from London to report that his new son-in-law Wroth had appeared for a man-to-man talk: "I find by him that there was somewhat that doth discontent him: but the particulars I could not get out from him: only that he protests that he cannot take any exceptions to his wife nor her carriage towards him. It were very soon for any unkindnesses to begin." While hoping that Barbara could help ameliorate the situation, Robert was still extremely anxious to keep the whole matter secret, "For mine enemies would be very glad for such an occasion to make themselves merry at me."[85] Most likely, Wroth's "discontent" arose from his new wife's refusal to consummate the marriage, because his "protests" that "he cannot take any exceptions to his wife nor her carriage towards him" imply that he was not willing to except or excuse his wife from conjugal relations, the debt every spouse was owed according to the church and the law.[86] Together, Wroth's "discontent" and Sidney's fear of "unkindnesses" (meaning the absence of affection, unthankfulness, even hostility) suggest

83. *CRS*, 122.

84. *CRS*, 122.

85. *CRS*, 123.

86. Hannay, *MSLW*, 107–8, speculates that Robert Wroth may have been displeased to discover that Mary Sidney and William Herbert had "sometime in the past, made a *de praesenti* wedding pact," or that she had refused to consummate the marriage, or that "Robert Wroth had discovered that his wife was not a virgin."

38 *Introduction*

that there was "somewhat" more to the story than Sidney knew—or was willing to commit to writing.

Together, the documents pertaining to Herbert's and Sidney's marriage negotiations leave us with questions we have not yet answered. Why did Herbert agree to a purely pragmatic marriage with Mary Talbot when a marriage for love was the happiest thing he could imagine? What did Hugh Sanford tell Barbara Sidney to make her so anxious to marry her daughter "hastily"? Why did Barbara's "grief" persist even after the wedding? And what did she then tell her husband that made him fear "it" could bring misfortune and dishonor to the entire family?

Herbert's "Elegy" and Wroth's "Penshurst Mount": The Poetics of Secrecy

The private manuscript versions of two poems, "Elegy" by William Herbert and "Penshurst Mount," written by Mary Sidney/Wroth in response to Herbert's "Elegy," help explain what Robert Sidney's letters simultaneously allude to and elide.[87] Together, the poems provide important corroboration that Herbert and Wroth carried on a private lyric dialogue that began before their respective marriages. Equally important, the poems provide a justification and methodology for reading "Pamphilia to Amphilanthus" as one side of a covert lyric dialogue between Mary Sidney/Wroth and her first cousin, William Herbert, third Earl of Pembroke.

Herbert's "Elegy" is an occasional poem, an intervention that seeks to influence events in which the poem is embroiled. "To engage Pembroke's poems," that is, Herbert's poems, "requires attentiveness to the social circumstances which prompted them, and to the social circumstances which they in turn prompted," Mary Ellen Lamb writes. "Pembroke's poems were meant to be read by a specific reader or readership for a specific purpose, perhaps to respond to an encounter or to manipulate a certain situation in the poet's favor."[88] Why then did Herbert write "Elegy," and what kind of response was he trying to elicit?

Herbert's account begins by stressing the confidential nature of their relationship and their intimate knowledge of each other's lives and families: "Wee have bynn private, and thou know'st of mine / (which is even all) as much as I of thine." The lovingly detailed description of their nighttime trysts in an enclosed garden room, concealed by a row of espaliered trees atop a mount or hill, matches

---

87. The unexpurgated manuscript versions of Herbert's "Elegy," Huntington Library, MS HM 198, Part 2, fol. 105r–v, and Wroth's "Penshurst Mount," British Library, MS Additional 23229, fol. 91r–92r, appear in appendix 1.

88. Lamb, "Poetry of William Herbert," *ARC*, 2:271.

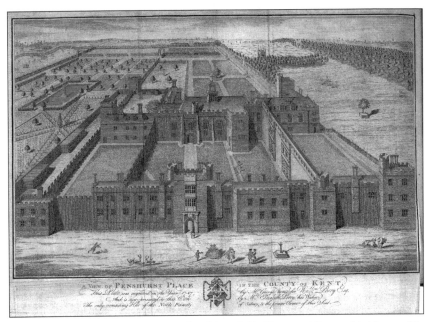

Figure 10. Penshurst Place in 1757. From Edward Hasted, *The History and Topographical Survey of the County of Kent* (Canterbury, 1778–1799). Reproduced by permission of the Folger Shakespeare Library, Washington, DC.

the topography of Penshurst, where Mary Sidney was raised and her cousin Will often visited, sometimes as often as three or four times a week.[89]

"Penshurst Mount," the title Wroth appended to the manuscript of her answer poem, confirms the location, though Wroth omitted the title when she published the poem in *Urania*.[90]

Most importantly, as Garth Bond has shown, the manuscript version of Herbert's "Elegy" describes a clandestine marriage contract: "whereon the powers of the night may oft have seene us, / and heard the contracts, that have binn betweene us."[91] The hushed secrecy acquires even greater significance from the fact that these key lines were omitted from the 1660 printed text, probably because, as the poem goes on to explain, they consummated their vows under the watchful eyes of heaven:

> and unrequired thou solemly did'st sweare
> (Of which avenging heaven can witness beare).
> That from the time, thou gav'st the spoiles to me

---

89. *Urania*, 1:lxxii.

90. Marion Wynne-Davies provides compelling reasons for connecting the setting to Penshurst in "'So Much Worth as Lives in You': Veiled Portraits of the Sidney Women," *SJ* 14 (1996): 45–56.

91. Bond, "Amphilanthus to Pamphilia," 72.

40 *Introduction*

> thou woudst mainetaine a spotles chastity
> and unprophain'd by any second hande
> from sport and love's delight removed stand

The religious language endows their erotic pleasures, their "sport and love's delight," with the exalted solemnity of clandestine nuptials, although the threat of an "avenging heaven" and the unsavory connotations of "spoiles" [meaning the spoils of war, pillage, plunder, and rapine] hint that something had gone terribly awry.

Herbert had been away only three days when she broke her solemn oath, or so he was told upon his return: "and gav'st the reliques of thy virgin head / upon the easiest prayers as could be said / Tis true?" Herbert's explicit reference to her "virgin head" leaves no doubt that she was a virgin when they consummated their vows. Male complaints about female inconstancy were a popular Renaissance poetic genre, as well as one of the most pervasive antifeminist stereotypes, but this is not at all the sort of language one expects to find in a Renaissance poem.

The printed text replaces the question mark with a comma—"Tis true,"— turning Herbert's original query into a statement of fact. But the manuscript version of the poem pivots on the question, "Tis true?" The stark brevity conveys Herbert's desperate hope that her reply will convince him it's *not* "true." Indeed, that lingering hope explains why Herbert spent the first twenty-three lines tenderly recounting their secret trysts and prompting her to recall ("Dost thou remember?") her promise to preserve herself from "any second hande." If "true," her betrayal cancelled the "contracts" they exchanged, but how could it be true? How could she have broken the solemn vows they made to each other?

What mystified Herbert almost as much as her alleged betrayal distressed him was her careless disregard for her reputation: "couldst thou not cover it from common tongues. / But cheapest eyes, must see thee tread amisse / my Rimes that wonn thee, never taught thee this." Herbert's remark that he wooed and won her in coded poetry and that she responded in kind, using cryptic language he "taught" her to conceal their intimacy and protect her honor, provides an important methodological directive for reading their poetry as a coded dialogue. Indeed, Herbert's "Elegy" practices the poetics of secrecy it propounds, for it omits her name and anything that could definitively connect the poem to her.[92]

After the tenderness of the opening lines, the nastiness of the ending comes as a shock:

---

92. Since "Elegy" does not identify the female lover, Bond speculates that Herbert could have originally written it for Mary Fitton and later readdressed it to Wroth, whose poem is clearly a response. However, the loving reminder of "the contracts, that have binn betweene us" and the poignant question, "'Tis true?," are completely at odds with Herbert's refusal to marry Fitton at all costs, even though he incurred the queen's wrath, and was imprisoned and banished from court as a result.

> Thus doe I leave thee to the multitudes
> that on my leavings hastily intrudes
> Injoy thou many or rejoice in one
> I was before them, and before me none /

It might be tempting to read these lines as vaunting male braggadocio, but if Herbert was thinking about seeking revenge by circulating the poem among his male friends, he must have changed his mind since there are only two extant manuscripts, and one ends at line 18 with the loving account of their clandestine courtship and her promise to "mainetaine a spotles chastity." In context, the ending sounds more like an uncontrolled burst of jealous anger and a desire to make her suffer as much as he has suffered.[93]

"Penshurst Mount," Wroth's lyric response, begins where Herbert's "Elegy" breaks off. Indeed, the opening lines make it absolutely clear that she has no desire to "Injoy" the multitudes to whom he bequeaths her or to "rejoice in" any "one" except him: "Sweete solitarines joy to those hartes / That feele the pleasure of brave Cupids darts." By echoing Herbert's language and adopting his iambic pentameter rhymed couplets, Wroth signals that her poem is a direct response to his. Indeed, everything in Wroth's answer poem is calculated to convince Herbert that the rumor he heard is *not* true. "Dost thou remember," Herbert's "Elegy" asks. Of course, she remembers. His poem turned her "once blest" memories into a "torment." The apostrophes, first to "Sweete solitarines" and then to "Remembrance," are a way of pleading with Herbert, showing him how much she still loves him and indicating how much his poem hurt her without blaming him overtly—a rhetorical strategy Wroth uses repeatedly in "Pamphilia in Amphilanthus."

In "Penshurst Mount," as in "Pamphilia to Amphilanthus," Wroth deploys the poetics of secrecy set forth in Herbert's "Elegy." Cognizant of his warning to "cover" her behavior "from common tongues," she alludes to but neither affirms nor denies his suggestion that she lost her virginity "here" in the walled garden atop Penshurst Mount: "You tell mee that I first did her[e] knowe love / And mayden Passions in thys roome did move." The verbs "know" (in the biblical sense[94]) and "move" were common circumlocutions for sexual intercourse, as the clandestine trysts dramatized in "Pamphilia to Amphilanthus" reveal. But, she responds, she has done nothing to betray their vows. It was he, not she, who sullied her "spotles chastity" by representing it as "spoiles" or "leavings" for "the multitudes," he, not she, who despoiled her "honor" (meaning chastity and reputation, as well as female genitalia), which she still sees as a treasure "given" to him and him alone.

---

93. I am indebted to Mary Ellen Lamb for this observation.

94. Cf. Raymond-Jean Frontain, "'Since that I may know': Donne and the Biblical Basis of Sexual Knowledge," *John Donne Journal* 30 (2011): 157–71.

42 *Introduction*

"Penshurst Mount" contains what is probably the earliest example of the worth/Wroth pun that Wroth uses in *Urania* and "Pamphilia to Amphilanthus" to simultaneously signal and encode the connection between herself and her persona:

> Or is itt that I noe way worthy was
> In so rich honor my past dayes to passe.
> Alas if soe and such a Treasun given
> Must I for thys to hell-like gaine be driven

Together, the worth/Wroth pun, the location on Penshurst Mount, and the time frame, poised between her premarital love affair and her marriage ("Must I ..."), suggest that Mary Sidney wrote her response to Herbert's "Elegy" when she was desperately hoping to convince him that she *was* "worthy" of the "rich honor" of becoming his wife but feared she would "be driven" to marry Robert Wroth because Herbert had been mistakenly led to believe that she was in "noe way worthy." The visual pun on "Treasun/r," which vacillates between treasure and treason,[95] shows how "hell-like" it was for her to see their treasured vows besmirched by traitorous untruth.

How might the events recounted in "Elegy" and "Penshurst Mount" relate to or illuminate the marriage negotiations examined above? And conversely, how might those negotiations illuminate the lyric dialogue between William Herbert and Mary Sidney/Wroth? Since "Elegy" recounts Herbert's return from a voyage to "a forraine kingdome," it was probably written after Herbert went to escort King James to the English court in April 1603.[96] Significantly, it was only a few months later, in September 1603, that Sanford reopened marriage negotiations with Shrewsbury. If Herbert had been led to believe that Mary Sidney (Wroth) broke "the contracts, that have binn between us," that would explain why he reluctantly agreed to let Sanford reopen negotiations with the Talbots even though, as the impassioned reminiscences that begin "Elegy" suggest, he was still deeply in love with his cousin Mary Sidney. Herbert would most likely have asked his trusted steward Hugh Sanford to deliver "Elegy" to her. We know she received it since she clearly wrote "Penshurst Mount" in response. But if her reply failed to reach Herbert, he might well have concluded that her silence confirmed the charges against her, which would explain why the poignant and pivotal question

---

95. I'm grateful to Steven May for this observation.

96. On Herbert's whereabouts, see Bond, "Amphilanthus to Pamphilia," 60–61. Since Herbert never reached Scotland, Bond does not think the poem refers to Herbert's journey to meet King James; however, his reservations are based on an overly narrow definition of the words "forraine kingdome" which aptly describe James' transition from king of Scotland to king of England, since "kingdom" meant, primarily, kingly function, authority, or domain, and "foreign" meant distant or situated outside an estate, manor, district, parish, province, country, or kingdom.

"tis true?" became a pained statement of fact, "tis true," in the expurgated, printed text. Indeed, there's such a disconnect between the tenderness Herbert expresses in lines 1–18 and the vituperation of the ending that I can't help but wonder whether Herbert added the final lines after failing to receive the reassurances he hoped to elicit by his question, "Tis true?"

Herbert's dashed hopes elucidate the surprisingly tactless and otherwise inexplicable letter he wrote to his future father-in-law a few weeks before his own marriage in which he reports "that which is as joyful unto me as any thing that ever fell out since my birth... . The matter in brief is that, after long love, and many changes, my brother on Friday last was privately contracted to my Lady Susan [de Vere], without the knowledge of any of his or her friends" (meaning family as well as friends). "On Saturday she acquainted her uncle [Cecil] with it, and he me."[97] If William Herbert and Mary Sidney had also exchanged "private" marriage "contracts" and subsequently received their family's blessing, that would explain why Herbert was so sure Robert Sidney would object to his marriage negotiations with Shrewsbury. If, moreover, Herbert was heartbroken by the breakup of his own lovers' "contracts," that would also explain why he was inordinately moved when his brother's clandestine betrothal succeeded as his own had not.

Herbert would almost certainly have asked Sanford to deliver "Elegy." If Sanford shared its contents with Barbara Sidney, she would have been readily persuaded of the need to arrange a marriage "hastily," before rumors of her daughter's sexual transgressions besmirched her honor and ruined her marriage prospects. Since it would have been virtually impossible to squelch rumors once they began to circulate, Barbara's "grief" would have naturally persisted even after the wedding, and the threat to the family's honor would surely have upset her husband, impelling him to write, "If it be so, I must confess it a great misfortune unto us all." Furthermore, if Mary Sidney made a sacred vow to remain true to Herbert—"thou solemly did'st sweare," Herbert's "Elegy" reminded her, "thou woudst mainetaine a spotles chastity / and unprophain'd by any *second* hande"— she would have felt honor-bound not to pay her conjugal debt to Robert Wroth, the "second" man to whom she gave her hand, who would have had every reason to complain that he would not make an "exception" for her.

Robert and Mary Wroth seem to have reached a peaceful accord by the time he wrote his will a decade later. Nonetheless, the marriage began so badly that it tore Mary Sidney/Wroth's life apart, haunted her memory, and fueled her imagination, producing seismic rifts that reverberated throughout her writing. The surviving documents reveal interlocking strands of a marriage plot, rife with secrets, rumormongering, betrayal, and villainy. And yes, despite its antique literary flavor, villainy is not too strong a word, as we shall see when we turn to *Love's Victory* and *Urania*. But first, we need to look more closely at Wroth's songs and

97. *Illustrations*, 1:100-01.

44 *Introduction*

sonnets. Herbert's "Elegy" and Wroth's "Penshurst Mount" comprise a pre-text, an ur-tale or backstory, that reverberates throughout Wroth's writing, especially, and most importantly for this edition, in the poems that begin "Pamphilia to Amphilanthus."

"Pamphilia to Amphilanthus" in Manuscript

Most English Renaissance lyric poems, including Sidney's "Astrophil and Stella," Spenser's "Amoretti," Shakespeare's *Sonnets*, and Donne's "Songs and Sonnets," were originally written not for print but for a private audience of family, friends, fellow writers, or patrons. Wroth's "Pamphilia to Amphilanthus" is firmly situated in this manuscript tradition. As indicated by the closural signs and distinctive numbering reproduced in this edition, Wroth's poems originally existed as individual lyrics and groups of lyrics that she collected and transcribed onto the paper that became MS V.a.104, which she then revised and culled for print.

"Pamphilia to Amphilanthus" opens with a haunting Petrarchan dream vision of "bright Venus Queene of love" and her son Cupid:

> Butt one hart flaming more then all the rest
> > the goddess held, and putt itt to my brest
> > deare sonne, now shute sayd she: thus must wee winn

> Hee her obay'd, and martir'd my poore hart,
> > I, waking hop'd as dreames itt would depart
> > Yett since: O mee: a lover have I binn $

Wroth's self-consciously artful portrayal of Venus and Cupid announces that her writings are imaginative constructions, rooted in literary tradition but capable of transformative metamorphosis. By invoking Venus, the iconic embodiment of elemental passion and the champion of erotic pleasure, Wroth differentiates Pamphilia from Stella and all the other Renaissance sonnet ladies who remained distant, unattainable objects of desire.[98] From the outset, Pamphilia is represented as "a lover"; she speaks and actively seeks the joys of reciprocal love, which is all the more astonishing when we remember that Renaissance women were brought up to guard their chastity as their life.

In "Astrophil and Stella" Cupid is a mischievous figure whose impish games inspire some of Sidney's wittiest sonnets. Astrophil tries to turn Stella into an

---

98. As Christine Kondoleon writes in the introduction to *Aphrodite and the Gods of Love*, ed. Christine Kondoleon with Phoebe C. Segal (Boston: MFA Publications, 2011), 11, Greek art depicts Venus's counterpart "Aphrodite in her multivalent roles as adulterous seductress; instigator of sexual desire; mother of the mischievous Eros and to the sexual outliers Hermaphrodite and Priapos; patroness of brides, seafarers, and warriors; and an agent of political harmony." Catherine Belsey, "The Myth of Venus in Early Modern Culture," *ELR* 42 (2012): 179–202, also explores Venus's many roles.

acolyte of Venus—"Onely to you her Scepter *Venus* granteth"—but the more he urges Stella to recognize and act on her Venerian impulses, the more adamantly she resists until he is forced to concede: "*Venus* is taught with *Dian's* wings to flie: / I must no more in thy sweet passions lie."[99] By contrast, Wroth begins her sonnet sequence by representing Venus as her muse and mentor. Cupid stokes Pamphilia's "burning," "flaming" heart, and he does so at Venus's command.

Venus's power over Cupid—and Pamphilia—emerges even more clearly in MS 4: "to shoote wthout her leave they [the gods] him [Cupid] forbid / hee this observ'd, and since obays her will." Since "will" means not only intention but also sexual desire, MS 4 playfully suggests what the mythological figures imply: Pamphilia's clandestine love for Amphilanthus is as sexual as Venus's love for Mars or Cupid's love for Psyche.[100] These lines become even more revelatory, and potentially scandalous, when we realize that "will" is one of many puns on Will that connect Amphilanthus with Wroth's cousin and lover, William Herbert, a coded allusion that, along with the paean to Venus, explains why this is one of six poems Wroth decided not to include either in the 1621 *Urania* or the printed collection of her poetry.

Most Wroth scholars have accepted and many have reiterated Roberts's claims that Amphilanthus is a shadowy figure and that the language of wooing is absent from *Pamphilia to Amphilanthus*. But that is a misapprehension. Wroth doesn't write *about* Amphilanthus because her poems are addressed *to* Amphilanthus, much as Donne's "Songs and Sonnets" do not describe his beloved because they are written to her and for her rather than about her. In Wroth's autograph manuscript, Pamphilia courts Amphilanthus in poetry, even as Mary Sidney/Wroth and William Herbert wooed each other in poetry.

When one conceptualizes "Pamphilia to Amphilanthus" not as a collection of poems written for the reading public but as individual poems or groups of poems written for a private lyric audience and assembled later, one begins to notice elocutionary cues that indicate the original dramatic situation and, especially, the target audience.[101] Many of Wroth's songs and sonnets are performative, designed to be read aloud, recited, or sung to her lover, a female confidant, or intim-

---

99. Quoted from *The Poems of Sir Philip Sidney*, ed. William A. Ringler, Jr. (Oxford: Clarendon Press, 1962), 2:4, *First song*: 16; 72:6–7.

100. Sandra Yaeger, "'She who still constant lov'd': *Pamphilia to Amphilanthus* as Lady Wroth's Indictment of Male Codes of Love," *Sidney Newsletter* 10 (1990), 89, argues that "like her uncle" Wroth "demonstrates the harms inherent in a society which devalues the wholesomeness of wedded sexual love." Yaeger does not even consider the possibility that Wroth's poems could have been about extramarital love.

101. For a review of anthropological studies of performance theory and elocutionary cues, see Richard Bauman and Charles L. Briggs, "Poetics and Performance as Critical Perspectives on Language and Social Life," *Annual Review of Anthropology* 19 (1990): 59–88.

46 *Introduction*

ate family and friends who have come together upon a specific occasion. Some are epistolary, to communicate with her lover during his absence. Some address him directly, using the second person pronouns "thou" and "you." Others address him indirectly, in ways that would be understood by him, or could be explained to him, while being concealed from unwitting readers. Some petition mythological figures such as Venus and Cupid or abstractions such as Love and Night, although these apostrophes generally morph into a lover's dialogue that is addressed either covertly or explicitly to "you." Some, like MS 3, are deeply private, meant to be hidden away, "Lodg[ed] in that brest" where she has already sent her heart. Still others, such as MS 7, address her listeners or readers indirectly through pastoral song that would have been understood one way by her lover and their confidants and another way by unwitting members of the lyric audience. The dialogic, covert nature of pastoral, combined with the self-conscious artistry and self-reflexivity of a pastoral persona who sings and writes about singing and writing, epitomizes the ways in which "Pamphilia to Amphilanthus" combines literary tradition with a poetics of secrecy to make something new.[102]

Like William Herbert's poems, Wroth's manuscript poems can be usefully understood as occasional—as interventions in circumstances and events they do not explain because their audience already knew what was happening, or because the poem was seeking an account of or a reaction to circumstances the speaker could not control or did not fully understand, or because the state of affairs was too sensitive to reveal.[103] Much as Robert Sidney's letters about his daughter's marriage allude to hopes, anxieties, and grievances they omit, Wroth's manuscript poems are at once allusive and elusive. When the dramatic situation blurs the literal and the symbolic, or a perfectly lucid octave culminates in a baffling sestet, or a seemingly conventional trope veers into mystifying obliquity, that is the tip-off that Wroth is negotiating something too vital and audacious to express openly.

Like so many of Wroth's manuscript poems, MS 10 couches the dramatic situation in abstraction, illustrating the ways in which Wroth's poems would have meant different things to different members of her lyric audience, depending on what they did or did not know. While the printed text seems to address us all, the manuscript poem addresses an intimate group of family and friends who have come together to celebrate a festive occasion:

> Bee you all pleas'd? your pleasures grieve nott mee;
> Doe you delight? I envy nott your joy;

---

102. See Lamb, "Poetry of William Herbert," and Ilona Bell, "'A too curious secrecie': Wroth's Pastoral Song and *Urania*," *SJ* 31 (2013): 23–50.

103. As Meredith Anne Skura writes in *Tudor Autobiography: Listening for Inwardness* (Chicago: University of Chicago Press, 2008), 9, "Tudor autobiography, in particular is occasional. It emerges from an act defined by a particular setting and a specific audience."

have you content? contentment w^t you bee:
hope you for bliss; hope still, and still injoye:

As indicated by the repeated "you"s, which are stressed by the iambic rhythm and the reinforcing "your"s, this is a performance piece. Indeed, *copia*, or repetition and variation to expand upon a point, is one of the most characteristic features of oral literature. The reiterated short questions and pointed answers make the point all too clear: The speaker wants her listeners to know that she does not share their happiness. But why not? And if their "pleasures" are not, as the first line declares, the cause of her grief, what is? Moreover, what is the tone: warmly welcoming or bitterly sarcastic?

The dramatic situation becomes clearer as the poem unfolds:

Joyes are beereav'd, and harmes doe only tarry;
dispaire takes place, disdaine hath gott the hand;
yett firme love holds my sences in such band
as since dispise'd, I, w^t sorrow marry;

Then if wth griefe I now must coupled bee
Sorrow I'le wed: Dispaire thus governs mee $

Modern readers encountering these lines in print would most likely read the contradictions as conventional Petrarchan oxymorons, and the conjugal diction as a metaphor or analogy for the universal frustrations of love. But when we construe MS 10 as a performance, addressed to a private lyric audience, the "hand"/"band" rhyme reinforces what the verbs, "marry," "coupled," and "wed" declare: The listeners have gathered to celebrate the speaker's impending wedding: "I now must coupled bee," "Sorrow I'le wed." Yet, the more carefully one tries to piece together the dramatic situation, the more puzzling it becomes. If her family and friends are "all" so full of "hope" for her "bliss," why does she feel "dispise'd"? And by whom? Moreover, if "firme love holds [her] sences in such band," why does she say, "Joyes are beereav'd"? And what purpose could such a performance serve?

Robert Sidney's letters indicate that William Herbert was at Penshurst for his cousin Mary's wedding. Let's imagine that Mary Sidney wrote and performed MS 10 at least in part for his benefit, since, under the circumstances, it would have been difficult if not impossible for her to speak with him in private: "dispaire takes place, disdaine hath gott the hand." As Herbert would have understood better than anyone, it was *his* "disdaine"—the disdainful fury he unleashed at the end of "Elegy" when he bequeathed "the spoiles" and "leavings" of her "spotles chastity" to the "multitudes"—that left her no choice but to marry someone else. The ambiguous syntax, puzzling logical and causal connections, and untethered abstract nouns and pronouns—stylistic features that recur throughout "Pamphilia to Amphilanthus" as well as *Urania*—add further layers of obliquity, merging his

48 *Introduction*

"disdaine" for her with her "disdaine" for the man to whom she is "now" about to give her "hand" in wedlock.

When we reread MS 10 in the context of the marriage negotiations examined above, the language looks less puzzling and more meaningfully multifaceted, less abstract and more urgently persuasive. The "hand"/"band" rhyme reprises and revises the "hand"/"stand" rhyme that connects "Elegy" (19–20) and "Penshurst Mount" (41–42), telling Herbert, and any family and friends who were privy to the "contracts, that have binn betweene us," that this impending marriage fills her with "griefe," "Sorrow," and " Dispaire " because her "firme love" for him still "holds my sences in such band." Herbert would have readily grasped the covert "sences" of her words, for he alone had aroused her senses. (According to the *OED*, "senses" in the plural was first used in 1600 to mean "the faculties of corporeal sensation considered as channels for gratifying the desire for pleasure and the lusts of the flesh.")

To Herbert the opening questions and pointed answers—"hope you for bliss; hope still, and still injoye "—constitute an invitation to love. Indeed, the abstract nouns that propel the opening quatrain, " pleasures," "bliss," "delight," "content," "contentment," and "joy," are some of Wroth's favorite terms for sexual pleasure. The repetition of "still" ("hope still, and still injoye") heightens the dramatic immediacy, suggesting that if he acts quickly, he can "still" "injoye " the "pleasures" of the "senses" that united them before he was wrongly convinced that she betrayed him.

The wedding guests have gathered, and her fate is about to be sealed. The final couplet makes one last fervent plea:

> Then if wth griefe I now must coupled bee
> Sorrow I'le wed: Dispaire thus governs mee $

Everything pivots on that little two-letter word, "if." "If" only her family and friends would come to her aid, the poem intimates, they could still save her from the "Sorrow" and "griefe" of this dread marriage. Even more importantly, "if" only her lover would understand that his "disdaine" for her is a terrible mistake, he, more than anyone, could avert the looming tragedy.

Of course, there are limits to any poem's persuasive power. There is no way to insure that a performance will have the desired effect any more than a letter writer can be sure that an epistle such as "Penshurst Mount" will reach its destination and elicit the answer it seeks. Indeed, one has to wonder whether Herbert ever received her answer poem since MS 10 makes much the same case as "Penshurst Mount," reiterating that he is terribly mistaken to think she betrayed the sacred vows she made to him.

When one pauses to imagine the ways in which Wroth's manuscript poems would have engaged the various members of her private lyric audience, her poems become less general and more individuated, less hazy and more knowingly multifaceted, less conventionally Petrarchan or Neoplatonic and more urgently, passionately persuasive. Indeed, it is their very specificity that makes Wroth's manuscript poems so groundbreaking and compelling. Wroth not only adapts familiar tropes of male literary tradition to express a female point of view, but she alters the discourse to confront pressing problems that troubled her and so many other early modern women.[104]

Some scholars have thought that Wroth wrote *Pamphilia to Amphilanthus* after her husband's death in 1614—a decade or more after the rage for sonnet writing had run its course. But if Wroth began to write her poetry around the time of her marriage in September 1604, as "Penshurst Mount," MS 10, and the other poems at the beginning of her autograph manuscript indicate, then "Pamphilia to Amphilanthus" emerged when English Renaissance love poetry was at its acme, around the time Donne was writing "Songs and Sonnets" and Shakespeare was writing "Sonnets."

The encoded drama of love and joy punctuated by periods of distrust, jealousy, and anger that unfolds in "Pamphilia to Amphilanthus" is far too protracted and convoluted to unpack here, but the moment-by-moment shifts in feeling that change as quickly as a cloud conceals the sun are among the great strengths of Wroth's poetry, as they are of Shakespeare's sonnets. Consider, for example, MS 76 where Pamphilia's love reemerges after a wintry hiatus:

> The springing time of my first loving
> finds yett noe winter of removing
> nor frost to make my hopes decrease
> butt w^t the sommer still increase $

The freshness and energy conveyed by the two simple words "springing time" transform a cliché (spring is the time for love) into a vital force that has an almost Wordsworthian power: "A motion and a spirit, that impels / All thinking things, all objects of all thought, / And rolls through all things."[105] The 1621 typesetter changed "springing time" to "spring time," but Wroth reinserted her original wording, one of only four corrections she wrote onto her copy of *Pamphilia to Amphilanthus*. In print, the movement from the first-person singular ("The springing time of *my* first loving") to first person plural ("The trees may teach *us*") sounds as if Pamphilia is singing to and for "us" all. In Wroth's autograph manuscript, however, the plural pronoun unites the lovers, telling Amphilanthus

---

104. See Ilona Bell, *Elizabeth I: The Voice of a Monarch* (Basingstoke, UK: Palgrave Macmillan, 2010), 117–43.

105. William Wordsworth, "Lines Composed above Tintern Abbey," *Selected Poems and Prefaces*, ed. Jack Stillinger (Boston: Riverside, Houghton Mifflin, 1965), 110.

50 *Introduction*

"The trees may teach us"—the two of us—"love's remaining / who suffer chang wth little paining."

That Pamphilia writes and sings to Amphilanthus, as Wroth wrote and sang to William Herbert, becomes even clearer in the next poem, the aubade (MS 77), which escaped the attention of modern readers because it was omitted from the 1621 printed sequence and from all modern editions except Roberts's, where it appears in a separate, disregarded section at the back. Whereas modern criticism of Wroth's printed poetry stresses Pamphilia's isolation, unfulfilled longing, and spiritual transcendence, the aubade leaves no doubt that Pamphilia is addressing her clandestine lover. What separates the aubade from Wroth's Petrarchan precursors is not only her speaker's female sex but also her celebration of erotic pleasure and her confidence (at least at this moment) that her love is reciprocated: "greete this faire morne wth thy faire eyes / wher farr more love, and brightnes lies." The loving tenderness is palpable, "arise, arise my only deere." The teasing playfulness arouses him in more ways than one! Morning is approaching. They need to hasten back before their absence is discovered. She is anxious for him to awaken so that they can "joye" in and make "farr more love" before parting. The word "joye," which connotes both heavenly bliss and erotic pleasure (*maiden of joy* was a common term for a courtesan), retains its erotic valence in the surrounding manuscript poems, though not in the 1621 printed text, where the omission of the aubade suppresses the double entendre.

The dramatic situation and the generic conventions of the aubade leave no doubt that the sexual pleasures promised by Venus in MS 4 and eagerly anticipated in "The springing time of love" have been fulfilled. Like Donne's "The Sun Rising" or "The Good Morrow," Wroth's aubade posits a private code of honor, of exalted physicality and eroticized spirituality that leaves Petrarchan literary convention far behind. The pun on rights/rites evokes the concept of "due benevolence" in marriage: "Let the husband render unto the wife due benevolence: and likewise also the wife unto the husband" (1 Corinthians 7.3). Wroth's lovers are justified in enjoying "theyr due rights" because, the pun implies, their love is sanctioned by a private lovers' contract like the one Herbert described in "Elegy" and Wroth recounted in the manuscript continuation of *Urania*.

"Pamphilia to Amphilanthus" contains numerous other poems that allude in carefully coded ways to nights spent making love with Amphilanthus and evading her jealous husband. MS 30 is one "Most blessed Night" when Venus has put Pamphilia's jealous husband to sleep—"Butt thou hast clos'd those eyes from pr[y]ing sight / that nourish jealousie more then joyes right,"—creating a "happy time for love" and for "joy's sports to move."[106] As the aubade confirms, both "moved" and "joye" refer to lovemaking. Furthermore, as Herbert's "Elegy"

---

106. For a very different reading of this poem based on the 1621 printed sequence, see Clare R. Kinney, "Turn and Counterturn: Reappraising Mary Wroth's Poetic Labyrinths," *RRMW*, 91–92.

Introduction 51

reveals, "sports" denotes not only entertainment and merriment but also amorous play and, specifically, sexual intercourse. Just as the aubade asserts the lovers' "due rights," "Most blessed Night" defends "joyes right," claiming that their secret love is "just" indeed—and in deed! Wroth's autograph manuscript uses the word "just" (meaning morally right; lawful, rightful; in accordance with reason and truth) and its cognates nineteen times and the word "right" or "rights" fourteen times to invoke a relationship that is at once sexual and spiritual, illicit and honorable, intermittent and long-lasting.

Of course, an aspiring poet will naturally desire more than a "dialogue of one" (to borrow a term from Donne's poem, "The Extasie"). One advantage of writing manuscript poems for performance or private circulation is that the poet could decide which lyrics to show to whom, though there was always the possibility that a poem would be read or overheard by someone for whom it was not originally intended. To "cover" their intimacy from prying eyes as Herbert advises in "Elegy," Wroth deploys enigmatic, ambiguous language so that her erotic joys would be concealed or could be denied should a poem or group of poems be read or circulated more widely. Some editors and critics have seen the evasions and ellipses that pervade Wroth's poems as poetic deficiencies—as thoughts and feelings wrenched or muddled to fulfill the demands of meter and rhyme. Instead, these moments of difficulty and obliquity are a signal to pause and look more closely. To maintain secrecy and deniability, and to enable her words to mean different things to different readers, Wroth developed a panoply of rhetorical and verbal strategies: 1) first and foremost, personae—Pamphilia and Amphilanthus and their pastoral stand-ins—that displace or veil connections between lyric and life; 2) syntactical ambiguities, logical gaps, and words with multiple, oftentimes contradictory, meanings; 3) formal devices such as the frame within a frame that comprises Song 1; 4) apostrophes to allegorical abstractions such as Joy, Hope, and Night or mythological figures such as Venus and Cupid that enable Pamphilia (and Wroth) to arrange or recall nighttime trysts while evading or deceiving prying eyes; and 5) generic conventions such as Petrarchan complaint, pastoral song, and Ovidian metamorphosis that impel and screen Wroth's most daring moves.

Wroth could have destroyed her earlier autograph manuscript once *Pamphilia to Amphilanthus* was printed in 1621, but she chose not to do so. Indeed, she may have kept her private poems safely locked away in her cabinet, as Pamphilia does in *Urania,* so that future generations like our own could read the lyric dialogue of clandestine, premarital or extramarital love that would have provoked calumny and censorship if a woman tried to publish it in 1621. By preserving what was omitted or concealed in the bowdlerized printed sequence, Wroth held open a door through which other women writers could someday stride.[107]

---

107. I am grateful to the poet Teresa Cader for this suggestion.

Pamphilia to Amphilanthus *in Print*

A premarital or extramarital love affair, presented with passionate urgency and recognizable autobiographical allusions, would have been potentially scandalous for any Renaissance poet. It was far more perilous for a woman writer because female honor was defined by chastity, by virginity before marriage and fidelity after marriage. Print called for even more vigilant methods of concealment. Having already veiled her private lyric dialogue in ambiguity, double entendre, circumlocution, metaphor, and allegory, Wroth was able to produce a version appropriate for print by making some astute, strategic changes. Together, the new poem, excised poems, targeted revisions, and reconfigured subsequences conceal the unfolding private dialogue and sexually consummated clandestine love affair dramatized in Wroth's manuscript poems.[108]

Wroth preserved the hauntingly beautiful, opening dream vision because the mythological figures and triumphal chariot create the impression of a traditional Petrarchan mythopoeia, but she removed MS 4 with its telltale pun on will/Will, along with several other references to Venus which hint that Pamphilia's love for Amphilanthus is a consummated love affair. By replacing MS 4 with Print 4, the only new poem added to the 1621 printed sequence, Wroth made the entire printed collection seem less dramatic and more meditative, less powered by youthful passion and more seasoned by woe, "All light of comfort dimb'd"—more like a classic Petrarchan equipoise of hope and fear, joy and despair, rooted in memory and perpetuated by art.

For readers privy to Wroth's manuscript poems, however, the new poem (Print 4) provides a retrospective explanation of a drama that is about to unfold in the following poems. Unlike Petrarch's anniversary poems which commemorate and perpetuate his originating vision of idealized, transcendent love, Wroth's "memory" "Of those best dayes, in former time I knew" contains a pointed acknowledgment that her poetry "change must know." The confidential wink warns readers familiar with her manuscript poems to be on the lookout for the "change" that her poems "must" now undergo.

"Most blessed night" (MS 30/Print 65) is just one example of the kinds of modifications Wroth made in reconceiving her private poems for public consumption. In MS 30 "Venus servants" are urged to ready themselves for their nocturnal tryst. By contrast, the revised printed version contains no mention of Venus, the proponent and guardian of erotic pleasure. By replacing "the Raigne of Venus servants" with "the raigne of Love for servants," and by amending "season" to "seasons," Wroth made this most intimate of poems look like a meditation on all Love's "servants" and "seasons." She then masked the poem's private meaning and purpose by resituating it amid a group of poems where Pamphilia is alone,

---

108. For a list of poems Wroth omitted or transposed in the printed sequence, see appendix 2.

bemoaning her separation from Amphilanthus whose behavior has left her feeling jealous and sad. The manuscript poems that follow "Most blessed Night" deploy and reconfigure traditional Petrarchan tropes to deal with the psychological after-effects of being discovered in flagrante delicto. By removing the precipitating event and inserting a celebration "Of pure and spotlesse Love" in its place (Print 30, formerly MS 68), Wroth made the poems that follow sound like a catalogue of classic Petrarchan woes—of frustrated "Hope," "killing griefe," "despaire," "lasting torments," "Absence more sad, more bitter then is gall," "death," and "unrest."[109] And much the same could be said for the sequence as a whole.

We have already reviewed the ways in which modern critics have interpreted the 1621 printed text of *Pamphilia to Amphilanthus*. It remains for future critics to examine the ways in which Wroth's manuscript poems alter or complicate these widely accepted assumptions.

Love's Victory

Wroth's play, *Love's Victory*, survived, unpublished until the twentieth century, in two versions. The longer Penshurst manuscript, which is still owned by the Sidney family, was printed for the first and only time in the elegant 1988 facsimile edited by Michael Brennan. The shorter Huntington manuscript, with numerous corrections and insertions in Wroth's informal italic hand, is more readily available, both in print and online.[110]

Love's Victory was probably written to be performed by and for Wroth's family and friends, among whom were several experienced, amateur players. The multilayered allusions to two generations of Sidneys would have made *Love's Victory* all the more resonant to Wroth's coterie audience. The heroine resembles the young Mary Sidney before her marriage to Robert Wroth, even as her name Musella, an amalgam of Muse and Stella, combined with puns on "rich," recalls Philip Sidney's adulterous courtship of Penelope Rich in "Astrophil and Stella." Musella's lover, Philisses, figures Wroth's own lover, William Herbert, while also

109. For a fuller reading of these poems, see Ilona Bell, "'Joy's Sports': The Unexpurgated Text of Mary Wroth's *Pamphilia to Amphilanthus*," *MP* 111 (2013): 231–52.

110. *Lady Mary Wroth's Love's Victory: The Penshurst Manuscript*, ed. Michael G. Brennan (London: Roxburghe Club, 1988). *Renaissance Drama by Women*, ed. S. P. Cerasano and Marion Wynne-Davies (London: Routledge, 1996), contains a composite text. A modernized text of the Huntington Manuscript is included in *Early Modern Women's Writing: An Anthology 1560–1700*, ed. Paul Salzman (Oxford: World's Classics, 2008). Facsimiles, with both original and modernized spelling transcriptions, also edited by Paul Salzman, are available online at the Early Modern Women's Research Network: http://hri.newcastle.edu.au/emwrn/da/index.php?content=marywroth. Marta Straznicky and Sara Mueller are currently editing the Huntington manuscript for The Other Voice in Early Modern Europe: The Toronto Series (Toronto: Iter Press and Tempe, AZ: ACMRS, in progress), with the title *Women's Household Drama: "Loves Victorie," "A Pastorall," and "The concealed Fansyes."*

54 *Introduction*

alluding to Philisides, Phili[p] Sid[ney's] anagrammatic alter ego in his romance, *Arcadia*.[111] The precedent of her uncle Philip's lyric courtship of a married woman would have been a way of enlisting the family's support for Wroth's own love affair.

The main marriage plot, Musella's love for Philisses, is illuminated by subplots that, like the subplots in Shakespeare's *As You Like It*, represent a variety of attitudes toward love.[112] The most important involves Simeana, who thinks she has been betrayed by Lissius, which recalls the allegations of betrayal that propel Herbert's "Elegy." Musella intervenes, telling the wrangling lovers over and over again what Wroth no doubt wished her poetic response to Herbert's "Elegy" had been able to convince him, that it was all a terrible mistake: "Sure some strang error is. / Learne you itt out... . Discover it"; "What so soddaine matter moves in you this woe?"; "Have no ill tongues reported fauls of you?"; "this can bee noe grownd to take / Soe great dislike upon one man's report, / [which] may well prove false?"[113]

The plot culminates in the machinations of the villainous steward Arcas, who parallels the character Forsandurus from *Urania*, whose name is an anagram for Herbert's tutor and steward Hugh Sanford, who was the moving force behind both Herbert's and Wroth's marriages. Having been falsely led to believe by Arcas that Musella was "wanton" with Philisses, "the mother" tries to hurriedly arrange Musella's marriage to Rustic, much as Barbara Sidney was induced by Sanford to "hastily" arrange her daughter's marriage to Robert Wroth.[114]

The conclusion of the longer Penshurst manuscript of *Love's Victory* brings the four couples together in marriage through a *deus ex machina*, though life failed to bring their real-life counterparts together so neatly. The comic tone and happy ending of the more complete Penshurst *Love's Victory* suggest that Wroth was looking back, imagining how she might have averted her own unwanted marriage. As Roberts aptly remarked of *Urania*, writing enabled Wroth "to narrate herself in the conditional or subjunctive mode, as she could have, should

---

111. See Marion Wynne-Davies, "'Here is a sport will well befit this time and place': Allusion and Delusion in Mary Wroth's *Love's Victory*," *WW* 6 (1999): 47–64, and Roberts, "Deciphering Women's Pastoral: Coded Language in Wroth's *Love's Victory*," in *Representing Women in Renaissance England*, ed. Claude J. Summers and Ted-Larry Pebworth (Columbia: University of Missouri Press, 1997), 163–74.

112. See Paul Salzman, "*Love's Victory*, Pastoral, Gender, and *As You Like It*," in *Mary Wroth and Shakespeare*, 125–36.

113. *Love's Victory*, ed. Brennan, 4:165–66; 4:180; 4:201; 4:233–35.

114. Rustic is usually associated with Robert Wroth, though Hannay argues, *MSLW*, 214, that Mary Wroth felt too much "affection and respect" for him to write such a satirical portrait. On the identity of "the mother," I agree with Roberts, "Deciphering," 170, rather than Wynne-Davies, "So Much Worth," who connects the mother to the Countess of Pembroke.

Introduction 55

have, or might have been."[115] If Musella and Philisses were performed by Mary Wroth and William Herbert as Alison Findlay suggests, the play "would have enacted a fantasy of paradise regained and hope for the future."[116]

Although it is difficult to date *Love's Victory*, it was almost certainly written sometime after Robert Wroth's death in 1614. Margaret Hannay suggests that it "would have been an appropriate entertainment for her sister Barbara's wedding" in 1619; however, the portrait of the mother is so negative, and her actions so misguided, that I think it was more likely written after Barbara Sidney's death in 1621.[117]

The longer Penshurst manuscript of *Love's Victory* has been generally seen as a later, more authoritative text because it contains most of the revisions written onto the Huntington manuscript along with four additional passages, most importantly, the frame in which Venus, goddess of Love, controls the action and the ending in which Venus resolves the lovers' misunderstandings and brings the four couples together in marriage. Marion Wynne-Davies argues that the Huntington manuscript is a later performance text, because the manuscript was owned by Sir Edward Dering who purchased over 220 playbooks between 1619 and 1624 and whose estate in Surrenden, Kent, was well known for amateur theatrical productions.[118] Paul Salzman has also questioned the relationship between the two manuscripts; because the Huntington manuscript ends abruptly, shortly after the climactic scene with Musella, Simeana, and Lissius, Salzman suggests that it is "a radically and … *consciously* unfinished text: just like *Urania*, just like *Arcadia*."[119]

Given the ways in which Wroth revised and expurgated the printed versions of "Penshurst Mount" and *Pamphilia to Amphilanthus*, the Huntington manuscript may well be another self-censored abridgement that omits those parts of the text that would have seemed inappropriate for performance outside the family: the framing device that gives Venus control over the plot; the passage mocking the clownish Rustic whom the mother tries to make Musella marry; the critique of the mother for succumbing to the steward's pressure to marry her daughter to Rustic rather than to the man she loved.

Intriguingly, Venus, who was known for her fiery love affair with Mars and her support of brides and clandestine lovers, reigns over the longer Penshurst

---

115. Roberts, "Knott," 126.

116. Findlay, "Lady Mary Wroth: *Love's Victory*," ARC, 2:216.

117. *MSLW*, 221. In "Love's Victory in Production at Penshurst," *SJ* 34 (2016): 107, Alison Findlay, explores "differences between individuals" that "work as a centrifugal force likely to tear the communal bonds of the coterie apart" and shows how "the pastoral settings, rooted in the soil of the Penshurst estate, provides fruitful spaces to exorcise conflicts and sow the seeds of regeneration."

118. For additional information, see Lennam, "Sir Edward Dering's Collection of Playbooks, 1619–1624," 145–53.

119. Salzman, *Reading*, 84.

56 *Introduction*

manuscript of *Love's Victory* as she presides over the longer private manuscript version of "Pamphilia to Amphilanthus." Since Venus's role is circumscribed in both the shorter Huntington manuscript of *Love's Victory* and the bowdlerized printed text of *Pamphilia to Amphilanthus,* the Huntington manuscript may also be a revised, expurgated text. Indeed, the Huntington manuscript omits precisely those aspects of the Penshurst manuscript that parallel the complicated love story that emerges from Herbert's "Elegy" and Wroth's "Penshurst Mount," Herbert's marriage negotiations with Shrewsbury, Robert Sidney's letters to Barbara, and, as we shall soon see, Forsandurus's deathbed confession in the manuscript continuation of Wroth's romance.

Since the Penshurst manuscript incorporates revisions written onto the Huntington manuscript, the Penshurst manuscript was probably *transcribed* later, but that does not mean it was *written* later. As Marta Straznicky explains, "A detailed comparison of the two manuscripts, however, reveals that their chronological relationship with one another is not self-evident, for while the Penshurst manuscript seems in many places to transcribe the Huntington text, there are also hundreds of substantive variants between the two versions, few of which are demonstrably superior to one another and do not therefore indicate a straightforward process of revision."[120] Wroth entered revisions onto the Huntington manuscript, just as she wrote revisions onto her autograph manuscript of "Pamplilia to Amphilanthus," which also began as fair copy and became a working draft. Wroth may well have revised and expurgated *Love's Victory* for performance outside the family just as she revised and expurgated her private poems for a public readership. What we can say with certainty is that Wroth transcribed the Penshurst Manuscript in order to preserve a more complete version of the play.

The front and back covers of the Penshurst *Love's Victory* are decorated with a cipher of interwoven letters that simultaneously spells out and conceals two sets of names: 1) Pamphilia and Amphilanthus; 2) Musella and Philisses.[121] The cipher connects the leading characters from "Pamphilia to Amphilanthus," *Love's Victory,* and *Urania,* offering an iconographic representation of the interconnections between Wroth's major works. Moreover, the cipher is surrounded by four *fermesses,* arranged in a diamond pattern like those surrounding Pamphilia's signature in the Folger manuscript after the first fifty-five poems, and again after MS 110, a second collection of fifty-five poems.

---

120. Straznicky, "Lady Mary Wroth's Patchwork Play: The Huntington Manuscript of *Love's Victory,*" *SJ* 34 (2016): 82. Straznicky suggests that Wroth may have been "at least partly transcribing from another, *third,* manuscript of the play, no longer extant, and thus preparing a coherent and continuous text for Dering rather than a rough draft for herself" (91).

121. Roberts, "Deciphering," 165ff.

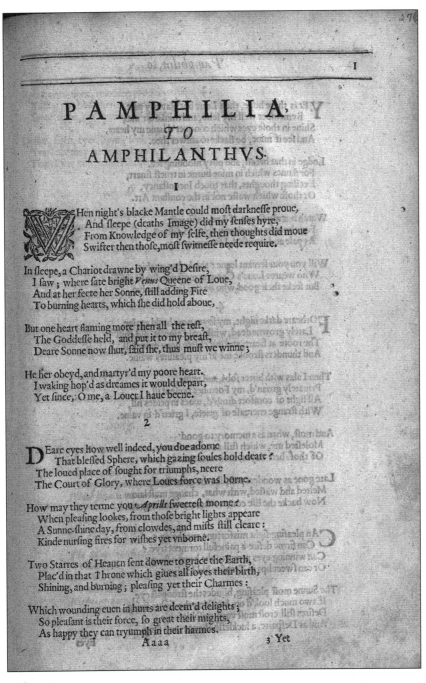

Figure 11. The first page of *Pamphilia to Amphilanthus*, as appended to *The Countesse of Mountgomeries Urania* (1621), sig. 4A1r. Reproduced by permission of the Folger Shakespeare Library, Washington, DC.

58 *Introduction*

The *fermesse*, or slashed s, which looks like a dollar sign ($), was used to symbolize constancy, particularly in clandestine love letters.[122] Thus it is probably a visual sign that the more complete Penshurst manuscript of *Love's Victory* was originally an intimate gift to Wroth's lover, William Herbert. Musella's remarks about "some strang error" and "ill tongues [that] reported fauls" would have reminded Herbert of the misprision that precipitated his "Elegy" and their respective marriages. Moreover, the similarity of the paper and watermarks suggests that the Penshurst manuscript of *Love's Victory* and the Folger manuscript of "Pamphilia to Amphilanthus" were companion manuscripts, prepared by Mary Wroth for her lover, William Herbert.[123] The cipher may also have appeared on the original cover of "Pamphilia to Amphilanthus," although there is no way to know since the manuscript was rebound before being acquired by the Folger Shakespeare Library.

The Countess of Montgomery's Urania (1621)

The first part of *Urania* was published in 1621 along with the revised, expurgated version of *Pamphilia to Amphilanthus*. The second part, which is often referred to as the manuscript continuation, survived in Wroth's autograph manuscript, ending up at the Newberry Library before being printed for the first time in 1999.

Wroth is thought to have begun writing part 1 between 1618 and 1620. It was entered into the Stationers' Register on July 13, 1621, and was being sold in Edinburgh five months later.[124] She probably read or showed episodes to family and friends while she was working on them, but the complete manuscript, comprising some 350,000 words and 300 characters, would have been far too lengthy for complete copies to circulate in manuscript. The only surviving text of part 1 is the one printed in 1621. It begins with signature B, suggesting that the printer expected but did not receive the usual dedicatory epistles that would have filled the missing signature A. The title page features an engraving by the Dutch artist Simon van de Passe commissioned by someone, most likely Wroth herself, who had an intimate understanding of the romance.

In constructing the fantastical, multifaceted plot of *Urania*, Wroth mined her own experiences along with the experiences of her family and friends, fracturing and fictionalizing their stories into multiple overlapping characters and plots.

---

122. For additional information about the *fermesse*, see Katherine R. Larson's perceptive essay, "Voicing Lyric: The Songs of Mary Wroth," *RRMW*, 121–22. I am grateful to Larson for calling my attention to Claude Dulong-Sainteny, "Les Signes Cryptiques dans la Correspondance d'Anne d'Autriche avec Mazarin, Contribution à l'emblématique du XVIIe Siècle," *Bibliothèque de l'école des chartes* 140 (1982): 61–83.

123. Alexander, *Writing*, 307.

124. *Urania*, 1:xvii, cv.

Family members and friends, including her husband, Robert Wroth, her lover, William Herbert, her aunt, Mary Sidney Herbert, and her cousin by marriage, Susan Herbert, the eponymous Countess of Montgomery, play fictionalized but discernible roles. Roberts observes in her introduction that Wroth's Spenserian "technique of including competing and often conflicting fictional representations of the same person necessarily leads to complexities of interpretation."[125] Mary Ellen Lamb further explains that in *Urania* "topicality became a sophisticated and even devious vehicle of meaning, able simultaneously to reveal and to unsettle its revelations."[126]

Wroth invited her readers to look for connections between art and life by giving her characters recognizable names: Bersindor for her father, Robert Sidney; Rosindy for her brother Robert Sidney; Lindamira for herself, Lady Mary; Treborius for her husband, Robert Wroth; Forsandurus for Herbert's steward, Hugh Sanford.[127] Some episodes reference particular, identifiable biographical details. For example, Lindamira's father, Bersindor, like Mary Wroth's father, Robert Sidney, is the "second sonne to a famous Nobleman ... who had great imployment under the King." Bersindor's marriage to "a great Heyre in little Brittany, of rich possessions," was facilitated by his brother-in-law, much as Robert Sidney's marriage to the Welsh heiress, Barbara Gamage, was backed by his brother-in-law, Henry Herbert, second Earl of Pembroke.[128] Bellamira, another of Wroth's autobiographical avatars, marries a nobleman chosen by her parents even though she loved someone else.[129] Bellamira's widowhood and subsequent loss of her young son shadow Wroth's own widowhood and son's death, as does the prophetic flash forward to Pamphilia's widowhood and son's death at the end of *Urania* part 2.[130] As Helen Hackett aptly observes, "What [Pamphilia] and Wroth require are consensual readers who will participate in the fiction that their fiction is merely fiction."[131]

By naming *Urania*'s central characters Pamphilia and Amphilanthus, and reprinting her sonnet sequence with the title *Pamphilia to Amphilanthus* and the signature Pamphilia after the first group of fifty-five poems (though not, as in

125. *Urania*, 1:xxi. In the section of her introduction entitled "Personal Contexts," *Urania* 1:lxix–xcviii, Roberts profiles "thirteen of the most important persons shadowed in the *Urania*."

126. *Urania Abr*, 22.

127. Roberts provides a brief biography of Sanford in *Urania*, 1:xcvi–xcviii.

128. *Urania*, 1:499.

129. As Clare R. Kinney writes in "'Beleeve this butt a fiction': Female Authorship, Narrative Undoing, and the Limits of Romance in *The Second Part of the Countess of Montgomery's Urania*," *ACE* 154–55, "The prose narrative of Lindamira's troubled affair ... is a complicated act of simultaneous masking and disclosure, eliding the distinction between fiction and fact, romance and autobiography."

130. See Roberts, "Marriage," 112, Lamb *Urania Abr*, 11–15, and Hannay, "Sleuthing," 28.

131. Hackett, "Lady Mary Sidney Wroth: *The Countess of Montgomery's Urania*", *ARC*, 2:137.

60   *Introduction*

the manuscript after a second group of fifty-five poems), Wroth invited the public to envision her sonnets and romance as interlocking texts. Unfortunately, the modern edition of *Urania* omits *Pamphilia to Amphilanthus* so the connection is less evident to modern readers. The romance identifies Pamphilia and Amphilanthus as first cousins, intimating that their relationship shadows Wroth's own clandestine love affair with her first cousin, William Herbert—a connection that is reinforced by numerous other love affairs between cousins. Hannay's biography cites the fact that Amphilanthus's marriage precedes Pamphilia's as evidence that Wroth altered the facts when she transformed her life into art, which she clearly did; however, the chronology is more psychologically true than their wedding dates might suggest because Herbert's decision to marry Mary Talbot precipitated Robert Sidney's hasty efforts to marry his daughter to Robert Wroth.

Together the embedded poems and the prose commentary of *Urania* constitute a poetics of secrecy that recalls Herbert's "Elegy." A Wrothian hermeneutics, or critical methodology, needs to recognize that both Wroth and Pamphilia deploy the ambiguities of love language to simultaneously express and conceal their deepest thoughts and feelings. At one point, for example, Amphilanthus learns that Pamphilia has been writing love poems. She takes him into her private closet where her poems are locked away in a cabinet. After reading them, he says, how amazing that you can write such moving poems when you aren't even in love. Wrong, she answers, I am in love, upon which Amphilanthus "caught her in his armes, she chid him not, nor did so much as frowne."[132] Pamphilia's words and actions confirm what her poems simultaneously express and conceal: her secret love for Amphilanthus. In this pivotal scene, the poems, as elucidated by the lovers' conversation, become a form of action—a precipitating event that initiates a more intimate, physical relationship.

In another scene, Pamphilia writes an encoded poem, and her friends, who know her cipher, tactfully pretend not to understand in order to maintain the fiction that her poems are a fiction.[133] Even more telling is the scene where Antissia, after seeing Pamphilia carve a poem on an ash tree, assumes that Pamphilia is in love: "'your owne hand in yonder faire Ash is witnes against you.' 'Not so,' said Pamphilia, 'for many Poets write aswell by imitation, as by sence of passion; therefore, this is no proofe against me.'"[134] But Antissia has watched Pamphilia sighing and crying while writing the poem and is therefore unconvinced. Not wanting to hurt Antissia, who also loves Amphilanthus, Pamphilia equivocates, using a series of rhetorical subterfuges to make it sound as if she is not in love with Amphilanthus. Even though "Antissia was with this answer thorowly

---

132. *Urania*, 1:320.

133. *Urania*, 1:490.

134. *Urania*, 1:94–95.

satisfied,"[135] we know differently. When we read the scene, we admire Pamphilia's cleverly formulated double meanings. The bowdlerized 1621 version of *Pamphilia to Amphilanthus* makes us all Antissias.

The inclusion of "Penshurst Mount" in the 1621 *Urania* epitomizes the ways in which the romance simultaneously incorporates and disguises Wroth's private lyric dialogue with Herbert. Wroth distances the painful personal experience that prompted her to write "Penshurst Mount" by omitting the telltale title and attributing the poem to a male character, Dolorindus, much as *Love's Victory* veils its autobiographical origins by giving the dramatic situation of Herbert's "Elegy" to a female character, Simeana. Significantly, *Urania* omits the key lines from the manuscript of "Penshurst Mount" that cite Herbert's claim that he took her "virgin head," lines that appear in the manuscript but not the printed text of Herbert's "Elegy."[136] And yet, for the cognoscenti, *Urania* hints at the poem's autobiographical origins because the prose commentary that follows the poem references the "mount" and even specific trees that locate the lovers' trysts on Penshurst Mount.

After reciting the poem, moreover, Dolorindus gives the manuscript to Amphilanthus, who shadows Herbert, the poem's original lyric audience. And most intriguingly of all, the poem prompts Amphilanthus to remember and correct the misprision Herbert himself expressed in "Elegy." Indeed, the thoughts and feelings Amphilanthus expresses immediately after reading the poem in *Urania* are precisely what Wroth hoped Herbert would think and feel after reading "Penshurst Mount": "My soule hath also eyes to see thy worth ... and this vow still will keepe, that onely thou art worthy and alone will I love thee."[137] By appropriating her poem's pointed pun on worth/Wroth ("Or is itt that I noe way worthy was") and citing the poem's apostrophe to memory, Wroth has Amphilanthus reaffirm the "vows" that she made and Herbert erroneously thought she broke when he wrote "Elegy."

Although many of the topical allusions to Jacobean society are less visible to modern readers, Wroth's contemporaries saw *Urania* as a roman à clef. In 1640, two decades after its publication, George Manners, Earl of Rutland, wrote to Wroth asking her to provide a key that would "interprete unto me the names as heere I have begunn them."[138] And shortly after *Urania* was published, Edward Denny, Baron of Waltham, created a stir by complaining to King James that Wroth had defamed him in *Urania*. Even if the story Wroth told was an accurate portrayal of Denny, as it seems to be, why would he want to associate himself with a character—the father-in-law of Sirelius—who is just barely prevented from killing his own daughter after hearing that she betrayed her husband? In his

135. *Urania*, 1:97.

136. Bond, "Amphilanthus to Pamphilia," 70.

137. *Urania*, 1:135.

138. *Poems*, 244.

62   *Introduction*

biting poetic satire, Denny refers to Wroth as Pamphilia, showing that Wroth's contemporaries equated her with her character.

To defend herself from Denny's charge of slander, Wroth wrote a mocking parody of his attack, as well as several extant letters disavowing "the strang constructions which are made of my booke contrary to my imagination, and as farr from my meaning as is possible."[139] Wroth maintained that she never intended to publish *Urania,* though her disclaimer seems to have been more rhetorical than literal since she neither halted sales nor withdrew the extant copies from circulation as she offered to do. As mentioned above, Wroth corrected numerous errors in the printed text of the romance, probably in anticipation of a second printing, but she only corrected four errors in the printed text of *Pamphilia to Amphilanthus,* leaving sixty errors uncorrected, most likely because her claim that she never had intended to publish *Urania* made further publication impossible.[140]

The 1621 *Urania* ends with the word, "And," which may have been an allusion to the ending of Sidney's *Arcadia,* or a sign meaning *to be continued,* or the printer's misleading representation of a catchword indicating the manuscript's next page. Whatever the reason, part 1 breaks off where part 2 begins, with "And." Wroth seems to have begun the second part of *Urania* even before part 1 was printed in 1621, because Wroth's sister Philip(pa) died after giving birth in September 1620 and *Urania* part 2 opens with Philistella's death "with a feaver in child bed."[141]

The Newberry manuscript of *Urania* part 2 survived, virtually unread except by family and friends, until it attracted the attention of modern scholars and was printed for the first time in 1999.[142] The manuscript is a working draft of about 240,000 words, with numerous corrections and revisions, written in a more informal italic hand than the Folger Manuscript of "Pamphilia to Amphilanthus." Changes in handwriting, paper, and ink suggest that Wroth worked on the romance continuation at different times. She wrote out the prose narrative first, leaving space to insert poems later, much as she left space for speeches by Venus and Cupid in *Love's Victory.*

Part 2 revisits characters from part 1, filling in more transgressive parts of their stories. The continuation alludes to poems Wroth and Herbert exchanged by giving Pamphilia a poem to sing, "Had I loved but att that rate," that was written

---

139. *Poems,* 236.

140. Roberts did not know about this copy when she edited *Poems* in 1983, but she added Wroth's corrections to the list of variants in the 1992 paperback.

141. *Urania,* 2:1.

142. Josephine Roberts was working on *The Second Part of the Countess of Montgomery's Urania* at the time of her death; it was completed by Suzanne Gossett and Janel Mueller.

by Herbert.[143] Most notably, part 2 recounts the clandestine marriage contract between Pamphilia and Amphilanthus mentioned above. Indeed, as the editors of part 2 suggest, a bifolium that was cut out of the manuscript at this point may well have been an act "of self-censorship (especially if the pages indicated that the per verba de praesenti marriage between Pamphilia and Amphilanthus had been consummated)."[144]

Part 2 also contains the dramatic deathbed confession of Amphilanthus's former tutor and steward, Forsandurus, aka Hugh Sanford, whose behind-the-scenes maneuvering played a key role in William Herbert's marriage to Mary Talbot and Mary Sidney's marriage to Robert Wroth. Forsandurus informs Pamphilia that he deceived Amphilanthus into marrying someone else by telling him she betrayed him: "I told him, and sware to him, you had left him, and taken the Tartarian." At first, Amphilanthus refused to believe that his beloved Pamphilia could have broken her vows. Forsandurus confesses that he secretly kept the letters Amphilanthus entrusted him to deliver to Pamphilia asking her whether the story was true, as well as the missive Pamphilia asked Forsandurus to deliver to Amphilanthus, assuring him of her continuing love.

Amphilanthus was convinced of Pamphilia's betrayal only when she failed to respond to his queries. We know that Mary Sidney (Wroth) received William Herbert's "Elegy" because she wrote "Penshurst Mount" in response. Did Hugh Sanford lead Herbert to believe that she betrayed him, and then fail to deliver her disavowal to Herbert, as Forsandurus's confession suggests? But why would Sanford have betrayed Herbert, whom he had tutored as a youth and served as a young man? In his deathbed confession, Forsandurus reveals that he was "soundly bribed by the Queene of Slavonia to make the match with my lord [Amphilanthus] and her eldest daughter."[145] Did the Countess of Shrewsbury pay Sanford to maneuver Herbert into marrying her daughter, as Forsandurus' confession implies? If so, the harsh portrait of the Mother who conspires with the steward to marry Musella to Rustic in the Penshurst *Love's Victory* may shadow not only Wroth's mother but also Mary Talbot's mother.

Many of the details of Forsandurus' deathbed confession were most likely fabricated or altered to heighten the drama; as Margaret Hannay observes, Wroth "often began with true events and veered into fantasy."[146] Nonetheless, the insist-

---

143. As Lamb explains, *ARC*, 2:273, "the sophisticated topicality of Wroth's romance implicates Wroth's relationship with Pembroke in the volatile affair between Pamphilia and Amphilanthus.... this connection rises to the surface of the text in the identification of Amphilanthus as the author of this poem by Pembroke." Larson, "Voicing Lyric," *RRMW*, 128, writes, "Pamphilia's performance ... exemplifies the disturbing excess and affective force associated with the singing body."

144. *Urania*, 2:xxvi.

145. *Urania*, 2:387.

146. *MSLW*, 234.

64   *Introduction*

ent, repeated puns on Wroth/worth that pepper this scene make it difficult to deny the autobiographical subtext: "I ame the Villaine abusd your worthe and ruind my deere (O most worthely to bee esteemed deere) master, his faithe, his truthe, his love, and yours."[147] Upon being told of Forsandurus' confession, Amphilanthus is outraged, claiming that his steward's "ba[s]er treachery" deprived him and Pamphilia "of that wee both soe lovingly, zealously, and most affectionately coveted." "[H]er Vowe beeing now safely concluded without breach," Amphilanthus affirms the loving vows Herbert described so powerfully in "Elegy."[148]

The dense thicket of allusions to "Elegy" and "Penshurst Mount"—especially to Herbert's pointed question, "Tis true?" and her answer that her "honor" was "a treasun given" to him and him alone—connect Forsandurus's "ba[s] er treachery" with the machinations Hugh Sanford deployed to trick them into breaking "the contracts, that have binn betweene us" when he reopened marriage negotiations with the Earl of Shrewsbury and then convinced Barbara and Robert Sidney "hastily" to marry their daughter to Robert Wroth.

In addition to filling in pieces missing from Pamphilia and Amphilanthus's love story, *Urania* part 2 follows the fortunes of the knight Faire Designe, "one of those youths whose mysterious parentage generates intense narrative interest." Wroth's hints that Faire Designe "is Amphilanthus's son" suggest that she was hoping to convince Herbert, who had no surviving legitimate children, to acknowledge their natural son Will as his heir.[149] Any such hopes were dashed in 1626 when Herbert agreed to leave his title and estate to his nephew Charles.

The manuscript continuation of *Urania* also breaks off with the final word "and," which may, as critics have variously suggested, be a tribute to Sidney's *Arcadia*, or the beginning of a sentence Wroth intended but never returned to complete when she learned that Herbert would not make their son his heir, or a sign of a radically, deliberately unfinished work.

The Afterlife of Wroth's Sonnets

Despite Denny's attack and Wroth's offer to recall the printed copies, the 1621 *Urania* continued to circulate with *Pamphilia to Amphilanthus* in a separately numbered section at the back, winning accolades during Wroth's lifetime and in the years following her death. Nonetheless, her writing was all but forgotten for four centuries. In fact, so little was known about Wroth by the eighteenth century that George Ballard claimed he could not find enough information to include her in his *Memoirs of Several Ladies of Great Britain*. In 1825 two songs from *Urania*,

147. *Urania*, 2:386–87.

148. *Urania*, 2:389.

149. See Lamb's influential discussion of Faire Designe in "The Biopolitics of Romance in Mary Wroth's *The Countess of Montgomery's Urania*," *ELR* 31 (2001): 121–30.

"Who can blame me, if I love?" and "Love, a child is ever crying" appeared in Alexander Dyce's *Specimens of British Poetesses*. Dyce noted that Wroth was well known in her day as the author of *Urania*, a romance with poems interspersed. In 1848 Frederic Rowton reprinted the same two poems in *The Female Poets of Great Britain*.[150]

Wroth's work resurfaced in the 1970s and 1980s with the resurgence of interest in early modern women writers such as Mary (Sidney) Herbert, Aemelia Lanyer, Elizabeth Cary, Lucy Hutchinson, and Katherine Philips. Gary F. Waller published the first modern edition of *Pamphilia to Amphilanthus* in 1977. A year later, Margaret A. Witten-Hannah discussed the poems in her doctoral dissertation, "Lady Mary Wroth's *Urania*: The Work and the Tradition." In 1982 May Nelson Paulissen published the first full-length critical study of Wroth's poetry, which stressed her debts to Petrarchan poetry and Neoplatonic philosophy.[151] In 1983 Josephine Roberts published *The Poems of Lady Mary Wroth*, which reproduced the 1621 collection of poems followed by the six unprinted manuscript poems and all the poems in *Urania* and *Love's Victory*. R. E. Pritchard's 1996 hardcover provided modernized texts of the 1621 sonnet sequence and the *Urania* poems but omitted MS 4, the aubade, and the four other unprinted manuscript poems.

Two anthologies published in 2002, Stephanie Hodgson-Wright, *Women's Writing of the Early Modern Period: 1588–1688,* and Marion Wynne-Davies, *Women Poets of the Renaissance,* included modernized texts of the complete, 1621 printed *Pamphilia to Amphilanthus*. In 2005 Jonathan Gibson edited fifteen sonnets and two songs from MS V.a.104 to be included in *Early Modern Women's Manuscript Poetry*.[152] The 2007 Benediction Classic reprint, *Pamphilia to Amphilanthus,* purportedly followed the Marriot and Grismand printing of 1621, but the unidentified editor frequently emended the 1621 text, mimicking the old spelling to conceal interpolated changes.

After being all but lost to English literary tradition, Mary Wroth has attained the status of a major English writer. She was described by Gary F. Waller as "the most important woman writer in English before Aphra Behn" and by Barbara Kiefer Lewalski as "the most prolific, most self-conscious, and most

150. Ballard, *Memoirs of Several Ladies* (Oxford, 1752); Dyce, *Specimens of British Poetesses* (London, 1825); Rowton, *Female Poets of Great Britain Chronologically Arranged* (Philadelphia, 1849).

151. Paulissen, *The Love Sonnets of Lady Mary Wroth: A Critical Introduction* (Salzburg: Institut für Anglistik & Amerikanistik, University of Salzburg, 1982).

152. Hodgson-Wright, *Women's Writing of the Early Modern Period, 1588–1688: An Anthology* (New York: Columbia University Press, 2002), 143–99; Wynne-Davies, *Women Poets* (1998; London: Routledge, 1999), 183–228; Gibson, ed., "Lady Mary Wroth: *Pamphilia to Amphilanthus,* Folger Shakespeare Library V.a.104," in *Manuscript Poetry,* ed. Millman and Wright (Manchester, New York: Manchester University Press, 2005), 35–56.

66   *Introduction*

impressive female author of the Jacobean era."[153] Wroth is regularly studied in Renaissance courses, in surveys of English literature, in poetry classes, and in courses on women writers. There are numerous book chapters and scholarly essays analyzing the 1621 printed sequence. As Paul Salzman observes, "Wroth has moved from comparative obscurity to something approaching a secure place in the canon of Renaissance poetry."[154] Now that the complete collection of Wroth's manuscript poems is finally available in print along with the original text of her printed poems, both versions of her poems can receive the attention they deserve.

Editorial Principles and Practices

As noted above, Folger MS V.a.104 and Wroth's 1621 romance, *The Countesse of Mountgomeries Urania* (STC 26051), are the primary textual witnesses to the two versions of her sonnet sequence. In addition, Wroth made six notations on the Kohler copy (K) of *Pamphilia to Amphilanthus* in the 1621 *Urania*.[155] She wrote two words in the margin of Print 22. She restored the manuscript's stanza divisions in Print 21, and she reinstated the manuscript reading of one word in Print 41:1, Print 58:18, Print 59:13, and Print 73:1. These changes are incorporated into this volume's printed text, and are cited as "Wroth's corrections" in the variants that appear below both the print and manuscript texts. Wroth's attention to the printed text of *Pamphilia to Amphilanthus* was highly selective, however, and numerous manifest errors remained uncorrected.[156] Appendix 3 contains a complete list of uncorrected errors as well as stop press corrections that appear in some copies of 1621 but not others.

Wroth's holograph manuscript, comprising 117 sonnets and songs, began as fair copy of earlier, no longer extant loose papers on which she originally composed and revised individual poems. Many of the manuscript poems lack catchwords, and many of the catchwords are simply "Song," suggesting that Wroth may have decided which song to insert where at a later date. The catchword at the

153. Waller, *Sidney Family Romance*, 192; Lewalski, *Writing Women*, 243.

154. In "Mary Wroth: From Obscurity to Canonization," *Reading*, 60–89, Salzman discusses Wroth's emergence as a canonical writer. For an earlier discussion of the factors affecting women writers and canonicity, see Elizabeth Hanson, "Boredom and Whoredom: Reading Renaissance Women's Sonnet Sequences," *ACE*, 409–435.

155. This copy, now at the University of Pennsylvania library, was owned by Charlotte Kohler, who identified the corrections as Wroth's. The corrections are difficult to make out in the 1996 facsimile edition cited above, but are crystal clear in the digital edition that is available at the University of Pennsylvania website: http://dla.library.upenn.edu/dla/print/pageturn.html?id=PRINT_3441687&rotation=0&size=2&currentpage=557.

156. For example, Wroth failed to correct "switnesse" to "swiftness" at Print 1.4, or "Sow" to "Snow" at Print 4.12, or "may" to "my" at Print 6.11.

Introduction 67

bottom of MS 19 is "O lett," but MS 20 begins, "W^ch." Since "O lett" is such a distinctive catchword, and there are no poems beginning, "O lett," Wroth apparently decided to omit the poem while transcribing the manuscript. Several groups of poems lack catchwords altogether. For example, the first coherently numbered sequence (MS 1-MS 55) is followed by ten poems (MS 56-MS 65) without catchwords, suggesting that Wroth arranged those poems in that order as she compiled or transcribed MS V.a.104.[157]

Wroth transcribed her poems on sixty-five leaves of paper now bound into a quarto volume measuring 19 x 14 mm (7.5 x 5.5 in). This paper's watermarks suggest that it was manufactured during the last decade or so of the sixteenth century.[158] On folios 1–54, the sheets were ruled along the left, top, and bottom margins in a rubricated ink, now faded to a deep pink, that formed a rectangular space for the text in the center of each page. After fol. 54, each page was ruled along the top and left-hand margins only. Wroth transcribed the text of the Penshurst House manuscript of *Love's Victory* on the same paper stock she used for the final eleven leaves of the Folger manuscript.[159] It became a working draft when she inserted numerous, multistage revisions that were then incorporated into the 1621 version. The printed text, comprising 103 poems, had to have been based on a lost, intervening manuscript because the order and selection of printed poems differs drastically from the Folger manuscript and includes one new sonnet, Print 4, not found in the manuscript.

The printer's copy, a lost manuscript containing the corrections in Wroth's manuscript, was most likely transcribed by Wroth herself rather than an amanuensis, because some of the 1621 readings suggest confusion caused by distinctive characteristics of Wroth's handwriting. For example, Wroth's *k*, which often differs from her *h* only in its slightly indented minim, could have led the compositor to set "heart-held" in Print 6.12, which reads "hart=kild" in MS 6:12.

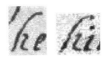   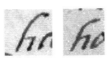

Wroth's minuscule k   Wroth's minuscule h

157. For additional details about the make-up of the manuscript, see the essays by Alexander, "Constant Works," Dubrow, "'And Thus Leave Off';" and Hannay, "The 'Ending End,'" cited above.

158. Roberts, *Poems*, finds similar watermarks on paper dated 1587 and 1602 (62).

159. Gavin Alexander noted that these two manuscripts shared "the same watermark and format," without specifying the distinctive ruling along two (rather than three) borders of each page that confirms that Wroth drew on the same stock of paper for both documents (*Writing After Sidney*, 307). Hannay concluded that both the watermark and ruling of the Penshurst manuscript matched that in Folger MS V.a.104 (*MSLW*, 218).

68   *Introduction*

The faulty reading in Print 5.9, "Eyes having none," may have resulted from Wroth's spelling of "won" as "wunn"–a spelling that the *OED* cites as a fifteenth-century Scottish or an eighteenth-century English form of the verb.

w'i(nn

This spelling appears sixteen times in F, fourteen as "wun/n" and twice in "wunder."[160] Thus the manuscript's "Eyes, hauing wunn" could plausibly have led the compositor to mistake Wroth's initial *w* for *n* and the minims following it for "onn," transliterated to "none." To what degree, if any, compositors were influenced by their copy text's spelling is uncertain and would no doubt have varied from one workman to another.[161] Nonetheless, the appearance in Print 91.4 of *"Summers pride is wun"* probably reflects Wroth's spelling in the lost manuscript she prepared for the printer (F reads "som*m*ers pride is wun*n*"). Wroth's somewhat unusual spelling of "shute" for "shoot" in MS 1.11 may likewise have influenced the 1621 reading "shut" at 1.11.

Whether or not Wroth herself transcribed the manuscript of "Pamphilia to Amphilanthus" used by the typesetter, she is the only person with plausible opportunity and motive to make the radical revisions entered onto the manuscript and incorporated into the printed text. She rearranged the poems, omitted fifteen of them,[162] added one to their number, and incorporated the final readings of F into the lost manuscript. In addition, she made numerous further revisions that do not appear in MS V.a.104. For example, she reduced the explicit references to Venus and Cupid, changed the second person pronouns from the familiar "thou" in MS 8 to the formal "you" in Print 8, converted numerous singular nouns and pronouns to plurals, and made other substantive changes in the wording, as recorded in the notes to our manuscript and printed texts. No printer would have attempted these kinds of changes. They are clearly authorial. Having gone to this

---

160. Wroth spells "won" as "wun/n" in MS 5.9, 27.9, 31.9, 35.8, 39.9, 51.3, 72.6, 75.4, 77.14, 92.11, 97.4, 101.12, 101.18, 110.12, 114.225. In MS 17.2, she spells "wonder" with an *o*, otherwise "wunder" at MS 23.6 and 55.4.

161. J. Dover Wilson argued, for example, that Shakespeare's spelling habits could be reconstructed from unusual spellings in the quartos, assuming that some of them were set from the author's holographs ("Bibliographical Links Between the Three Pages and the Good Quartos" in *Shakespeare's Hand in the Play of Sir Thomas More*, ed. W. W. Greg (1923; repr. Cambridge: Cambridge University Press, 1967), 113–41).

162. The nine "Pamphilia to Amphilanthus" poems that Wroth incorporated into the *Urania* narrative are, in order: MS 58/*Urania* 1:212; MS 63/ *Urania* 1:173–74; MS 65/ *Urania* 1:171–72; MS 80/ *Urania* 1:172–73; MS 100/ *Urania* 1:490; MS 111/ *Urania* 1:460–61; MS 114 / *Urania* 1:614–23; MS 116/ *Urania* 1:198; MS 117/ *Urania* 1:326–27. Wroth omitted MS poems 4, 77, 96, 112, 113, and 115 from the 1621 print altogether.

Introduction 69

much trouble, however, the number of errors in both accidentals and substantive readings remaining in the printed copies of *Pamphilia to Amphilanthus* show that Wroth did not read proofs as the book was being set in print.

"Pamphilia to Amphilanthus" offers the rare textual luxury of a Renaissance poet's holograph copy of her work. The present edition of Wroth's manuscript poetry therefore reproduces her holograph as closely as possible, preserving Wroth's original transcription along with her revisions so that readers can trace her development as a poet. Since Wroth did not oversee the printing of the 1621 text, we have silently corrected obvious printer's errors, incorporated Wroth's handwritten corrections from the Kohler copy, and emended other readings that would, we think, have differed from those set forth in the lost manuscript Wroth prepared for the press. These variants (based on the readings of F) are recorded in the notes so that readers can judge Wroth's final intentions for themselves. Otherwise, this edition adheres to the overall format of the 1621 first edition, presenting that text as much as possible as it appeared to Wroth's contemporaries.

Both sequences are reproduced here with the following editorial interventions. Wroth's early modern usage of *i* for *j* and *u* for *v*, as well as her long or "swash" *s*, and her doubled miniscule *ff* for the capital letter *F*, have been modernized. Line numbers have been added at ten-line intervals in the right margin to help readers discuss and cite Wroth's longer poems, though her fourteen-line sonnets are unnumbered to accommodate marginal glosses. Wroth's numbers, along with her periods and slashed S ($) are reproduced here as they originally appeared, centered above each poem, since they are important signifiers of poems Wroth intended to separate or group together. Since Wroth's original numbers are repetitive and confusing, consecutive numbers for both sequences have been added in brackets above the poems—for example, [MS 1] and [Print 1]—to help readers locate and cite a specific poem, or cross-reference a manuscript and printed poem. Bracketed folio numbers appear at the beginning of each new page so that readers can locate poems in the Folger manuscript. Scholars can use bracketed signature numbers to find poems in the original 1621 text since the printed page numbers contain several errors.[163] Appendix 2 enables readers to find and cross-reference poems using the various numbering systems: consecutive manuscript numbers provided by this edition; Wroth's original manuscript numbers; folio numbers for V.a.104; consecutive numbers for the 1621 printed text; page numbers for poems moved to *Urania*; Roberts's numbers; original poem numbers for the 1621 printed text.

Wroth's language can be quite mysterious and puzzling. The annotations do not analyze all the multitudinous ambiguities created by Wroth's lexicon, syntax, and punctuation since the goal of this edition is not to interpret the poems but to enable readers to have the pleasure of working out their own interpretations. To

163. Several copies have pages erroneously numbered 17, 20, 21 and 23, 24, 25, 24, 25.

70   *Introduction*

that end, the notes provide definitions, adapted generally though not exclusively from the *Oxford English Dictionary*, for words that are no longer in common usage; for words that meant something else or something additional in Wroth's day; for words that were commonly used in various, oftentimes contradictory ways; and for words that acquire a specific meaning in Wroth's writing. A superscript o (°) indicates glosses in the right margin that provide brief definitions or modern spellings for words that might be confusing. More elaborate or complicated annotations appear beneath the text, with semicolons to distinguish one definition from another. Since it is impossible to include every possible meaning, the annotations provide the definitions that seem most appropriate for a particular line of verse. As a result, definitions of a given word may vary from one poem, or even one line to another. Readers should consult the *OED* for additional meanings that could illuminate or substantiate their own interpretations of a particular poem. Readers of the 1621 printed text should turn to the manuscript for glosses and annotations.

In accordance with the Other Voice series guidelines, both annotations and textual notes appear in running footnotes, one set for the manuscript and a second, separately numbered set for the printed poems. Footnotes for the manuscript text include: annotations too long or complex for marginal glosses; variants from the 1621 printed text; changes Wroth wrote onto the manuscript, including numerous places not noted in Roberts's list of variants where Wroth overwrote letters, either to correct a transcription error or to form a new word. Footnotes to the printed text list differences between the manuscript and printed text, including places where overwritten letters from the manuscript produced new words that were incorporated into the printed text. Both sets of footnotes omit overwritten letters where the writing is not sufficiently clear to discern a substantive revision. Variant readings listed in the footnotes record substantive differences between the manuscript and printed texts of Wroth's sonnet sequence as well as Herbert's "Elegy" and Wroth's "Penshurst Mount." Readers should compare the texts for themselves to discern variants in spelling and punctuation, which are too numerous to be reproduced in the space available at the bottom of the page.

Folger Manuscript V.a.104 has never been edited in print. The text is laid out to look as much as possible like Wroth's handwritten transcription. Each new poem appears on a new page except for songs that are too long to fit on one page and the fourteen separately numbered, interlocking poems entitled "a crowne of sonnets" (MS 82-MS 95) which Wroth transcribed with only minimal spacing between one sonnet and the next. The title and distinctive appearance of "a crowne of sonnets" indicate that these sonnets should be read as a unit.

Contracted forms with *y* for lowercase thorn (*th*) in abbreviations such as y^e for "the" are reproduced as they appear in Wroth's handwriting. However, italic font replaces the superscript macrons (or tildes) for the letters *m* and *n*. The text replicates Wroth's use of slanted lines below poems and the *fermesse,* or slashed *s* ($) that she used variously to mark the end of a stanza or poem and to demarcate groups of poems.[164] The text does not replicate Wroth's swash *s,* her double *ff,* or her ligatures, the lines that routinely connect some letters of her italic script. Features of the manuscript that cannot be represented in the text, such as tears or holes in the paper, inkblots, visual signs, and other anomalies, are described in the footnotes.

Wroth's manuscript contains numerous, multistage corrections and revisions, which are reproduced here as closely as possible so that readers can follow her process of revision—a process that continued as she prepared the lost manuscript used by the press. In addition to the corrections listed in Roberts's edition, the manuscript contains numerous places where Wroth made corrections or revisions by writing over individual letters, which offered an efficient way to alter a line or poem without having to recopy the entire manuscript. In some cases the original letters are no longer legible, but in many cases they can still be reconstructed. Whenever possible both the original and the revision are included within the text of the poem, including the carat (^) Wroth used to signal corrections entered above the line and a strikethrough to indicate places where she crossed out and rewrote letters or words. Multistage revisions that would be too complicated or distracting to reproduce within the text are described in the footnotes.

Spacing creates additional editorial problems. For example, Wroth often placed commas a space or two after the word and somewhat below the line, which makes them easy to mistake for apostrophes in the line below. This edition places punctuation marks squarely on the line and silently eliminates extra spaces, with the exception of Wroth's characteristic spaces before and after parentheses, which we have included throughout, even though the spacing is sometimes ambiguous.

The spacing between stanzas of the songs is quite consistent, but Wroth's use of indentation and line breaks to designate rhyming units within the sonnets produces additional problems. Here she seems to have combined the practice of her uncle Philip, who used several patterns of indentation in accord with the varied rhyme schemes of his "Astrophil and Stella" sonnets, and that of her father, Robert, who did not indent the lines of his sonnets but used stanza breaks aligned with the rhyme scheme.[165] Where a sonnet ends with different rhyme sounds, Wroth

---

164. On occasion (e.g., fols. 3v, 7v, 11, 11v, and 18v), the closural line appears without a catchword. Some catchwords (e.g., fols. 4, 6, 27v, 28v) lack lines above them, and on a few pages (fols. 22v, 42v) Wroth omitted both line and catchword.

165. These patterns are preserved in *The Poems of Sir Philip Sidney*, ed. William A. Ringler, Jr. (Oxford: Clarendon Press, 1962). Ringler analyzes the indentation patterns of the "Astrophil and Stella" sonnets and their importance in establishing relationships among the various texts on p. 448. Robert Sidney's use of line spacing to create stanzas in his holograph manuscript is reproduced in Crofts' edition.

72 *Introduction*

indents lines 2–4, 6–8, 10–11, and 13–14, with spaces after lines 4, 8, and 11 to create a 4.4.3.3 pattern (two quatrains followed by two triplets). Sonnets that end with couplets, however, indent lines 2–4, 6–8, and 10–12, with spaces after lines 4, 8, and 12, producing a 4.4.4.2 pattern (three quatrains and a couplet). Wroth often failed to leave a clear space between these stanzas when transcribing the sonnets, although that seems to have been her overall intent, as indicated (again, without absolute consistency) by her practice of capitalizing the beginning of lines flush with the left margin and beginning the indented lines with minuscules. Stanza divisions are retained in accord with Wroth's normal practice even where the spaces between stanzas are ambiguous or imperceptible.

The 1621 text is the only edition of *Pamphilia to Amphilanthus* printed during Wroth's lifetime. There are twenty-eight known copies. The thirty errors that were not corrected in any of the extant copies argue strongly that Wroth did not read proofs but left the volume's production entirely in the hands of the printer. The remaining twenty-eight errors, corrected in some copies but not in others, show that the pages were proofread in the printing house by the press corrector as the sheets were being printed. Several copies of a given page might be run before the proofreading was finished, the press stopped, and the type reset to correct an error. Paper and printing time were valuable, so it was normal printing house practice to retain the uncorrected pages and collate them at random with the corrected sheets to assemble final copies of the book. All twenty-eight extant copies (the final forty-six pages containing the sonnet sequence are missing from a twenty-ninth copy at New York University) have been collated to identify the corrected and uncorrected pages in each copy. This edition's text of the 1621 *Pamphilia to Amphilanthus* is based on Folger Library, copy 2, which has only four of the errors that are corrected in some copies but not others. Folger Library, copy 1, which is widely available from *Early English Books Online*, has seven more errors than copy 2. Corrected and uncorrected errors for all twenty-eight extant copies are listed in appendix 3.

Printer's errors in spacing, turned letters, and other minor accidentals have been silently corrected, and catchwords at the bottom of each printed page omitted. Otherwise, the text has been set forth to look as much as possible like the original 1621 printed text. Italicized type is retained, even though the manuscript contains no evidence that Wroth made such distinctions. More importantly, the layout follows the printer's lead by entering as many lines of poetry as fit onto a page—an understandable effort to conserve paper since the edition already contained the 558 pages of Wroth's romance. The variant readings in the footnotes record only substantive differences between MS V.a.104 and Folger Library copy 2 of the printed text. Where Wroth used a caret to superscript a word or words in the manuscript, the passage is placed between two carets in the footnotes to the 1621 text, for example, ^doe^.

FOLGER MS V.a.104

[MS 1]   [Print 1]

$ Pamphilia to Amphilanthus $ [fol. 1r]

.1.

When nights black mantle could most darknes prove,
    and sleepe deaths Image did my senceses hiere°   senses hire, engage
    from knowledg of my self, then thoughts did move
    swifter then° those most swiftnes need require: than

In sleepe, a Chariot drawne by wing'd desire
    I sawe: wher sate bright Venus Queene of love,
    and att her feete her sonne,[1] still adding fire
    to burning hearts wch she did hold above,

Butt one hart flaming more then all the rest
    the goddess held, and putt itt to my brest
    deare sonne, now shute° sayd she: thus must wee win*n*   shoot

Hee her obay'd, and martir'd my poore hart,
    I, waking hop'd as dreames itt would depart
    Yett since: O mee: a lover have I[2] bin*n* $

                        Deare=

---

1. Cupid, god of love, son of Venus and Mars, wounds his victims with an arrow to make them fall in love.

2. have I] I have 1621

74 Mary Wroth

[MS 2]   [Print 2]

.2.   [fol. 1v]

Deare eyes how well (indeed) you doe adorne
    that blessed sphære,[3] wch gazing eyes[4] hold deere:
    the loved place of Cupids[5] triumph's neere:
    the court of glory, wher his[6] force was borne:

How may they terme you Aprills sweetest morne
    when pleasing looks, from those bright lights apeere:
    A sun=shine day; from clouds, and mists still cleere
    kind nursing fires for wishes yett unborne!

Too[7] starrs of Heaven,[8] sent downe to grace the Earthe,
    plac'd in that throne wch gives all joyes theyr birthe;
    shining, and burning; pleasing yett theyr charmes;

W^{ch} wounding, yett[9] in hurts are deem'd delights,
    soe pleasant is ther force! Soe great theyr mights
    As, happy, they can triumph in theyr harmes $

yett is=

---

3. The vault of heaven; Amphilanthus's face.

4. eyes] soules 1621

5. Cupids] sought for 1621

6. his] Loves 1621

7. Too] Two 1621

8. Amphilanthus's eyes; Venus and Mars, the two brightest stars in the night sky.

9. yett] even 1621

Manuscript Text 75

[MS 3] [Print 3]

.3. [fol. 2r]

Yett is ther hope: Then Love[10] butt play thy part
    remember well thy self, and think on mee;
    shine in those eyes wch conquer'd have my hart;
    and see if mine bee slack° to answere thee!   remiss, slow

Lodg in that brest, and pitty move[11] to bee[12]
    for flames wch in mine burne in truest smart[13]
    exiling thoughts that touch[14] inconstancie,
    or those wch waste nott[15] in the constant art,[16]

Watch butt my sleepe, if I take any rest
    for thought of you, my spiritt soe distrest
    as pale, and famish'd, I, for mercy cry?

Will you yor servant° leave? think butt on this;   devotee; lover
    who weares loves crowne, must nott doe soe amiss,[17]
    butt seeke theyr good, who on thy force rely:[18] $

Venus=

10. Cupid; Amphilanthus; the emotion of love.

11. Induce compassion or mercy. After "move," Wroth has erased "for" and written "to" over it; the *b* in "bee" appears to have been written over the last minim in an original *m*.

12. move to bee] mooving see 1621

13. Sharp intense pain; mental suffering; grief.

14. Produce a particular feeling; border on; speak or write about.

15. Are not occupied or consumed with.

16. In the skill, practice, or study of constancy.

17. Erroneously; wrongly; so as to incur blame.

18. rely] doe lye 1621

76 MARY WROTH

[MS 4]   [Print omitted]

.4.   [fol. 2v]

Venus unto the Gods a sute° did move,   suit
    that since she was of love the godess stil'd[19]
    she only might the pouer have of love,
    and nott as now a partner wth her child,

The cause to this wch stird the Godess milde
    was that of late her servant[20] faulse did prove
    hurt as she sayd afresh by Cupid[21] wilde,
    and to a Nimph[22] his passions did remove;

Or els that they would eyes[23] unto him give
    that hee might see, how hee his shafts° did drive: arrows
    this they deny'd:° For if hee blind did ill   refused

What would hee seeing? Butt thus much they did
    to shoote wthout her leave they him forbid
    hee this observ'd, and since obays her will.[24] $

Can=

---

19. Named; honored with the title.

20. The mythological reference is unclear, perhaps referring to Mars, who upon being shot by a stray arrow from Cupid's bow, betrayed Venus, or to Cupid himself, who, having cut himself with his own arrow while gazing at Psyche, fell in love, and disobeyed Venus's orders to make Psyche fall in love with a monster.

21. Wroth has erased a terminal *s* on "Cupid."

22. Semi-divine creature; beautiful young woman.

23. Would give him eyesight since Cupid was blind.

24. Command; inclination or erotic desire; possible allusion to Wroth's clandestine lover, Will[iam] Herbert.

Manuscript Text 77

[MS 5] [Print 5]

.5. [fol. 3r]

Can pleasing sight,[25] misfortune ever bring?
 can firme desire, ever, torments[26] try?[27]
 can win*n*ing eyes prove to the hart a sting?[28]
 Or can sweet lips in treason hidden ly?° lie

The Sun most pleasing blinds the strongest eye
 if to[29] much look'd on, breaking the sights string;[30]
 desires[31] crost,[32] must unto mischiefes[33] hye,° hasten, speed
 and as dispaire, a luckles chance may fling.

Eyes, having wunn,[34] rejecting proves a sting
 killing the bud beefor the tree doth[35] spring
 sweet lips nott loving doth[36] as poyson prove° turn out to be

Desire, sight, Eyes, lips, seeke, see, prove,[37] and find
 you love may win*n*, butt curses if unkind[38]
 Then show you harmes dislike, and joye in Love.[39] $

Ô strive=

25. Ability to see; thing seen; appearance; mental or spiritual vision.

26. ever, torments] a painefull torment 1621

27. Afflict with; test by means of.

28. Acute pain or wound; goad to action; sharp stimulus or incitement.

29. to] two 1621

30. Ligament, nerve, tendon.

31. desires] Desires still 1621

32. Thwarted, frustrated, opposed. *OED* cites Wroth's *Urania* (1621), 203, "All fortunes pass'd in my cross'd love," as the first such usage.

33. Misfortunes; harms; injuries; wrongs.
 mischiefes] mischiefe 1621

34. wunn] none 1621

35. The *d* in "doth" is written over an original letter.

36. doth] do 1621

37. Test or demonstrate by action.

38. Unnatural; hurtful; villainous; hostile; ungrateful.

39. Take pleasure in love or making love.

78 MARY WROTH

[MS 6]   [Print 6]

:6.   [fol. 3v]

Ô strive nott still to heape disdaine on mee
     nor pleasure take your cruelty to show
     on haples° mee, on whom all sorrowes flow,   unfortunate
     and byding make:° as given, and lost by thee,   stay or remain

Alas, ev'ne griefe is growne to pitty mee;
     scorne cries out 'gainst itt self such ill to show,
     and would give place for joyes delights to flow;
     yett wreched I, all torturs[40] beare from thee,

Long have I suffer'd, and esteem'd itt deere
     sincc you soe willd;[41] yett grew my paines[42] more neere:[43]
     wish you my[44] end? say soe, you shall itt have;

For all the depth of my hart=kild[45] dispaire
     is that for you I feele nott death[46] for care;[47]
     Butt now I'le seeke itt, since you will nott save $

---

40. torturs] torture 1621

41. you soe willd] such thy will 1621. Possible pun on wild/willed/Will. Wroth added the second *l* in "willd" as a correction.

42. paines] paine 1621

43. Close in proximity; closely related.

44. my] may 1621

45. hart=kild] heart-held 1621

46. Common circumlocution for sexual pleasure since it was believed that reaching sexual climax subtracted a day from your life.

47. Sorrow, lamentation; concern; protection; solicitude.

Manuscript Text 79

[MS 7]   [Print 7]

Song 1.   [fol. 4r]

The spring now come att last
    to trees, fields, to flowers,
And medowes makes to tast[48]
    his pride,[49] while sad showers
W^ch from my[50] eyes do flow
    makes knowne w^t cruell paines
    colde winter yett remaines
Noe signe of spring I[51] know $

The Sunn wch to the Earth
    gives heate, light, and pleasure,   10
joyes in spring, hateth dearth,
    plenty makes his treasure
His heat[52] to mee is colde,
    his light all darknes is
    since I am bar'd^o[53] of bliss[54]   bared/barred
I heate nor light beeholde $

A sheapherdess[55] thus sayd
    who was w^t griefe oprest
for truest love beetraid
    bard her from quiett rest   20
And weeping thus sayd she
    my end aprocheth neere
    now willow[56] must I weare
My fortune soe will bee $

W^th=

48. Feel, touch; experience; please; know carnally.

49. High opinion; luxuriant growth; splendor, magnificence; pleasure; sexual organ; sexual desire.

50. my] mine 1621

51. I] wee 1621

52. Wroth changed an original "hi" to "he" in "heat."

53. bar'd] barr,d 1621

54. Perfect pleasure, spiritual or physical.

55. Wroth feminizes the stock pastoral figure of the singer shepherd.

56. Conventional symbol for the grief of unrequited love.

80 Mary Wroth

Wth branches of this tree   [fol. 4v]
   I'le dress my haples head
wch shall my wittnes bee
   my hopes in love ar dead;
My clothes imbroder'd° all   embroidered
   shall bee w^t Gyrlands round   30
some scater'd, others bound
some ti'de,° some like to fall $ tied

The barck my booke shall bee
   wher dayly I will wright
this tale of haples mee
   true slave to fortunes spight;
The roote shall bee my bed
   wher nightly I will lye,
   wayling inconstancy
since all true love is dead, $ 40

And thes lines I will leave
   if some such lover come
who may them right conseave,[57]
   and place them on my tombe
she who still constant lov'd
   now dead w^t cruell care
   kild w^t unkind dispaire,
And change, her end[58] heere prov'd[59] $

       Love

---

57. Conceive; form or have a (correct) conception of.

58. Death; aim, purpose.

59. Suffered; tested; demonstrated.

Manuscript Text 81

[MS 8]   [Print 8]

.7.   [fol. 5r]

Love leave° to urge, thou know'st thou hast yᵉ hand;[60]   cease
   'T'is cowardise, to strive wher none resist:
   Pray thee leave of,° I yeeld unto thy band;[61]   off
   Doe nott thus, still, in thine owne powre persist,

Beehold I yeeld: lett forces bee dismist;
   I ame your[62] subiect, conquer'd, bound[63] doe[64] stand,°   remain steadfast
   never your[65] foe, butt did your[66] claime assist
   seeking your[67] due of those who did wᵗ=stand;[68]

Butt now, itt seemes, you would[69] I should you[70] love;
   I doe confess, t'was you, made mee first[71] chuse;
   and yoʳ[72] faire showes[73] made mee a lover prove[74]
   when I my freedome did, for paine refuse[75]

Yett this Sʳ God, yoʳ boyship[76] I dispise;
Your charmes[77] I'obay, butt love nott want of eyes[78] $

           Led=

60. Power; possession; reference to the marriage ceremony.

61. Moral, spiritual, or legal bond; wedding band.

62. your] thy 1621

63. The "o" and "n" in "bound" overwrite erased letters with descenders.

64. doe] to 1621

65. your] thy 1621

66. your] thy 1621

67. your] thy 1621

68. Those who did resist or oppose what is due to you.

69. you would] thou would'st 1621

70. you] thee 1621

71. you made mee first] thy will made mee 1621

72. yoʳ] thy 1621

73. Physical attractions; splendid displays; enticing dissemblings.

74. Demonstrate or prove my love by action.

75. Abandon or forsake something valued; reject an offer, lover, or marriage proposal.

76. Title of mock respect for a boy or young man.

77. Magical spells; qualities, traits, or features exciting love or admiration.

78. Reference to Cupid's blindness; possible pun on *ayes.*

82 MARY WROTH

[MS 9] [Print 9]

.8. [fol. 5v]

Led by the powre of griefe, to waylings brought
    by faulce consiete[79] of change fall'ne on my part,
    I seeke for some smale ease by lines, wch bought[80]
    increaseth[81] paine; griefe is nott cur'd by art:[82]

Ah! how unkindnes moves w^t in the hart
    wch still is true, and free from changing thought
    What unknowne woe itt breeds; what endles smart[83]
    wth ceasles teares wch causelessly ar brought.[84]

Itt makes mee now to shunn all shining light,
    and seeke for blackest clouds mee light to give,
    wch to all others, only darknes drive,
    they on mee shine, for sunn disdaines my sight

Yett though I darke do live I triumph may
Unkindnes,[85] nor this wrong shall love allay° $ destroy

Bee=

79. Conception, idea, thought.

80. Paid a penalty for or suffered the consequences of; obtained by making a sacrifice.

81. increaseth] Increase the 1621

82. Skill; learning; creativity; pretence. The reference to her poetry aligns Pamphilia with Wroth.

83. Sharp intense pain; mental suffering; grief.

84. Wroth wrote "ai wrought," which she changed to "ar brought."] are wrought 1621

85. Unnatural conduct; lack of affection; ingratitude; hostility.

[MS 10]   [Print 10]

.9.   [fol. 6r]

Bee you all pleas'd? your pleasures grieve nott mee;
    Doe you delight? I envy nott your joy;
    have you content? contentment[86] w^t you bee:
    hope you for bliss; hope still, and still injoye:

Lett sad misfortune, haples mee destroy,
    leave crosses° to rule mee, and still rule free,   trials, afflictions
    while[87] all delights theyr contrairies[88] imploy
    to keepe good back, and I butt torments see,

Joyes are beereav'd,[89] and harmes[90] doe only tarry;
    dispaire takes place, disdaine[91] hath gott the hand;
    yett firme° love holds my sences in such band[92]   unwavering
    as since dispise'd, I, w^t sorrow marry;[93]

Then if wth griefe I now must coupled bee
Sorrow I'le wed: Dispaire thus governs mee $

The=

---

86. Contentedness; satisfaction; pleasure.

87. Wroth has written the "whi" of "while" over an initial "W" followed by three other letters.

88. Opposites; opposing forces or enemies.

89. Robbed, plundered; taken away by violence.

90. and harmes] me, harmes 1621

91. Scorn; anger; loathing.

92. The repetition of the hand/band rhyme from MS 8 strengthens the reference to marriage.

93. I marry sorrow; I sorrowfully marry another.

84 MARY WROTH

[MS 11]   [Print 11]

.10.   [fol. 6v]

The weary traveller who tired sought
 In places distant farr, yett found noe end
 of paine, or labour, nor his state to mend,
 att last wᵗ joy is to his home back brought;

Finds nott more ease, though hee wᵗʰ joy bee fraught;° laden, furnished
 when past is[94] feare, content° like soules assend; pleasure, delight
 then I, on whom new pleasures doe dessend
 wᶜʰ now as high as first borne bliss is wrought;[95]

Hee tired wᵗ his paines,[96] I, wᵗ my mind;
 hee all content receaves by ease of limms;° limbs
 I, greatest hapines that I doe find
 beeleefe for fayth, while hope in pleasure swimms;

Truth says[97] t'was wrong conseite° bred my despite[98] false conception
wᶜʰ once acknowledg'd, brings my harts delight; $

you=

---

94. is] his 1621

95. Created, made; characterized by heightened emotion.

96. Physical or mental sufferings; physical or sexual exertions.

97. says] saith 1621

98. Offended pride; scorn, hatred, or spite; contemptuous treatment; opposition; indignation.

Manuscript Text 85

[MS 12]   [Print 12]

.11.   [fol. 7r]

You endless torments that my rest opress
  how long will you delight in my sad paine?
  will never love[99] yor favour more express?
  shall I still live, and ever feele disdaine?

Alass now stay,° and lett my griefe obtaine   cease, desist
  some end; feede nott my hart wth sharpe distress:
  lett mee once see my cruell fortunes gaine
  att least[100] release, and long felt woes redress;[101]

Lett nott the blame of cruelty disgrace
  the honor'd title of your Godhed,[102] Love:
  give nott just cause for mee to say a place
  is found for rage alone on mee to move;[103]

O quickly end, and doe nott long debate
my needfull ayde, least help do come to late; $

       Cloyde=

---

99. Emotion of love; Cupid; Amphilanthus.

100. Wroth at first wrote "last," then squeezed in the *e* between *l* and *a*.

101. Abolish; rectify, make amends; resolve a disagreement.

102. Deity, divine personality; synecdoche for Cupid or Amphilanthus.

103. Keep in continuous motion; progress, develop.

86 MARY WROTH

[MS 13]   [Print 13]

.12.   [fol. 7v]

Cloy'd[104] wth the torments of a tedious night
    I wish for day; w[ch] come, I hope for joy:
    When cross[105] I finde new tortures to destroy
    my woe=kil'd hart, first hurt by mischiefs[106] might,

Then cry for night, and once more day takes flight
    and brightnes gon; what rest should heere injoy
    Usurped is; hate will her force imploy;
    Night can nott griefe intombe though black as spite[107]

My thoughts are sad; her° face as sad doth seeme: night's
    My paincs arc long; Her houers tædious are:
    My griefe is great; and endles is my care:
    Her face, her force, and all of woes esteeme:

Then wellcome Night, and farwell flattring day
wch all hopes breed, and yett our joyes delay; $

---

104. Encumbered, weighed down; weary.

105. Contrarious; contrary, opposed.

106. Powerful misfortunes, harms, injuries, or wrongs suffered by a person in distress.

107. Harm, injury; contempt, hatred, ill will.

Manuscript Text 87

[MS 14]   [Print 14]

.Song 2.   [fol. 8r]

All night I weepe, all day I cry, Ay mee;[108]
I still doe wish though yett deny, Ay mee;
I sigh, I mourne, and[109] say that still
I only ame the store for ill,[110] Ay mee;

In coldest hopes I freeze, yett burne Ay mee;
From flames I strive to fly, yett turne Ay mee;
From griefe I haste butt sorrowes hy,°   hasten
and on my hart all woes doe ly Ay mee;

From contraries[111] I seeke to runn Ay mee;
butt contraries I can nott shunn Ay mee;   10
For they delight theyr force to try,
and to despaire my thoughts doe ty Ay mee;

Whether° (alas) then shall I goe Ay mee;   whether; wither
When as dispaire all hopes outgoe Ay mee;
Iff to the Forest, Cupid hyes,
and my poore soule to his lawe ties Ay mee;

To the' Court? O no. Hee crys fy Ay mee;
ther no true love you shall espy Ay mee;
Leave that place to faulscest lovers
yor true love all truth discovers Ay mee;   20

Then quiett rest, and noe more prove Ay mee;
All places ar alike to love Ay mee;
And constant bee in this beegunn
Yett say, till lyfe w^t love be dunn° Ay mee; $ done

Deere=

108. Alas for me; ever or always me.

109. and] I 1621

110. Storehouse or repository of injuries or misfortunes.

111. Opposites; the reverse of what has been mentioned; wrongs; opponents, enemies.

88 Mary Wroth

[MS 15]   [Print 15]

.13.   [fol. 8v]

Deare fam*m*ish nott what you your self gave food,
    destroy nott what your glory is to save;
    kill nott that soule to wch you spiritt gave;
    In pitty, nott disdaine your triumph stood;

An easy thing itt is to shed the blood
    of one, who att your will, yeelds to the grave;
    butt more you may true worthe by mercy crave
    when you preserve, nott spoyle, butt nurrish good;

Your sight is all the food I doe desire;
    then sacrifics° mee nott in hidden fire,   sacrifice
    Or stop that[112] breath wch did your prayses move:

Think butt how easy t'is a sight to give;
    nay ev'n deserte;[113] since by itt I doe live,
    I butt Camælion=like[114] would live, and love; $

Am I =

---

112. that] the 1621

113. Due reward, recompense; excellence, worth.

114. Chameleons were thought to live on the air, since they could go long periods of time without food.

Manuscript Text 89

[MS 16]   [Print 16]

.14.   [fol. 9r]

Am I thus conquer'd? have I lost the powers
    that to w^{th}stand,[115] wch joy's to ruin mee?
    must I bee still while itt my strength devowres
    and captive leads mee prisoner, bound, unfree?

Love first shall leave mens phant'sies to them free,
    desire shall quench loves flames, spring hate sweet showres,
    Cupid shall loose[116] his darts, have sight, and see
    his shame, and Venus[117] hinder happy howres;

Why should wee nott loves purblind° charmes resist?   completely blind
    must wee bee servile, doing what hee list?
    Noe, seeke some hoste to harbour thee: I fly

Thy babish° trickes, and freedome doe profess;   babyish
    butt ô my hurt, makes my lost hart confess
    I love, and must: So farwell liberty; $

                Love

---

115. Resist the attraction or influence of; abstain from doing something; refuse to allow a person to take possession.

116. Cupid shall loose] Love shall loose all 1621

117. Venus] wishings 1621

90 MARY WROTH

[MS 17]   [Print 64]

.15.   [fol. 9v]

Love like a jugler,[118] comes to play his prise,[119]
    and all minds draw his wonders to admire,
    to see how cuningly hee, wanting° eyes,   lacking
    can yett deseave° the best sight of desire: deceive

The wanton[120] child, how hee can faine[121] his fire
    so pretely as° none sees his disguise!   so that; while
    how finely doe his tricks, while wee fooles hire[122]
    the marke[123] and service[124] of his tirannies,

For in the end, such jugling° doth hee[125] make   playful trickery
    as hee our harts, in stead of eyes doth take
    for men can only by theyr slieghts° abuse   sleights; slights

The sight wth nimble, and delightfull skill;
    butt if hee play, his gaine is our lost will:[126]
    yett childlike, wee can nott his sports[127] refuse: $

My=

---

118. Jester, buffoon; magician; trickster or deceiver.

119. Play his part; participate in a sporting match.

120. Playful, carefree; undisciplined, reckless; lascivious, promiscuous; spoiled or pampered; luxurious, extravagant, profligate; without regard to justice, propriety, or others' feelings; malevolent.

121. Pretend, deceive; invent a story or fiction. Also *fain:* rejoice in; pretend kindness.

122. Engage the services of someone for reward or payment; bribe; lease.

123. Wroth has crossed out a word, possibly "sonnge" or "sonnage," meaning the status of a son, or sonship, and written "marke" above the line. marke] badge 1621.

124. Condition of being a servant, or serving a master.
service] office 1621

125. doth hee] he doth 1621

126. Desire, specifically carnal desire; intention; power of choice.

127. Athletic competition; amorous dalliance or intercourse.

Manuscript Text 91

[MS 18]   [Print 68]

.16.   [fol. 10r]

My paine, still smother'd in my grieved brest,
    seekes for some ease, yett cannott passage[128] finde
    to bee discharg'd of this unwellcome ghest;°   guest
    when most I strive, more fast° his burdens bind,   firmly

Like to a ship, on Goodwines[129] cast by wind
    the more she strives,[130] more deepe in sand is prest
    till she bee lost; so am I, in this kind
    sunk, and devour'd, and swallow'd by unrest,

Lost, shipwrack't, spoyl'd,[131] debar'd of smallest[132] hope
    nothing of pleasure left; save thought's have scope,
    wch wander may: Goe then, my thoughts, and cry

Hope's perish'd; Love tempest=beaten; Joy lost
    killing dispaire hath all thes blessing[133] crost°   thwarted, opposed
    yett faith still cries, Love will nott falsefy: $

                    Poore=

128. Opportunity to get beyond.

129. Perilous sandbar off the coast of Kent, England.

130. strives] strive 1621

131. Pillaged, plundered; ravaged, despoiled.

132. Wroth wrote "swallest"] smallest 1621

133. blessing] blessings 1621

92 MARY WROTH

[MS 19]   [Print 70]

.17.   [fol. 10v]

Poore Love in chaines, and fetters like a thiefe
    I mett led forthe, as chast Diana's[134] gaine,°   booty; prey
    Vowing the untaught Lad should noe reliefe
    from her receave, who glory'd in fond paine,[135]

She call'd him theife; w^t Vowes hee did maintaine
    hee never stole; butt some slight touch[136] of griefe
    had given to those who did his powre disdaine,
    in wch reveng, his honor, was the chiefe:

She say'd hee murder'd, and therfor must dy;
    hee, that hee caus'd butt love: did harmes deny
    butt, while she thus discoursing w^t him stood

The Nimphs unty'd him, and his chaines tooke of°   off
    thinking him safe; butt hee, loose,° made a scofe°   let loose ... scoff
    smiling, and scorning them, flew to the wood. $

                    O Lett=

---

134. Roman goddess of the moon, depicted as a huntress, and symbol of chastity.

135. The pain of infatuated, doting lovers.

136. slight touch] sadd slight 1621

Manuscript Text 93

[MS 20]   [Print 20]

.18.   [fol. 11r]

W^{ch} should I better like of, day, or night
　　since all the day I live in bitter woe
　　injoying light more cleeere my wrongs to know,
　　and yett most sad, feeling in itt all spite;[137]

In night, when darknes doth forbid all light
　　yett see I griefe aparant to the show
　　follow'd by jealousie whose fond tricks flow°   gush forth
　　and on unconstant waves of doubt allight,

I can beehold rage cowardly to feede
　　upon foule error wch thes humours° breed   feelings; fancies
　　shame, doubt, and feare, yett boldly will think ill,

All thes[138] in both I feele, then wch is best
　　darke to joy by day, light in night oprest
　　Leave both, and end, thes butt each other spill:° $ kill, destroy

137. Outrage, injury, reproach; hatred; ill-will.

138. thes] those 1621

94 MARY WROTH

[MS 21]   [Print 21]

Song 3.   [fol. 11v]

Stay,° my thoughts, do nott aspire   cease, halt
    to Vaine hopes of high desire:
    see you nott all meanes bereft°   snatched away
    to injoye? noe hope[139] is left;
    yett still mee thinks my thoughts doe say
    some hopes do live amid dismay;

Hope, then once more hope for joy;
    bury feare wch joyes destroy;
    thought hath yett some comfort giv'ne,
    wch dispaire hath from us drivn;   10
    therfor deerly my thoughts cherish
    never lett such thinking perish;

'Tis an idle thing to plaine°   complain
    odder farr to dy[140] for paine,
    thinke, and see how thoughts do rise
    winning wher ther noe hope lies:
    wch alone is lovers treasure
    For by thoughts wee love doe measure:

Then kinde thought my phant'sies[141] guide
    lett mee never hopeles[142] slide;   20
    still maintaine thy force in mee,
    lett my[143] thinking still bee free:
    nor leave thy might untill my death
    butt lett mee, thinking yeeld up breath $

139. Wroth wrote "hope" over an original "joye"] joy 1621

140. Expire; reach sexual climax.

141. phant'sies] fant'sie 1621

142. hopeles] haplesse 1621

143. my] me 1621

[MS 22]   [Print 22]

.19.   [fol. 12r]

Come darkest night, beecoming° sorrow best;   befitting
    light; leave thy light; fitt for a lightsome soule;
    darknes doth truly sute° wᵗ mee oprest   suit
    whom absence power doth from mirthe controle:°   restrain, hold back

The Very trees wᵗ hanging heads condole
    sweet sommers parting, and of leaves distrest
    in dying coulers° make a griefe=full role;   colors
    soe much (alas) to sorrow are they prest

Thus of dead leaves her farewell carpett's made;
    theyr fall, theyr branches, all theyr mournings prove;
    wᵗʰ leavles,° naked bodies, whose huese Vade°   leafless ... hues fade
    from hopefull greene, to wither in theyr love,

If trees, and leaves for absence, mourners bee
Noe mervaile° yᵗ I grieve, who like want see $ marvel

The

96 MARY WROTH

[MS 23]   [Print 23]

                           20.   [fol. 12v]

The Sunn wch glads, the earth att his bright sight
   When in the morne hee showes his golden face,
   and takes the place from tædious drowsy night
   making the world still happy by[144] his grace;

Shewes° hapines remaines nott in one place,   shows
   nor may the heavens, alone to us give light,
   butt hide that cheerfull face, though noe long space,
   yett long enough for triall of theyr might;

Butt never sunn=sett could bee soe obscure
   no desart ever have[145] a shade soe sadd,
   nor could black darknes ever prove soe badd
   as paines wch absence makes mee now indure;

The missing of the sunn awhile makes night
butt absence of my joy[146] sees never Light $

               When I=

---

144. by] in 1621

145. have] had 1621

146. Delight; sexual pleasure; lover. Cf. MS 77.

Manuscript Text 97

[MS 24]   [Print 24]

21.   [fol. 13r]

When I last[147] saw thee, I did nott thee see,
    itt was thy[148] Image, wch in my thoughts lay
    soe lively figur'd, as noe times delay
    could suffer mee in hart to parted bee;

And sleepe soe favorable is to mee,
    as nott to lett thy lov'd remembrance stray,
    least° that I waking might have cause to say   lest
    ther was one minute found to forgett thee;

Then since my faith is such, soe kind my sleepe
    that gladly thee presents into my thought;
    and still true lover like thy face doth keepe
    soe as some pleasure shadowe=like is wrought

Pitty my loving, nay of consience give
reward to mee in whom thy[149] self doth[150] live, $

                        Cupid=

---

147. I last] last I 1621

148. thy] thine 1621

149. After "whom," Wroth erased a word beginning with *g,* then wrote "thy" (thy 1621), apparently over "my."

150. Wroth at first wrote "doe," erased the "e," and transformed the word into "doth"] doth 1621

98 MARY WROTH

[MS 25]   [Print 72]

22.   [fol. 13v]

Cupid[151] would needs make mee a lover bee
    when I did litle thinke of loving thought
    or ever to bee ty'de;° till hee[152] told mee   tied
    that non can live, butt to his[153] bands are brought;

I, ignorant, did grant, and soe was bought,
    and solde againe to lovers slaverie;
    the duty to the god of love[154] once taught
    such band is, as wee will nott seeke to free,

Yett when I well did understand his might
    how hee inflam'de, and forc'd one to[155] affect
    I lov'd, and smarted, counting itt delight
    soe still to wast, which reason did reject.

When love came blindfold, and did chaleng mee
Indeed I lov'd butt wanton boy nott hee. $

When=

---

151. Cupid] Folly 1621

152. till hee] while shee 1621

153. his] these 1621

154. the god of love] that vanity 1621

155. Wroth has crossed out "cuningly" and written above it, "forc'd one to"] forc'd one to 1621

[MS 26]   [Print 26]

                      23.   [fol. 14]

When every one to pleasing pastime hies°   hastens
    some hunt, some hauke,[156] some play,° while, some delight gamble
    in sweet discourse, and musique showes joys might
    yett I my thoughts doe[157] farr above thes prise°   value, esteem

The joy wch I take, is that free from eyes
    I sitt, and wunder att this[158] daylike night
    soe to dispose themselves, as Voyd of right;
    and leave true pleasure for poore Vanities:[159]

When others hunt, my thoughts I have in chase;
    if hauke, my minde att wished end doth fly,
    discourse, I, w^t my spiritt tauke,° and cry   talk
    while others, musique is theyr[160] greatest grace

O God, say I, can thes fond pleasures[161] move?
Or musique bee butt in deere[162] thoughts of love? $

                            Once=

156. Hawk, meaning to hunt game with a trained hawk or falcon.

157. Wroth has written "doe" over an original "did"] doe 1621

158. Wroth at first followed "th" with a descender, then wrote "is" over it.

159. Vain or unprofitable activities.

160. is theyr] choose as 1621

161. Foolish pleasures, or pleasures that have lost their savor.

162. deere] sweet 1621

100 MARY WROTH

[MS 27]   [Print 27]

24.

[fol. 14v]

Once did I heere an aged father say
    unto his sonn who w^t attention hears
    what age, and wise experience ever clears
    from doubts of feare, or reason to betray,

My Sonn sayd hee, beehold thy father, gray,
    I once had as thou hast, fresh tender years,
    and like thee sported, destitude° of feares   destitute, lacking
    butt my young faults made mee too soone decay,

Love once I did, and like thee fear'd my love,
    led by the hatefull thread of Jelousy,
    striving to keepe, I lost my liberty,
    and gain'd my griefe wch still my sorrowes move,

In time shunn this; To love is noe offence
butt doubt in youth, in age breeds penitence; $

Song

Manuscript Text 101

[MS 28]   [Print 28]

Song 4.   [fol. 15r]

Sweetest love returne againe
        make nott to long stay.°   too long delay
killing mirthe, and forceing paine
        sorrow leading way:
lett us nott thus parted bee
love, and absence ne're° agree;   never

Butt since you must now[163] depart,
        and mee haples° leave,   unfortunate
in your journey take my hart
        wch will nott deseave°   10   deceive
Yo^rs itt is, to you itt flyes
joying in those loved eyes.

Soe in part,[164] wee shall nott part
        though wee absent bee;
time, nor place, nor greatest smart[165]
        shall my bands[166] make free
ty'de° I ame, yett thinke itt gaine;   tied
in such knotts I feele noe paine.

Butt can I live having lost
        chiefest part of mee   20
hart is fled, and sight is crost°   thwarted
        these my fortunes bee
yett deere hart goe, soone returne
as good there, as heere to burne $

Poore=

163. now] needs 1621

164. Partly, to some extent.

165. Sharp intense pain; mental suffering; grief.

166. Bonds; promises, pledges.

102 MARY WROTH

[MS 29]   [Print 29]

25.   [fol. 15v]

Poore eyes bee blind, the light behold noe more
    since that is gon wch is your deere delight
    ravish'd° from[167] you by greater powre, and might   stolen, taken away
    making yor loss a gaine to others store,[168]

Oreflowe, and drowne, till sight to you restore
    that blessed star,[169] and as in hatefull spite
    send forth your teares in flouds, to kill all sight,
    and looks, that lost, wherin you joy'd before

Bury those[170] beames, wch in some kindled fires,
    and conquer'd have theyr love=burnt=harts desires
    loosing,[171] and yett noe gaine by you esteem'd,

Till that bright starr doe once againe apeere
    brighter then Mars[172] when hee doth shine most cleere
    see nott: then by his might bee you redeem'd $.

Most=

167. Wroth has written the "ro" in "from" over two original letters and in doing so blotted the superscript *r* in "yor" in the line below.

168. Treasure; possession; abundant supply or reserves.

169. Amphilanthus, Venus, Cupid. Cf. MS 2:9.

170. those] these 1621

171. Releasing, letting go.

172. Mars, Roman god of war and clandestine lover of Venus, was thought to be Cupid's father. When the planet Mars orbits closest to the earth, only Venus, the sun, and the moon are brighter than Mars.

Manuscript Text 103

[MS 30]   [Print 65]

26.   [fol. 16r]

Most blessed Night, the happy time for love,
    the shade for Lovers, and theyr loves delight,
    the Raigne of Venus[173] servants, free from spite,°   harm, malice
    the hopefull season,[174] for joy's sports° to move;   lovemaking

Now hast thou made thy glory higher prove
    then did the God,[175] whose pleasant reede did smite
    all Argus eyes into a deathlike night
    till they were safe, that love could non[176] reprove.

Butt[177] thou hast clos'd those eyes from priing° sight   prying
    that nourish jealousie more then joyes right
    While Vaine suspition fosters theyr mistrust,

Making sweet sleepe to master all suspect°   suspicion
    wch els° theyr privatt feares would nott neglect   otherwise
    butt would imbrace both blinded, and unjust[178] $

Fy=

---

173. Venus] Love for 1621

174. season] seasons 1621

175. Hermes, disguised as a shepherd, was employed by Zeus to blind and kill Argos, the one-hundred-eyed mythological giant employed by Hera to guard the nymph Io, whom Zeus seduced and turned into a white heifer to protect her from Hera.

176. love could non] none could Love 1621

177. Butt] Now 1621

178. Unfair; improper; faithless; dishonest.

104 Mary Wroth

[MS 31]   [Print 31]

27.   [fol. 16v]

Fy[179] treacherous[180] Hope, why doe you still rebell?
    is itt nott yett enough you flatterd[181] mee?
    butt cuningly you seeke to use a spell
    how to beetray, must thes[182] your trophies bee?

I look'd from you farr sweeter fruite to see
    butt blasted[183] were your blossoms when they fell,
    and those delights expected late° from thee[184]   recently
    wither'd, and dead, and what seem'd bliss proves Hell,

Noe towne[185] was wunn° by a more plotted slight°   won … deception
    then I by you, who may my fortune write
    in embers of that fire wch ruind mee,

Thus Hope, your faulshood calls you to bee tride
    you're loth° I see the triall to abide   loathe
    prove true att last, and I will sett thee free[186] $

Griefe=

179. Exclamation of disgust or indignant reproach.

180. treacherous] tedious 1621

181. Courted, caressed; deceived with false praise.

182. Pamphilia's sorrows, heartaches, disappointed hopes.

183. Blighted; cursed, damned.

184. late from thee] from hands free 1621

185. Circumlocution for a woman's lost virginity.

186. I will sett thee free] gaine your liberty 1621

[MS 32]   [Print 32]

                    28.   [fol. 17r]

Griefe, killing griefe; have nott my torments bin*n*
    allreddy great, and strong enough: butt still
    thou dost increase, nay glory in my[187] ill.[188]
    and woes new past affresh new woes beegin*n!*

Am I the only purchase[189] you can[190] winn?
    was I ordain'd to give dispaire her fill
    or fittest I should mounte misfortunes hill
    who in the plaine of joy can=nott live in?

If itt bee soe: Griefe come as wellcome ghest°   guest
    since I must suffer, for an others rest:
    yett this good griefe, lett mee intreat of thee,

Use still thy force, butt nott from those I love
    lett mee all paines, and lasting torments prove°   experience, put to
    soe I miss thes, lay all thy waits[191] on mee $ the test

                    Fly=

---

187. my] mine 1621

188. Misfortune, calamity; pain, misery; wrongdoing.

189. Taking something by force; gaining something at the cost of suffering or sacrifice.

190. you can] thou canst 1621

191. Waitings, delays; burdens, weights.

106 Mary Wroth

[MS 33]   [Print 33]

29.   [fol. 17v]

Fly hence O! joy noe longer heere abide
    to great thy pleasures ar, for my dispaire
    to looke on, losses now must prove my fare
    who nott long since, on better foode relide;

Butt foole, how oft had I heavns changing spide°   spied
    beefore of my[192] owne fate I could take[193] care,
    yett now past time, too late I can[194] beeware
    now[195] nothing's left butt sorrowes faster tyde;°   tied

While I injoy'd that sunn whose sight did lend
    mee joy, I thought, that day, could have noc cnd
    but O![196] a night came cloth'd in absence darke,

Absence more sad, more bitter then is gall[197]
    or death, when on true lovers itt doth fall
    whose fires of love, disdaineth[198] rests poore[199] sparke $

                              You=

192. my] mine 1621

193. take] have 1621

194. too late I can] I can too late 1621

195. now] When 1621

196. O!] soone 1621

197. Bile; bitterness of spirit.

198. disdaineth] disdaine 1621

199. poore] poorer 1621

Manuscript Text 107

[MS 34]   [Print 34]

30.   [fol. 18r]

You blessed shades,[200] wch give mee silent rest,
    wittnes butt this when death hath clos'd mine eyes,
    and separated mee from earthly ties,
    beeing from hence to higher place adrest;[201]

How oft in you° I have laine heere oprest,   in shadows or dark
    and have my miseries in woefull cries
    deliver'd forth, mounting up to the skies
    yett helples back returnd to wound my brest,

W^ch wounds did butt strive how, to breed more harme
    to mee, who, can bee cur'de° by noe one charme   cured
    butt that of love, wch yett may mee releeve

If nott, lett death my former paines redeeme,
    and you my, trusty freinds, my faith esteeme[202]
and wittnes I ~~well~~ could[203] love, who soe could greeve° $ grieve

Song=

---

200. Shadows, darkness; specters, phantoms, ghosts.

201. Guided toward heavenly or uplifting thoughts.

202. and you my, trusty friends, my faith esteeme] My trusty friends, my faith untouch'd, esteeme 1621

203. I well could] I could 1621

108 Mary Wroth

[MS 35]   [Print 35]

Song 5.   [fol. 18v]

Time only cause of my unrest
by whom I hop'd once to bee blest
    how cruell art thou turned;
That first gav'st lyfe unto my love,
and still a pleasure nott to move
    or chang though ever burned;
Have I thee slack'd, or left undun
one loving rite, and soe have wunn
    thy rage or bitter changing?
That now noe minute[204] I shall see,   10
wherin I may least happy° bee   the least bit happy
    thy favor[205] soe estranging.
Blame thy self, and nott my folly,
time gave time butt to bee holly;°   holy; wholly
    true love such ends best loveth,
Unworthy love doth seeke for ends
a worthy love butt worth pretends[206]
    nor other thoughts itt proveth:
Then stay thy swiftnes cruell time,
and lett mee once more blessed clime°   20   climb
    to joy, that I may prayse thee
Lett mee pleasure sweetly tasting
joy in love, and faith nott wasting,
    and on fames wings I'le rayse thee:
Never shall thy glory dying
bee untill thine owne untying[207]
    that time noe longer liveth;
T'is a gaine such tyme to lend;°   grant, bestow
since soe thy fame shall never end
    Butt joy for what she giveth $ 30

---

204. minute] minutes 1621

205. favor] favours 1621

206. A worthy love only presents or claims what is truly valuable. The reiteration of "worth" calls attention to the pun on Wroth.

207. Dissolving or release from a union or bond.

[MS 36]   [Print 36]

                   31.   [fol. 19r]

After long trouble in a tædious way
    of loves unrest, lay'd downe to ease my paine
    hopeing for rest, new torments I did gaine
    possessing mee as if I ought t'obay:

When Fortune[208] came, though blinded, yett did stay,
    and in her blessed armes did mee inchaine;
    I, colde wth griefe, thought noe warmth to obtaine
    or, to dissolve that ice of joyes decay;

Till, rise sayd she, Venus[209] to thee doth send
    by mee the servante of true lovers, joy
    bannish all clowds of doubt, all feares destroy,
    and now on Fortune, and on Love depend

I, her obay'd, and rising felt that love
Indeed was best, when I did least itt move $.

                   How=

208. Fortuna, the Roman goddess of fortune, was often represented as blind.

209. Venus] Reward 1621

110 MARY WROTH

[MS 37]   [Print 37]

32.

[fol. 19v]

How fast thou fliest, O Time, on loves swift wings
    To hopes of joy, that flatters° our desire   encourages, gratifies
    wch to a lover, still, contentment° brings!   satisfaction, pleasure
    yett, when wee should injoy thou dost retire

Thou stay'st° thy pace faulse time from our desire,   haltest; lingerest
    When to our ill thou hast'st w^t Eagles wings,
    slowe, only to make us see thy retire
    was for dispayre, and harme, wch sorrowe brings;

O! slacke thy pase,° and milder pass to love   pace
    bee like the Bee,[210] whose wings she doth butt use
    to bring home profitt, masters good to prove[211]
    laden, and weary, yett againe pursues,

Soe lade° thy self wth honnye of sought[212] joye,   load
And doe nott mee the Hive of love destroy $

How=

---

210. The image of the bee, which brings profit to others, was often used in illustrations of Philip Sidney's motto: *sic vos non vobis*. See Emma M. Denkinger, "Some Renaissance References to Sic Vos Non Vobis," *Philological Quarterly* 10 (1931): 151–62.

211. For the sake of her master.

212. sought] sweet 1621

Manuscript Text 111

[MS 38]   [Print 38]

33.

[fol. 20r]

How many eyes hast thou poore Love[213] to guard
    thee, from thy most desired[214] wish, and end
    is itt because some say thou'art blind, that bard°   barred
    from sight, thou should'st noe hapines attend?[215]

Who blame thee soe, smale° justice can pretend[216]   simple, plain
    since 'twixt thee, and ye sunn noe question hard
    can bee, his[217] sight butt outward, thou canst bend
    the hart, and guide itt freely; thus unbard

Art thou, while wee[218] both blind, and bold thus[219] dare
    accuse thee of the harmes, our selves should find
    who led wth folly, and by rashnes blind
    thy sacred powre, doe w^t a childs compare

Yett Love this boldnes pardon: for admire
thee sure wee must, or bee borne wth out fire[220] $

Take=

213. hast thou poore Love] (poore Love) hast thou 1621

214. Wroth corrected "desir'd" to "desired."

215. Take charge of; minister to; expect; intend.

216. Claim; offer, present; bring a claim at law; allege, feign.

217. Wroth has written the "is" of "his" over one or more original letters.

218. Pamphilia and Amphilanthus.

219. thus] oft 1621

220. Passion, love.

112 MARY WROTH

[MS 39]   [Print 39]

                        34.   [fol. 20v]

Take heed mine eyes, how you yo[r] lookes doe cast
    least° they beetray my harts most secrett thought;   lest
    bee true unto your selves for nothings bought
    more deere then doubt w[ch] brings a lovers fast.

Catch you all waching° eyes, ere they bee past,   watching
    or take yours fixt wher your best love hath sought
    the pride of your desires; lett them bee taught
    theyr faults w[th221] shame, they could noe truer last;

Then looke, and looke w[t] joye for conquest wunn
    of those that search'd your hurt in double kinde;°   duplicitously
    soe you kept safe, lett them themselves looke blinde
    watch, gaze, and marke till they to madnes runn,

While you, my[222] eyes injoye full sight of love
contented° that such hapinesses move,[223] $ delighted

                        My=

---

221. w[th]] for 1621

222. my] mine 1621

223. Here, as elsewhere, a coded allusion to making love.

Manuscript Text 113

[MS 40]   [Print 95]

35.   [fol. 21r]

My hart is lost, what can I now expect,
    an ev'ning faire; after a drowsie day?
    (alas) fond phant'sie[224] this is nott the way
    to cure a morning[225] hurt,[226] or savle[227] neglect,

They who should help, doe mee, and help reject,
    imbrasing looce desires, and wanton play,
    while Venus[228] bace delights doe beare the swaye,°   govern, rule
    and impudencie° raignes w^t out respect: shamelessness

O Cupid! lett thy mother know her shame
    't'is time for her to leave this youthfull flame
    wch doth dishoner her, is ages blame,
    and takes away the greatnes of thy name;

Thou God of love, she only Queene of lust,[229]
yett strives by weakning thee, to bee unjust[230] $

Juno

---

224. A foolishly credulous fancy or imagined benefit.

225. morning] mourning 1621

226. hurt] heart 1621

227. savle] salve 1621

228. Venus] wanton 1621

229. Desires of the flesh, either positive or negative.

230. Unfair; faithless; dishonest.

114 MARY WROTH

[MS 41]   [Print 97]

36.   [fol. 21v]

Juno[231] still jealouse of her husband Jove[232]
　　desended from above, on earth to try
　　whether she ther could find his chosen love
　　wch made him from the heaven[233] so often fly;

Close by the place, wher I for shade did ly
　　she chafeing° came; butt when she saw mee move   irritated, scolding
　　have you nott seene this way sayd shee to hy°   hasten
　　one, in whom Vertue never ground did prove,°   never held sway

Hee, in whom love doth breed to stirr more hate,
　　courting a wanton Nimph for his delight
　　his name is Jupiter, my Lord by fate
　　who, for her leaves mee, heav'n, his throne, and light,

I sawe nott him, sayd I,[234] although heere are
Many in whose harts love hath made like° warr $ similar

Song=

231. Roman goddess of women and marriage.

232. Also called Jupiter, the king of the gods, brother and husband of Juno.

233. heaven] Heav'ns 1621

234. nott him, sayed I] him not 1621

Manuscript Text 115

[MS 42]   [Print 42]

Song vj.   [fol. 22r]

You happy blessed eyes,
wch in that ruling place
have force both to delight, and to disgrace,
whose light allures, and ties
all harts to yor command
O! looke on mee, who doe att mercy stand:

'T'is you that rule my lyfe
't'is you my comforts give;
then lett nott scorne to mee my ending drive,
nor lett the frownes of stryfe   10
have might to hurt those lights
wch while they shine they are true loves delights;

See butt when Night appears,
and Sunn hath lost his force
how his loss doth all joye from us divorce;
And when hee shines, and cleares
the heav'ns from clowds of night
how happy then is made our gazing sight,

Butt more then Sunns faire light
your beames doe seeme to mee,   20
whose sweetest lookes doe tye and yett make free;
Why should you then soe spite
poore mee as to destroy
the only pleasure that I taste of joye?

Shine then, O deerest lights
wth favor, and wth love,
and lett noe cause, yor cause of frownings move
butt as the soules delights
soe bless my then=bless'd eyes
wch unto you theyr true affection tyes.   30

=

Then shall the Sunn give place   [fol. 22v]
as to yor greater might,
yeelding that you doe show more parfect light,
O, then, butt grant this grace

116 Mary Wroth

Unto yor love=tied slave
to shine on mee, who to you all fayth gave;

And when you please to frowne
then use your[235] killing eyes
on them, who in untruth, and faulcehood lyes;
butt (deare) on mee cast downe   40
sweet lookes for true desire
that bannish doe all thoughts of fayned° fire $ feigned

235. then use your] Use your most 1621

Manuscript Text 117

[MS 43]   [Print 43]

37.[236]   [fol. 23r]

Night, welcome art thou to my mind destrest
    darke, heavy, sad, yett nott more sad then I
    never could'st thou find fitter company
    for thine owne humor then I thus oprest.

If thou bee[237] dark, my wrongs still unredrest[238]
    saw never light, nor smalest bliss can spy;
    If heavy, joy from mee too fast doth hy°   hurry away
    and care outgoes my hope of quiett rest,

Then now in freindship joine w^t haples mee,
    who ame as sad, and dark as thou canst bee
    hating all pleasure, or delight in[239] lyfe;

Silence, and griefe, wth thee I best doe love
    and from you three, I know I can nott move
    Then lett us live companions wth out strife $

What=

236. Wroth has written "37" over an original "38."

237. bee] beest 1621

238. Unsettled; unatoned for.

239. in] of 1621

118 Mary Wroth

[MS 44]   [Print 44]

38   [fol. 23v]

What pleasure can a bannish'd creature have
    in all the pastimes that invented arr°   are
    by witt or learning, absence making warr
    against all peace that may a biding[240] crave;

Can wee delight butt in a wellcome grave
    wher wee may bury paines, and soe bee farr
    from lothed company who allways jarr
    upon the string of mirthe that pastime gave;

The knowing part of joye is deem'd the hart
    if that bee gon,[241] what joy can joy impart,
    when senceless is the feeler of our mirthe,

Noe I ame bannish'd, and no good shall find
    butt all my fortunes must wth mischief bind°   join with trouble or
    Who butt for miserie did gaine a birth; $ grief

If=

---

240. Expectation, awaiting; staying here.

241. Since she has previously sent her heart to Amphilanthus.

Manuscript Text 119

[MS 45]   [Print 45]

39.   [fol. 24r]

Iff I were giv'n to mirthe 't'wowld bee more cross
    thus to bee robbed of my chiefest joy;
    butt silently I beare my greatest loss
    Who's us'd to sorrow, griefe will nott destroy;

Nor can I as thes[242] pleasant witts injoy
    my owne fram'd words,° wch I account the dross   my poems
    of purer thoughts, or recken them as moss
    while they (witt sick[243]) them selves to breath imploy,

Alas, think I, yor plenty shewes your want,
    for wher most feeling is, words are more scant,
    yett pardon mee, Live and your pleasure take,

Grudg nott, if I neglected, envy show
    't'is nott to you that I dislike doe owe
    butt crost° my self, wish some like mee to make $ thwarted

Itt is nott=

---

242. thes] those 1621

243. Their wisdom, good judgment, or discretion corrupted and spoiled.

120 MARY WROTH

[MS 46]   [Print 46]

40.   [fol. 24v]

Itt is nott love which you poore fooles do deeme
    that doth apeare by fond and outward showes
    of kissing, toying,[244] or by swearings glose,[245]
    o noe thes farr are of[246] from loves esteeme;

Alas thes ar nott them[247] that can redeeme
    love lost, or wining° keepe those chosen blowes   winning/whining
    though oft w^t face, and lookes love overthrowse
    yett soe slight conquest doth nott him beeseeme,°   suit, befit

'T'is nott a showe of sighes, or teares can prove
    who loves indeed: which blasts of fained°love   feigned, pretended
    increase, or dy as favors from them slide;°   slip away

Butt in the soule true love in safety lies
    guarded by faith wch to desart° still hies,°   desert … hastens
    and yett true[248] lookes doe many blessing[249] hide $

                  Late=

---

244. Doting displays of love that have lost their appeal.

245. Discourse upon; flatter; talk smoothly or speciously.

246. farr are of] are farre off 1621

247. thes … them] they … such 1621

248. true] kinde 1621

249. blessing] blessings 1621

Manuscript Text 121

[MS 47]   [Print 96]

41.   [fol. 25r]

Late in the Forest I did Cupid see
    colde, wett, and crying hee had lost his way,
    and beeing blind was farder° like to stray: farther
    wch sight a kind compassion bred in mee,

I kindly tooke, and dride him, while that hee
    poore child complain'd hee sterved was w^t stay,°   waiting; standing still
    and pin'de° for want of his accustom'd^{250} pray,   pined
    for non in that wilde place his hoste would bee,

I glad was of his finding, thinking sure
    this service should my freedome still procure,
    and in my armes I tooke him then unharm'de,

Carrying^{251} him^{252} unto a Mirtle^{253} bowre
    butt in the way hee made mee feele his powre,
    burning my hart who had him^{254} kindly^{255} warmd $

If ever=

---

250. Wroth has written the *o* in "accustom'd" over an original two minims.

251. Wroth has corrected "Carryng" to "Carrying."

252. him] him safe 1621

253. Evergreen shrub sacred to Venus. Myrtle garlands were ceremonial symbols of love, peace, honor, poetic glory, or immortality.

254. Wroth has written the "im" of "him" over an original four minims.

255. In accordance with nature or the natural course of things; spontaneously; affectionately, lovingly; pleasingly.

122 MARY WROTH

[MS 48]   [Print 48]

42.

[fol. 25v]

If ever love had force in humaine° brest?   human, humane
    If ever hee could move in pensive° hart?   sorrowful
    Or if that hee such powre could butt impart
    to breed those flames whose heat brings joys unrest

Then looke on mee. I ame to thes adrest,[256]
    I, ame the soule that feeles the greatest smart;[257]
             hartles trunk of harts depart[258]
    I, ame that ^ ~~body lives deprived of hart~~;
    and I, that one, by love, and griefe oprest;[259]

Non ever felt the truth of loves great miss°   lack
    of eyes, till I deprived was of bliss;
    for had hee[260] seene, hee must have pitty[261] show'd

I should nott have bin made the[262] stage of woe
    wher sad disasters have theyr open showe
    O noe, more pitty hee had sure beestow'd $

                      Song=

---

256. To these I address my words.

257. Sharp intense pain; mental suffering; grief.

258. That body, whose heart has departed.
~~body lives deprived of hart~~ ^hartles trunk of harts depart^] heartlesse Trunck of hearts depart 1621
Wroth's interlinear substitution is written with a different pen and ink.

259. An ink blot obscures "< > des" written in the left margin.

260. Blind Cupid; absent, inattentive Amphilanthus.

261. Compassion; tenderness; mercy.

262. the] this 1621

[MS 49]   [Print 49]

Song vij.   [fol. 26r]

Sorrow, I yeeld, and greive that I did miss:[263]
will nott thy rage be satisfied wth this?
    As sad a Divell as thee,
    made mee unhapy bee.
        yett[264]
Wilt thou nott^ consent to leave, butt still
strive how to showe thy cursed, devilsh skill;

I mourne, and dying am; what would you more?
my soule attends,° to leave this wreched[265] shore°   expects … earth
    Wher harmes doe only flow
    wch teach mee butt to know   10
The sadest howres of my lives unrest,
and tired minutes W^th griefs hand oprest:

Yett all this will nott pacefy thy spite;
no, nothing can bring ease butt my last night.
    then quickly lett itt bee
    while I unhappy see
That time, soe sparing to grant Lovers bliss
will see for time lost, ther shall noe grief miss.°   be lacking

Nor lett mee ever cease from lasting griefe,
butt endless lett itt bee w^t out reliefe: 20
    To winn againe of love,
    the favor I did prove;[266]
And wth my end please him; since living[267] I
have him offended, yett unwillingly $

        O dearest=

---

263. Go wrong; fail to attain a goal or desire; fail to make contact with someone.

264. ^yett^] yet 1621

265. wreched] cursed 1621

266. The favors she experienced in the past, or the favors she demonstrated by her actions.

267. living] dying 1621

124 Mary Wroth

[MS 50]   [Print 50]

43.[268]   [fol. 26v]

O dearest eyes the lights, and guids of love,
 the joyes of Cupid who himself borne blind
 to yor bright shining doth his triumphs bind
 for in yor seeing doth his glory move;

How happy are those places wher you prove
 yor heavnly beames wch makes the sun*n* to find
 envy,[269] and grudging hee soe long hath shind
 /and[270] your cleer light showld mach° his beames above match
 ~~now to bee match'd on earth wher you doe move~~

Butt now, Alas, your sight[271] is heere forbid
 and darknes must thes poore lost roomes[272] possess
 soe bee all blessed lights from henceforth hid
 that this black deed[273] in[274] darknes have excess,[275]
 should[276]
For why^ heaven afford least light to those
who for my misery this[277] darcknes chose $

How fast=

---

268. Wroth has written "43" over an original "42."

269. Malice; opprobrium; jealousy; admiration, emulation.

270. and] for 1621

271. Your appearance or presence; a glimpse of you.

272. Rooms (and stanzas in a poem) that have been deprived of you, or that have been morally and spiritually ruined.

273. Banishing Amphilanthus; making love to him in the dark of night.

274. in] of 1621

275. Literally, the action of going forth; also, beyond what is necessary or right.

276. ^should^] should 1621

277. Wroth has written "this" over an original *h* and a second, blotted letter, with the same pen and ink used for the rewritten l. 8.
this] such 1621

Manuscript Text 125

[MS 51] [Print 51]

44. [fol. 27r]

How fast thou hastst (o spring°) w^t swiftest[278] speed source of a stream
    to catch thy waters[279] wch befor are runn,
    and of the greater rivers wellcom wunn,
    êre° thes thy new borne streames thes places feed, before

Yett doe yow[280] well least° staying heere might breed lest
    dangerous fluds° yor sweetest banks t 'o'rerunn, floods
    and yett much better my distress to shunn
    wch makes my teares butt yor course to[281] succeed,° follow

Butt best you doe when wth soe hasty flight,
    you fly my ills wch now my self outgoe,[282]
    whose broken hart can testify such woe,
    w^ch[283] soe o'recharg'd my lyfe blood wasteth quite

Sweet spring then keepe your way, Bee never spent
and my ill days, or griefs assunder rent[284] $

               Good now=

278. swiftest] sweetest 1621

279. waters] water 1621

280. doe yow] you doe 1621

281. butt yor course to] your swiftest course 1621

282. Go forth; surpass.

283. w^ch] That 1621

284. Tear apart, rip open; destroy.

126 MARY WROTH

[MS 52]   [Print 52]

45.   [fol. 27v]

Good now bee still, and doe nott mee torment
    wᵗ multituds²⁸⁵ of questions, bee att rest,
    and only lett mee quarrell wᵗ my brest
    wᶜʰ still letts in new stormes my soule to rent;°   tear asunder

Fy, will you still my mischiefs° more augment?   misfortunes; injuries
    you say I answere cross,° I that confest   contrary; ill tempered
    long since, yett must I ever bee oprest
    wᵗʰ yoʳ toungue torture wᶜʰ will ne're bee spent?°   ended

Well then I see noe way butt this will fright
    that Divell speach; Alas I ame possest,
    and mad folks senceles ar of wisdomes right,

The hellish speritt° absence doth arest°   spirit … commandeer
    all my poore sences to his cruell might
    spare mee then till I ame my self, and blest $

Love=

---

285. multituds] multitude 1621

Manuscript Text 127

[MS 53]   [Print 53]

46.   [fol. 28r]

Love,[286] thou hast all, for now thou hast mee made
    soe thine, as if for thee I were ordain'd;
    then take thy conquest, nor lett mee bee pain'd
    more in thy sunn, when I doe seeke thy shade,

Noe place for help have I left to invade,[287]
    that show'de° a face wher least ease might bee gain'd;   showed
    yett found I paine increase, and butt obtain'd
    that this noe way was to have love allayd,°   quelled, assuaged

When hott, and thirsty to a well I came
    trusting by that to quench part of my flame,[288]
    butt ther I was by love afresh imbrac'd;

Drinke I could nott, butt in itt I did see
    my self a living glass° as well as shee   mirror
    for love to see him self in truly plac'd; $

O stay=

286. Cupid/Amphilanthus; emotion of love.

287. Seize upon; enter.

288. flame] paine 1621

128 MARY WROTH

[MS 54]   [Print 54]

47.   [fol. 28v]

O stay mine eyes, shed nott thes fruitles teares
　　since hope is past to win*n* you back againe
　　that treasure wch beeing lost breeds all yor paine,
　　cease from this poore° betraying of yor feares,　　　　unworthy

Think this to childish is, for wher griefe reares
　　soe high a powre, for such a wreched gaine;
　　sighs, nor laments should thus bee spent in Vaine:
　　true sorrow, never outward wayling beares;°　　　　demonstrates

Bee rul'd by mee, keepe all the rest in store,°　　　　in reserve
　　till noe roome is that may containe one more,
　　then in that sea of teares, drowne haples mee,

And I'le provide such store° of sighs as part　　　　abundance
　　shalbee enough to breake the strongest hart,
　　This dunn, wee shall from torments freed bee $

How=

Manuscript Text 129

[MS 55]   [Print 55]

48.   [fol. 29r]

How like a fire doth love increase in mee,
    the longer that itt lasts, the stronger still,
    the greater purer, brighter, and doth fill
    noe eye w[t] wunder more, then hopes still bee

bred in my brest, wher[289] fires of love are free
    to use that part to theyr best pleasing will,
    and now impossible itt is to kill
    the heat soe great wher Love his strength doth see.

Mine eyes can scarce sustaine the flames my hart
    doth trust in them my longings[290] to impart,
    and languishingly strive to show my love;

My breath nott able is to breathe least part
    of that increasing fuell of my smart;°   emotional suffering
    Yett love I will[291] till I butt ashes prove $

$

$ Pamphilia $

$

289. wher] when 1621

290. longings] passions 1621

291. Here as in line 6 above, Roberts suggests there is an allusion to Wroth's lover, Will[iam]Herbert.

130 MARY WROTH

[fol. 29v blank]

Manuscript Text 131

[MS 56]

[Print 56]

Sonett; $

[fol. 30r]

Lett griefe as farr bee from your deerest brest
    as I doe wish, or in my hands to ease;
    then showld itt bannist bee, and sweetest rest
    bee plac'ed to give content° by love to please,
              satisfaction, pleasure

Lett those disdaines wch on your hart doe seaze°   seize
    doubly returne to bring her soules unrest,
    since true love will nott that beelov'd displease
    or lett least smart° to theyr minds bee adrest,[292]   pain, anguish

Butt often times mistakings bee in love,
    bee they as farr from faulce accusing right,
    and still truthe governe wth a constant might,
    soe shall you only wished pleasures prove°   experience

And as for mee, she that showes you least scorne[293]
wth all despite, and hate bee her hart torne; $

$

---

292. Be framed for or directed to a particular audience.

293. Even the least bit of scorn.

132 Mary Wroth

[MS 57]   [Print 57]

Song $.

[fol. 30v]

O mee the time is come to part,
and wth itt my lyfe=killing smart[294]
fond hope leave mee my deer must goe
to meet more joy, and I more woe;

Wher still of mirth injoye thy fill
one is enough to suffer ill
my hart soe well to sorrow us'd°   accustomed
can better bee by new griefe[295] brus'd;°   bruised, crushed

Thou whom the heav'ns them selves like made
showld never sitt in mourning shade   10
noe I alone must mourne, and end
who have a lyfe in grief to spend,

My swiftest pace to wayling[296] bent
shews° joye had butt some[297] short time lent   shows
to bide in mee wher woes must dwell,
and charme mee wth theyr cruell spell,

And yett when they theyr wichrafts try
they only make mee wish to dy[298]
butt e're my faith in love they change
in horrid darknes will I range;° $ 20   wander

---

294. Sharp intense pain; mental suffering; grief.

295. griefe] griefes 1621

296. wayling] wailings 1621

297. some] a 1621

298. Expire; circumlocution for orgasm.

[MS 58]   [*Urania* 1:212]

Song $ [fol. 31r]

Gon is my joy while heere I burne
    in paines of absence, and of care,°   sorrow, grief
the heav'ns for my sad grief doe turne
    theyr face to stormes, and show dispayre;

The days ar dark, the nights oprest,
    wth cloudlike weeping for my paine,
wch in theyr acting seeme destrest
    sighing like griefe for absent gaine,

The Sunn gives place, and hids° his face   hides
    that day can now bee hardly knowne,   10
nor will the starrs in night yeeld grace
    to sunn=lost heav'n by woe o'rethrowne;

Our light is fire in fearfull flames,
    the aire tempestious blasts of winde
for warmth wee have forgott those names
    such colde, and stormes are us assinde.°   assigned

And still you blessed heav'ns remaine
    distemperd while this cursed powre
of absence rules, wch breeds my paine
    lett yor care bee more still to lowre.°   20   scowl

Butt when my sunn doth back returne
    call yours againe to give his light
that they in flames of joye may burne
    Both shining equall in our sight $
$

134 MARY WROTH

[MS 59]   [Print 58]

Song $ [fol. 31v]

Say Venus how long have I lov'd, and serv'd you heere
yett all my passions scorn'd or doubted allthough cleere
alas thinke love deserveth love, and you have lov'd
looke on my paines, and see if you the like have prov'd;°   experienced

Remember then you ar the Goddess of desire,
and that your sacred powre hath touch'd, and felt this fire,
parswade° thes flames in mee to cease, or them redress   persuade
in mee, poore mee who stormes of love have in excess.

My restles nights may show for mee how much I love
my sighs unfain'd can wittnes what my hart doth prove°   10   show; experience
my saddest looks doe show the greife my soule indures
yett all thes torments from your hands noe help procures

Command that wayward child your sonn to grant yo[r] right,
and y[t] his bowe, and shafts hee yeeld to your fayre sight
to you who have the eyes of joye the hart of love,
and then new hopes may spring y[t] I may pitty move

Lett him nott triumph that hee can both hurt, and save,
and more brag y[t] to you yo[r][299] self a wound hee gave[300]
rule him, or what shall I expect of good to see
since hee that hurt you, hee alas may murder mee $ 20
                    $

299. you yo[r]] your 1621] you your *Wroth's correction*
300. See note to MS 4.

Manuscript Text 135

[MS 60]   [Print 59]

Song $ [fol. 32r]

I, that ame of all most crost°   thwarted, forced to suffer
having, and that had, have lost,
may wth reason thus complaine
since love breeds love, and lovs paine;[301]

That wch I did most desire
to allay° my loving fire   alleviate, relinquish
I may have, yett now must miss
since an other ruler is:

Would that I noe ruler had,
or the service nott soe bad,   10
then might I, wth blis injoy
that wch now my hopes destroy;

And that wished[302] pleasure gott
brings w^t itt the sweetest lott
I, that must nott taste the best
fed must sterve, and restles rest $
                                    $

301. The ambiguous spelling could mean, love is pain, love's pain, or love favors pain.

302. wished] wicked 1621] wished *Wroth's correction*

136 Mary Wroth

[MS 61]

[Print 60]

Song, $

[fol. 32v]

Love as well can make abiding[303]
    in a faythfull sheapheards brest
as in Princese whose thoughts sliding
    like swift rivers never rest
chang to theyr minds is best feeding
    to a sheapheard all his care°   concern, suffering
Who when his love is exceeding
    thinks his faith his richest fare;

Beauty butt a slight inviting
    can nott stirr his hart to chang   10
constancy his chiefe delighting
    strives to fly[304] from phantsies strang
fairnes° to him is noe pleasure   beauty; honesty
    if in other then his love
nor can esteeme that a tresure
    wch in her smiles doth[305] nott move:

This a sheapheard once confessed
    who lov'd well butt was nott lov'd
though wth scorne, and griefe opressed
    could nott yett to chang bee mov'd   20
butt him self thus hee[306] contented
    While[307] in love hee was accurst
this hard hap° hee nott repented   fortune, mischance
    since best lovers speed° the wurst $ fare
        $

---

303. Pausing, stopping; remaining; delaying; awaiting, expecting.

304. fly] flee 1621

305. Wroth has over-written the *t* in "doth" in a darker ink.

306. thus hee] he thus 1621

307. Wroth has over-written the "il" in "While" in a darker ink.

Manuscript Text 137

[MS 62]   [Print 61]

Song $ [fol. 33r]

Deerest if I by my deserving
may maintaine in your thoughts my love,
    Lett mee itt still injoy
        nor faith destroy
Butt, pitty love wher itt doth move,
     new[308]
Lett noe other ^ love invite° you   entice
to leave mee who soe long have serv'd,
    Nor lett yor powre decline
        butt purely shine
On, mee, who have all truth preserv'd;   10

Or had you once found my hart straying[309]
then would nott I accuse your chang,°   inconstancy
    Butt beeing constant still
        itt needs must kill
One, whose soule knowes nott how to rang;[310]

Yett may you loves sweet smiles recover
since all love is nott yett quite lost
    Butt tempt nott love to long
        least° soe great wrong   lest
Make him think hee is too much crost° $ 20 thwarted, opposed
$

308. ^new^] new 1621

309. Wroth wrote the *y* in "straying" over two minims, perhaps joined as an *n*.

310. Rove, wander; change affections, be inconstant.

138 MARY WROTH

[MS 63]   [*Urania* 1:173–74]

Song $

[fol. 33v]

Who can blame mee if I love
since love beefore the world did move?

When I lov'd nott, I dispaird;
scarce for hansomnes I car'd,
since, soe much I ame refin'd
as new form'd of state, and mind;
Who can=

Some, in truth of love beeguil'de°   charmed; deceived
have him blinde, and childish stil'de,°   styled
butt lett non in thes persist   10
since soe judging, judgment mist;°   missed
Who can=

Love in Chaose did appeere,
when nothing was, hee seem'd cleere,
nor when light could bee descride°   descried, perceived
to his crowne a light was ty'de;°   tied
Who can=

Love is truth, and doth delight
wher as honor shines most bright,
Reasons self doth love aprove   20
wch makes us, our selves to love;
Who can=

Could I my past time[311] beeginn
I would nott committ such sinn
to live howre, and nott to love
since love makes us[312] parfaite prove; $
Who can= $

311. Either *past time* or *pastime*.

312. Wroth has written "vs" over two original letters.

[MS 64]   [Print 62]

Song $ [fol. 34r]

Fairest, and still truest eyes
can you the lights bee, and the spies
  of my desires?
Can you shine cleere for loves delight,
and yett the breeders bee of spite,
  and jealous fires?

Mark what lookes doe you beehold,
such as by jealousie are told
  they want your love:
See how they sparcle in distrust   10
wch by a heat of thoughts unjust[313]
  in them doe move;

Learne to guide your course by art[314]
chang your eyes into your hart,
  and patient bee
Till fruitles jealousie gives[315] leave
by safest absence to receave
  what you would see;

Then lett love his triumph have,
and suspition such a grave   20
  as nott to move,
While wished freedome brings that bliss
      all[316]
that you injoy what ^ joy is
  happy to love; $
        $

---

313. Unjustified; unfair; faithless, dishonest; improper.

314. Skill derived from knowledge or experience; artifice or deception.

315. gives] give 1621

316. ^all^] all 1621

140 Mary Wroth

[MS 65]

[*Urania* 1:171–72]

Dialogue $
Sheapherd, and sheapherdess $

[fol. 34v]

She: Deare how doe thy wining° eyes   winning
         my sences wholy ty?
sh:2. sence of sight wherin most lies
         chang, and Variety,
she: chang in mee?
sh: 2 choyse in thee some new delight to try;
she: When I chang, or chuse butt thee
         then changed bee mine eyes;
sh: 2 If you absent see nott mee
         will you nott breake thes tyes?   10
she: how can I
         from thence fly wher such parfection lies?
she 2 I must yett more try thy love
         how if y^t I should chang?
she: in thy hart can never move
         a thought soe ill, soe strang,
sh: 2 say I dy?
she: never I would from thy love estrang;
sh:2 Dead what couldst thou love in mee
         when hope, w^t lyfe were fled?   20
she: Beauty, worth,[317] and fayth in thee
         wch live will,[318] though thou dead:
sh: 2 beauty dies.
she: nott wher lies a minde soe richly sped;[319]
sh: 2 Thou dost speake soe faire, soe kind
         I can nott chuse butt trust:
she: none unto soe chaste° a minde   undefiled; free from guilt
         should ever bee unjust°   unfair; unjustified
[s]h:2 Then thus rest
         true possest of love w^t out mistrust $ 30
              $

---

317. Possible pun on Wroth's name.

318. Possible pun on Will[iam Herbert].

319. So successful in fulfilling its desires.

[MS 66]   [Print 63]

Sonett $ 1.   [fol. 35r]

In night yett may wee see some kind of light
    when as the Moone doth please to show her face,
    and in the sunns roome yeelds her sight,[320] and grace
    wch otherwise must suffer dullest night,

Soe ar my fortunes, bard from true delight
    colde, and unsertaine, like to this strang° place,   alien, unfamiliar
    decreasing, changing in an instant space,
    and even att full of joy[321] turn'd to despite;°   contempt, disdain

Justly on Fortune was beestow'd the wheele[322]
    Whose favors ficle, and unconstant reele;
    drunk wth delight of chang, and sodaine paine;

Wher pleasure hath noe settled place of stay
    butt turning still for our best hopes decay,
    And this (alas) wee lovers often gaine; $

                       Truly=

---

320. Wroth converted an original *l* to *s* in "sight."

321. At the point of satisfaction.

322. The wheel of fortune was an emblem of mutability.

142 MARY WROTH

[MS 67]   [Print 17]

2.   [fol. 35v]

Truly poore Night thou wellcome art to me:
    I love thee better in this sad attire
    then y^t wch raiseth some mens phant'sies° higher   fantasies
    like painted[323] outsids wch foule inward bee;

I love thy grave, and saddest lookes to see,
    wch seems my soule, and dying hart intire,
    like to the ashes of some happy fire
    that flam'd in joy, butt quench'd° in miserie;   burned out

I love thy count'nance, and thy sober pace
    wch evenly goes, and as of loving grace
    to uss, and mee among the rest oprest

Gives quiet, peace to my poore self alone,
    and freely grants day leave when thou art gone
    to give cleere light to see all ill redrest;° $ rectified

Deare=

---

323. Colored; artificial, feigned; made up with cosmetics.

Manuscript Text 143

[MS 68]   [Print 30]

                    3.   [fol. 36r]

Deare cherish this, and wth itt my soules will,
  nor for° itt rann away doe itt abuse,   because
  alas itt left poore mee your brest to chuse
  as the blest[324] shrine wher itt would harbour still;

Then favor shew,° and nott unkindly kill   show
  the hart wch fled to you, butt doe excuse
  that wch for better, did the wurse refuse,
  and pleas'd I'le bee, though hartles my lyfe spill,° kill

Butt if you will bee kind, and just[325] indeed,° in truth; in deed
  send mee your hart wch in mines place[326] shall feed
  on faithfull love to your devotion bound;

Ther shall itt see the sacrifises made
  of pure, and spottles love wch shall nott Vade° fade or decay
  while soule, and body are together found; $

       Cruell=

---

324. blest] best 1621

325. Upright, righteous, correct; corresponding exactly or equally; fully, in all respects.

326. In the place of mine. The exchange of hearts was a conventional trope of Renaissance poetry.

144 Mary Wroth

[MS 69]   [Print 66]

4.   [fol. 36v]

Cruell suspition, O! bee now att rest
    lett dayly torments bring to thee some stay[327]
    alas make nott my ill thy ease=full[328] pray,°   prey
    nor give loose raines to rage when loves oprest

I ame by care° sufficiently distrest   sorrow, worry
    noe rack° can strech my hart more, nor a way   an instrument of torture
    can I find out for least content° to lay   pleasure
    one happy foote of joye, one step that's blest;

Butt to my end thou fly'st w^t greedy eye,
    secking to bring griefe by bace° jealousie,   base
    O in how strang a cage ame I kept in?

Noe little signe of favor can I prove
    butt must bee way'de, and turnd to wronging love,
    and wth each humor[329] must my state begin; $

How=

---

327. Cessation of hostilities; peace; restraint, self-control.

328. Comforting; easy; careless.

329. Mental quality; mood.

Manuscript Text 145

[MS 70]   [Print 67]

5.   [fol. 37r]

How many nights have I w^t paine indur'd
  wch as soe many ages I esteem'd
  since my misfortune? yett noe whitt redeem'd
  butt rather faster tide,° to griefe assur'd?°   tied ... bound

How many howrs have my sad thoughts indur'd
  of killing paines? yett is itt nott esteem'd[330]
  by cruell love, who might have thes redeem'd,
  and all thes yeers of howres to joy assur'd:[331]

Butt fond° child, had hee had a care to save   foolish; infatuated
  as first to conquer, this my pleasures grave
  had nott bin now to testify my woe;

I might have bin*n* an Image of delight,
  as now a Tombe for sad misfortunes spite,
  W^{ch} Love unkindly for reward[332] doth showe $

Sleepe fy=

330. Wroth began the last word in this line with "red," anticipating "redeem'd" in the following line.

331. Secured against incursions; made sure for marriage, betrothed.

332. Punishment; recompense for hardship endured.

146 MARY WROTH

[MS 71] [Print 18]

6. [fol. 37v]

Sleepe fy possess mee nott, nor doe nott fright
    mee wth thy heavy, and thy deathlike might
    for counterfettings Vilder° then deaths sight,   more vile
    and such deluding more my thoughts doe spite

Thou suff'rest faulsest shapes my soule t'affright
    some times in liknes of a hopefull spright,°   spirit
    and oft times like my love as in dispite[333]
    Joying thou canst w^t mallice kill delight,

When I (a poore foole made by thee) think joy
    itt is while[334] thy fond shadows doe destroy
    my that while senceles self, then left[335] to thee,

Butt now doe well, lett mee for ever sleepe,
    and soe for ever that deare Image keepe,
    Or still wake, that my sences may bee free $

An end=

---

333. Notwithstanding the adverse effects.

334. itt is while] Doth flow, when 1621

335. then left] left free 1621

Manuscript Text 147

[MS 72]

[Print 69]

7.

[fol. 38r]

An end fond° jealousie alas I know   foolish, dazed
    thy hiden*n*est, and thy most secrett art°   skill, artistry; artifice
    thou canst noe new invention frame butt part
    I have allreddy seene, and felt w^t woe,

All thy dissemblings wch by fained° show   feigned
    wunn my beeleefe, while truth did rule my hart
    I, wth glad mind imbrace'd, and deemd my smart
    the spring of joy, whose streames wth bliss should flow;

I thought excuses had bin reasons true,
    and that noe faulcehood could of° thee ensue;   from; about
    soe soone beeleefe in honest minds is wrought;

Butt now I find thy flattery, and skill,
    wch idly made mee to observe[336] thy will;
    thus is my learning by my bondage bought $

Sweet=

336. Wroth has written over the *o* in "'observe" in darker ink.

148 MARY WROTH

[MS 73]   [Print 19]

8.   [fol. 38v]

Sweet shades why doe you seeke to give delight
　　to mee who deeme delight in this Vilde° place   vile; wild
　　butt torment, sorrow, and mine owne disgrace
　　to taste of joy, or your Vaine[337] pleasing sight;

Show them your pleasures who saw never night
　　of griefe, wher joyings fauning,° smiling face   fawning, admiring
　　　　　　　　　wher
　　appeers as day, ∧[338] griefe found never space
　　yett for a sigh, a grone, or envies spite;

Butt O. on mee a world of woes doe ly,
　　or els on mee all harmes strive to rely,
　　and to attend like servants bound[339] to mee,

Heat in desire, while frosts of cares[340] I prove,°   experience
　　　　　　　　　　　　　　　wᵗ[341]
　　wanting my love, yett surfett[342] doe ∧ love
　　burne, and yett freeze, better in hell to bee; $

Pray=

337. Vacant, void; senseless; futile, ineffectual. The modern allusion to "vanity" was not yet in use.

338. Wroth crossed out an initial *w* and then entered "'wher" above the line.

339. Indentured servants were legally bound to serve for a given period.

340. cares] care 1621

341. ∧wᵗ∧] with 1621

342. Surfeit, indulge to excess; suffer from or become weary of overabundance; lose by immoderate behavior.

Manuscript Text 149

[MS 74]   [Print 71]

9.   [fol. 39r]

'Pray doe nott use thes words I must bee gone,
    alas doe nott fortell my[343] ills to come,
    lett nott my care° bee to my joyes a tombe,   sorrow; concern
    butt rather finde my loss wth loss alone;

Cause mee nott thus a more distressed one
    nott feeling blis for feare[344] of this sad dombe°   doom
    of present cross, for thinking will orecome,
    and loose° all pleasure, since griefe breedeth none;   let loose; lose

Lett the misfortune come att once to mee,
    nor suffer mee wt paine[345] to punnish'd bee,
              bee[346]
    lett mee^ ignorant of mine owne ill

Then now wth the foreknowledg quite to lose
    that wch wth soe much care, and paines love chose
    for his reward, butt joye now, then mirth kill; $

Like to=

343. my] mine 1621

344. for feare] because 1621

345. paine] griefe 1621

346. ^bee^] be 1621

150 Mary Wroth

[MS 75]   [Print 25]

10.   [fol. 39v]

Like to the Indians, scorched wth the sunne,[347]
    the sunn wch they doe as theyr God adore
    soe ame I us'd by love, for ever more
    I worship him, less favor°[348] have I wunn,   good will; affection,
                                                   kindness

Better are they who thus to blacknes runn,[349]
    and soe can only whitenes want° deplore   lack
    then I who pale, and white ame w^t griefs store,° abundance
    nor can have hope, butt to see hopes undunn;°   undone

Beesids theyr sacrifies° receavd's[350] in sight   sacrifices
    of theyr chose° sainte: Mine hid as worthles rite; chosen
    grant mee to see wher I my offrings give,

Then lett mee weare the marke° of Cupids might   badge or banner
    in hart as they in skin doe[351] Phœbus° light   Apollo, the sun god
    Nott ceasing offrings to love while I Live $
                                    $

---

347. Roberts suggests that this poem was inspired by Wroth's performance at court in Ben Jonson's *Masque of Blackness* in 1606.

348. favor] favours 1621

349. Who tend toward dark skin.

350. receavd's] receiv'd 1621

351. doe] of 1621

Manuscript Text 151

[MS 76]   [Print 73]

Song $.   [fol. 40r]

The springing[352] time of my first loving
finds yett noe winter of removing
nor frost[353] to make my hopes decrease
butt w^t the sommer still increase $

The trees may teach us loves remaining
who suffer chang wth little paining
though winter make theyr leaves decrease
yett wth the sommer they increase $

As Birds by silence show theyr mourning
in colde, yett sing att springs returning   10
soe may love nipt° awhile decrease   nipped by cold
butt as the sommer soone increase $

Those that doe love butt for a season
doe faulcefy both love, and reason,
for reason wills if love decrease
itt like the sommer should increase $

Though love some times may bee mistaken
the truth yett ought nott to bee shaken,
or though the heate awhile decrease
itt wth the sommer may increase $ 20

And since the spring time of my loving
found never winter of removing
nor frost[354] to make my hopes decrease
shall as the sommer still increase $
$

352. springing] Spring 1621] springing *Wroth's correction*

353. frost] frosts 1621

354. frost] frosts 1621

152 Mary Wroth

[MS 77] [Print omitted]

Song; $ [fol. 40v]

The birds doe sing, day doth apeere[355]
arise, arise my only deere,
greete this faire morne wth thy faire eyes
wher farr more love, and brightnes lies,

All this long night noe sleepe, nor rest
my love commanded soule possest
butt wachfully° the time did marck watchfully
to see those starrs[356] rise in the darck,

Arise then now, and lett those lights
take Pheabus[357] place as theyr due rights[358] 10
for when they doe together shine
the greater light is still held thine,

Then wth those eyes inrich thy love
from whose deere beams my joye doth move[359]
shine wth delight on my sad hart,
and grace the prize wun by theyr dart $
$

---

355. The conventional aubade, or dawn song, celebrates the joy of lovers awakening after spending the night together.

356. Amphilanthus' eyes; Mars and Venus (Cf. MS 2).

357. Apollo, the sun god; Amphilanthus, the sun personified.

358. The pun on rights/rites suggests the concept of "due benevolence" in marriage: "Let the husband render unto the wife due benevolence: and likewise also the wife unto the husband" (1 Corinthians 7.3).

359. Here and throughout the manuscript, "joy" and "move" suggest the pleasures of making love.

Manuscript Text 153

[MS 78]   [Print 74]

Song: $ [fol. 41r]

Love a child is ever criing,[360]
　　please him, and hee straite is flying,
　　give him hee the more is craving
　　never satisfi'd w^t having;

His desires have noe measure,
　　endles folly is his treasure,
　　what hee promiseth hee breaketh
　　trust nott one word that hee speaketh;

Hee Vowes nothing butt faulce matter,
　　and to cousen[361] you hee'l flatter,　　　　10
　　lett him gaine the hand° hee'll leave you,　　the upper hand
　　and still glory to deseave you;

Hee will triumph in your wayling,
　　and yett cause bee of your fayling,
　　thes his Vertus ar, and slighter[362]
　　ar his guifts, his favors lighter,

Feathers[363] ar as firme in staying
　　woulves noe fiercer in theyr praying
　　as a child then leave him crying[364]
　　nor seeke him soe giv'n to flying $　　　　20
　　　　　　　$

360. Wroth failed to dot the second *i* in "cri[i]ng," so that the word appears on the page as "crimg."

361. To deceive, beguile. Possibly, another coded reference to Wroth's first cousin and clandestine lover, William Herbert.

362. Unworthy of confidence or trust.

363. Feathers] Fathers 1621

364. Cf. MS 47 where Pamphilia did not leave him crying.

154 MARY WROTH

[MS 79]   [Print 75]

Song.   [41v]

Beeing past the paines of love
freedome gladly seekes to move,
says that loves delights were pritty[365]
butt to dwell in them 't'were pitty,°   regrettable

And yett truly says that love
must of force in all harts move
butt though his delights are pritty
to dwell in[366] them were a pitty.

Lett love slightly pas like love
never lett itt to deepe move   10
for though loves delights are pritty
to dwell in them were great pitty;

Love noe pitty hath of love
rather griefes then pleasures move,
soe though his delights are pritty
to dwell in them would bee pitty

Those that like the smart of love
in them lett itt freely move
els though his delights are pritty
doe nott dwell in them for pitty: $ 20

---

365. Wroth changed an original *e* to *i* in "pritty."

366. in] on 1621

Manuscript Text 155

[MS 80]   [*Urania* 1:172–73]

Song;   [fol. 42r]

Love what art thou? A Vaine° thought   foolish, idle, fruitless
    in our minds by phant'sie wrought,
    idle smiles did thee beegett
    while fond° wishes made that nett   doting; foolish
    wch soe many fooles have caught;

Love what art thou? light, and faire,
    fresh as morning clear as th'Aire,
    butt too soone thy evening chang
    makes thy warmth wth coldenes rang°   seek new lovers
    still thy joy is mixt wth care: 10

Love what art thou? A sweet flowre
    once full blowne dead in an howre,
    dust in winde as stayd remaines
    as thy pleasure, or our gaines
    if thy humor chang, to^{367} lowre.°   lower, scowl

Love what art thou? childish, Vaine,
    firme as bubbles made by raine
    wan*n*tones thy greatest pride
    thes foule faults thy Vertues hide
    butt babes can noe staydnes° gaine.   20   staidness, constancy

Love what art thou? causeles curst°   perverse, cantankerous
    yett alas thes nott the wurst
    much more of thee may bee say'd
    butt thy law I once obay'd
    therfor say noe more att first $
$

O pardon=

---

367. Wroth has written "to" over an earlier reading.

156 Mary Wroth

[MS 81]   [Print 76]

                                                           [fol. 42v]

O pardon, Cupid I confess my fault
    then mercy grant mee in soe just a kind
    for treason never lodged in my mind
    against thy might soe much as in a thought,

And now my folly I have deerly° bought   tenderly, at great cost
    nor could my soule least rest, or[368] quiett find
    since rashnes did my thoughts to error bind
    wch now thy fury, and my harme hath wrought;

I curse that thought, and hand wch that first fram'd[369]
    for wch by thee I ame most justly blam'd,
    butt now that hand shall guided bee aright,

And give a crowne[370] unto thy endless prayse
    wch shall thy glory, and thy greatnes raise
    more then thes poore things° could thy honor spite[371] $

---

368. or] of 1621

369. Formulated. Probably an apologetic reference to the previous poem, suggesting that it framed, or falsely accused, the addressee.

370. Symbol of sovereignty or victory.

371. More than these slight poems could offend thy honor or greatness.

Manuscript Text 157

[MS 82]

[Print 77]

A crowne of Sonetts[372]

[fol. 43r]

dedicated to Love $

In this strang° labourinth[373] how shall I turne?[374]

alien, unfamiliar

            on[375]

wayes are^ all sids while the way I miss;

if to the right hand, ther in love I burne;

lett mee goe forward, therin danger is;

If to the left, suspition hinders bliss,

lett mee turne back, shame cries I ought returne

nor fainte though crosses° wth[376] my fortunes kiss;

adverse or opposing events

stand still is harder, allthough sure to mourne;

Thus lett mee take the right, or left hand way;

goe forward, or stand still, or back retire;

I must thes doubts indure w^t out allay° relief

or help, butt traveile[377] find for my best hire;°

reward; recompense for labor

Yett that wch most my troubled sence doth move

is to leave[378] all, and take the thread[379] of love,

372. The crown of sonnets, or corona, was a conventional poetic form in which the last line of the first poem becomes the first line of the following poem, coming full circle when the final line of the last poem reprises the first line of the first poem. Petrarch, Spenser, Wroth's uncle, Philip Sidney, and father, Robert Sidney, all wrote crowns of sonnets, though her father's broke off, unfinished.

373. Cf. *Urania* 2:416, which echoes phrases from this poem: "I have confidence to love, and yett that is master'd with dispaire. In this strange labourinth, help, and aide poore afflicted mee."

374. With an allusion to the poetic line, which turns from one line to the next.

375. ^on^] on 1621

376. wth] which 1621

377. traveile] travell 1621 Both readings apply. This is the first of many allusions to giving birth that appear throughout "a crowne of sonnets."

378. Leave behind or relinquish; abandon or forsake; agree to be controlled or decided by another.

379. Ariadne gave Theseus a thread so that he could find his way out of the labyrinth after killing the Minotaur.

158 MARY WROTH

[MS 83]   2.   [Print 78]

Is to leave all, and take the thread of love
      line
    w^ch ~~path~~[380] straite leads unto the soules content
    wher choyce delights on[381] pleasures wings doe move,
    and idle phant'sie never roome had lent,[382]

When chaste[383] thoughts guide us then owr minds ar bent
    to take that good wch ills from us remove,
    light of true love, brings fruite wch none repent
    butt constant lovers seeke, and wish to prove;

Love is the shining starr of blessings light;
    the fervent fire of zeale, the roote° of peace,   source or cause
    the[384] lasting lampe fed w^t the oyle° of right;[385]   oil
    Image of fayth, and wombe for joyes increase

                =
             Love

Love is true vertu, and his ends delight   [fol. 43v]
his flames ar joyes, his bands true lovers might,

[MS 84]   .3.   [Print 79]

His flames ar joyes, his bands true lovers might,
    noe staine[386] is ther butt pure, as purest white,
    wher noe clowde can apeere to dim*m* his light,
    nor spott defile, butt shame will soone requite,

---

380. path] line 1621. Wroth crossed out "path" and wrote "line" above it in different ink.

381. Wroth has written "on" over an original "W^th."
W^th] with 1621.

382. Where idle fancies, void of real worth had never been given a place.

383. Undefiled; restrained; morally pure; free from guilt.

384. Wroth has written "the" over an original "that."
that] The 1621

385. Righteousness; justice, fairness, or equitable treatment; an obligation that is incumbent on one to fulfill.

386. No disgrace or stigma that casts another person into the shadows.

are[387]
Heere ^affections, tri'de ~~are~~[388] by loves just might
    as gold by fire, and black desernd° by white,   discerned
    Error by truthe, and darknes knowne by light,
    wher faith is Vallwed° for love to requite,°   valued...repay

Please him, and serve him, glory in his might,
    and firme hee'll bee, as innosencye white,
    cleere as th'ayre, warme as sunn[389] beames, as day light,
    just as truth, constant as fate, joy'd to requite,

Then love obay, strive to observe his might,
and bee in his brave court a glorious light;

[MS 85]   4.   [Print 80]

And bee in his[390] brave court a gloriouse light,
    shine in[391] the eyes of faith, and constancie,
    maintaine the fires of love still burning bright
    nott slightly sparkling butt light flaming bee

Never to slack° till earth noe stars can see,   slacken
    till sunn, and Moone doe leave[392] to us dark night,
    and secound Chaose once againe doe free
    us, and the world from all devisions spite,

Till then, affections wch his followers are
    governe our harts, and prove his powers gaine

                        =

    to taste this pleasing sting seek w^t all care   [fol. 44r]
    for hapy smarting is itt wth smale paine,

such as although, itt pierce your[393] tender hart
and burne, yett burning you will love the smart;

387. ^are^] are 1621

388. tri'de are] tryde 1621

389. sunn] Sun's 1621

390. Wroth has written the *h* in "his" over an original letter.

391. Wroth apparently corrected an original *w* to "in."

392. Wroth has written the *le* in "leave" over an original *b*.

393. Wroth has written the *y* in "your" over an original *n*.

160 Mary Wroth

[MS 86]   5.   [Print 81]

And burne, yett burning you will love the smart,
  when you shall feele the weight[394] of true desire,
  soe pleasing, as you would nott wish your part
  of burden showld bee missing from that fire;

Butt faithfull, and unfained° heate aspire[395]   unfeigned, truthful
  wch sin*n* abolisheth, and doth impart
  savlves° to all feares,[396] w^t Vertues wch inspire   salves
  soules w^t devine love, wch showes his chaste° art,   virtuous, pure;
                                                             guiltless
And guide hee is to joyings; open eyes
  hee hath to hapines, and best can learne°   teach
  us means how to deserve, this hee descries,
  who blind yett doth our hidenest thought[397] deserne°   discern

Thus may wee[398] gaine since living in blest love
hee may our profitt,°[399] and owr Tuter[400] prove,[401]   profit/prophet

[MS 87]   6.   [Print 82]

Hee may owr profitt,[402] and our Tuter prove
  in whom alone wee doe this power finde,
  to joine tow° harts as in one frame to move;   two
  tow bodies, butt one soule to rule the minde;[403]

Eeyes w^t much[404] care to one deere object bind
  eares to each others speech as if above

394. Responsibility, obligation; persuasive power.

395. Ascend; ardently seek to attain.

396. feares] feare 1621

397. thought] thoughts 1621

398. may wee] we may 1621

399. profitt] Prophet 1621

400. Possible allusion to the Tudor dynasty and to William Herbert's increasingly powerful position at the Jacobean court.

401. Become; show by trial, action, or experience.

402. profitt] Prophet 1621

403. An allusion to the marriage service, which unites two souls into one.

404. w^t much] which must 1621

Manuscript Text 161

all els they sweet, and learned were; this kind° · natural, rightful
content° of lovers wittniseth true love, · satisfaction, happiness

Itt=

Itt doth inrich the witts,[405] and makes[406] you see · [fol. 44v]
    that in your self wch you knew nott before,
    forcing you to admire such guifts showld bee
    hid from your knowledg, yett in you the store;° · in reserve for your
      future use

Millians of thes adorne the throne of Love
how blest bee[407] they then, who his favours prove° · test; experience

[MS 88]   7.   [Print 83]

How blest bee they then, who his favors prove
    a lyfe wherof the birth is just desire,
    breeding sweet flames[408] wch hearts invite to move
    in those[409] lov'd-eyes wch kindles[410] Cupids fire.

And nurse his longings w^t his thoughts intire,
    fixt on the heat of wishes formd by love,
    yett as wher[411] fire distroys this doth respire,[412]
    increase, and foster all delights above;

Love will a painter make you, such, as you
    shall able bee to drawe your only deere
    more lively,[413] parfett,° lasting, and more true · perfect
    then rarest woorkmen,[414] and to you more neere,[415]

405. Minds; faculties of thinking and reasoning.

406. makes] make 1621

407. bee] are 1621

408. flames] flame 1621

409. those] these 1621

410. kindles] kindle 1621

411. as wher] whereas

412. breathe life into; respire] aspire 1621

413. Wroth has written the second *l* in "lively" over an original *r*.

414. woorkmen] Workeman 1621

415. More closely related by blood or kinship.

162 MARY WROTH

Thes be the least, then needs must all[416] confess
Hee that shunns love doth love him self the less

[MS 89] 8. [Print 84]

Hee that shunns love doth love him self the less
    and cursed hee whos spiritt nott admires
    the worth of love, wher endles blessednes
    raines,° and commands, maintaind by heavnly fires   reigns

made of Vertu, join'de by truth, blowne by desires   [fol. 45r]
    strengthned by worth, renued by carefullnes°   solicitude
    flaming in never changing thoughts, briers
    of jelousie shall heere miss wellcomnes;°   find no welcome here

nor coldly pass in the pursuites of love
    like one longe frozen in a sea of ise,
    and yett butt chastly lett your passions move
    noe thought from Vertuouse love your minds intise

Never to other ends your phant'sies[417] place
butt wher they may returne w^t honors grace,

[MS 90] 9. [Print 85]

Butt wher they may returne w^t honors grace
    wher Venus follyes can noe harbour winn
    butt chased° ar[418] as worthles of the face   chaste
    or stile of love who hath lasiviouse binn

Oure harts ar subjects[419] to her sunn;[420] wher sinn
    never did dwell, nor[421] rest one minutes space
    what faults hee hath, in her did still begin,
    and from her brest hee suckd his fleeting pace,°   vacillating, transitory journey

416. needs must all] all must needs 1621

417. Wroth at first wrote "phant'siss," which she corrected to "phant'sies."

418. After "chased," Wroth began to write "as" (anticipating its appearance in the line), then over-wrote the half-formed s with r.

419. subjects] subject 1621

420. Both Venus's son, Cupid, and Pamphilia's sun, Amphilanthus.
sunn] Sonne 1621

421. nor] or 1621

Manuscript Text 163

if lust[422] bee counted love t'is faulcely nam'd
    by wikednes a fayrer gloss[423] to sett
    upon that Vice, wch els makes men asham'd
    in the owne frase° to warrant[424] butt beget   phrase

This childe for love, who ought like monster borne[425]
bee from the court of Love, and reason torne;

[MS 91]   10.   [Print 86]

Bee from the court of Love, and reason torne
                           for=
    for Love in reason now doth putt his trust,   [fol. 45v]
    desert, and liking are together borne[426]
    children of love, and reason parents just,

Reason adviser is, love ruler must
    bee of the state wch crowne hee long hath worne
    yett soe as neither will in least mistrust
    the government wher noe feare is of scorne,

Then reverence[427] both theyr mights thus made butt[428] one,
    butt wantones, and all those errors shun,
    wch wrongers bee, impostures, and alone°   only
    maintainers of all follyes ill begunn;

Fruit of a sowre, and unwholsome ground°   overly acidic soil
unprofitably° pleasing, and unsound   unworthily, wickedly

---

422. "Lust" was used both positively, to describe physical pleasure or desire, and negatively, as in the Bible, to describe sins of the flesh.

423. Lustre; explanation; deceptive appearance; disingenuous interpretation.

424. In their own words to attest to the truth of. Both the manuscript and 1621 read 'the' in this line, an apparent error for 'their'. If so, as she transcribed MS V.a.104, Wroth may have misread the abbreviation for the possessive pronoun 'y^r' as the abbreviation for the definite article 'y^e', but failed to correct this error in the manuscript she sent to the printer.

425. Like an aborted fetus, or deformed birth.

426. Deserving, or worth, and pleasure, or sexual desire, are sustained together.

427. Wroth changed "reverance" to "reverence."

428. butt] of 1621

164 Mary Wroth

[MS 92] 11. [Print 87]

Unprofitably pleasing, and unsound
　　when heaven gave liberty to frayle dull earth
　　to bringe[429] forth plenty that in ills abound
　　w^{ch}[430] ripest yett doe bring a sertaine dearth

A timeles, and unseasonable birth
　　planted in ill, in wurse time springing found,
　　wch hemlock like° might feed a sick-witts mirthe　　poisonous
　　wher unruld° Vapors swim[431] in endles rounde,　　unruly, uncontrolled

Then joy wee nott in what wee ought to shun
　　wher shady[432] pleasures showe, butt true borne° fires　　borne/born
　　ar quite quench'd out, or by poore ashes wunnn
　　awhile to keepe those coole, and wann desires

　　　　　　　　　　=

O noe lett love his glory have, and might　　[fol. 46r]
bee given to him who triumphs in his right

[MS 93] 12. [Print 88]

Bee given to him who triumphs in his right
　　nor Vading[433] bee, butt like those blossooms fayre
　　wch fall for good, and lose theyr coulers bright
　　yett dy nott, butt wth fruite theyr loss repaire

soe may love make you pale w^{t} loving care°　　suffering, worry
　　when sweet injoying shall restore that light
　　more cleare in beauty then wee can compare
　　if nott to Venus in her chosen night[434]

And who soe give them selves in this deere kind
　　thes hapinesses shall attend them still

429. Wroth imposed the *i* in "bringe" over an original letter, added the final *e*, and rewrote the descender loop of the *g* in "gave" in the line above.

430. Wroth changed "W^{ch}" to "w^{ch}."

431. Wroth has written the *w* in "swim" over an original letter or letters.

432. Wroth's negative use of the word "shady" to mean defective precedes the first OED citation by a century.

433. fading away, transitory; Vading] fading 1621

434. night] might 1621

Manuscript Text 165

to bee suplyd wth joys, inrichd in^435 mind
wth treasures of contents,^436 and pleasures^437 fill,

Thus Love to bee devine doth heere apeere
free from all fogs butt shining faire, and cleere;

[MS 94]   13   [Print 89]

Free from all fogs butt shining faire, and cleere
    wise in all good, and innosent in ill^438
    wher holly° freindship is esteemed deere   holy
    wth truth in love, and justice in our will,°   intentions; desires

In love thes titles only have theyr fill
    of hapy lyfe maintainer, and the meere
    defence of right, the punnisher of skill,
    and fraude; from whence directnes^439 doth apeere,
                      To thee

to thee then Lord commander of all harts   [fol. 46v]
    ruller of owr affections kinde, and just
    great king of Love, my soule^440 from fained smarts
    or thought of change I offer to your trust

This crowne, my self, and all that I have more
except my hart wch you beestowd beefore;

[MS 95]   i4.^441   [Print 90]

Except my hart wch you beestow'd before,
and for a signe of conquest gave away
as worthles to bee kept in your choyse store^442
yett one more spotles wth you doth nott stay

435. Wroth has written "in" over an original letter or letters.

436. With reference to the "contents" of her poems.
 contents] content 1621

437. Wroth has written *ea* in "pleasures" over two original letters.

438. Free from evil or wrongdoing.

439. directnes] directions 1621

440. Wroth wrote "soule" over an original "sence."

441. Wroth wrote "i" instead of "1" in "14."

442. Repository of treasures or possessions.

166 MARY WROTH

The tribute wch my hart doth truly pay
    faith untouch'd is,[443] pure thoughts discharge ye score
    of debts for mee, wher constancy bears sway,
    and rules as Lord, unharm'd by envyes sore,

Yett other mischiefs faile nott to attend,
    as enimies to you, my foes must bee;
    curst jealousie doth all her forces bend
    to my undoing; thus my harmes I see

Soe though in Love I fervently doe burne,
In this strange labourinth how shall I turne? ! $
                             $

---

443. faith untouch'd is] Is faith untouch'd 1621

Manuscript Text 167

[fol. 47r, blank]

168 Mary Wroth

[MS 96]   [Print omitted]

Sonett $.   [fol. 47v]

Eyes, can you tell mee wher my hart remaines?
have you nott seene itt in those lovely eyes
wth pride showe you the place itt ther retaines,
and baby=like still passtime as itt lies?

Or can you in that blessed brest surprise
the run*n*-away? when itt new triumph gaines
to lodg wher greatest harts for mercy cries?
have you nott seene itt ther joye att theyr paines?

Iff neither wher? wher lives itt? wher abides
this careles sprite° who from mee closely slides,[444]   spirit
and hartles leavs mee? O, alas I knowe

Itt is petitioning for pitty's place
wher love hath purest, and still during° grace;   enduring
Thus while I thought itt sor'de,° itt creeps beelowe; /   soared

$

444. Slips away silently or secretly.

Manuscript Text 169

[MS 97]   [Print 91]

                         1.   [fol. 48r]

Sweet lett mee injoye thy sight
    more cleere, more bright then morning sun*n*,
wch in spring time gives delight
    and by wch som*m*ers pride is wun*n*

Present sight doth pleasures move
    wch in sad absence wee must miss,
butt when mett againe in love
    then twise redoubled is our bliss,[445]

Yett this comfort absence gives,
    and butt[446] faithfull loving tries°   10   tests
that though parted, loves force lives
    as just[447] in hart[448] as in our eyes,

Butt such comfort bannish quite
    farr sweeter is itt still to finde
favour in thy loved sight
    wch present° smiles wth joyes combind   when you are present

Eyes of gladnes, lips of love,
    and harts from passion nott to turne,
butt in sweet affections move
    in flames of faith to live, and burne,   20

Deerest[449] then this kindnes give,
    and grant mee lyfe wch is your sight
wherin I more blessed live
    then graced wth the sun*n*s faire light $
                $

445. These opening stanzas echo the language of the aubade [MS 77].

446. butt] only 1621

447. As appropriate; as accurately copied, or reproduced.

448. hart] hearts 1621

449. Wroth wrote "Deerest" over an original "Bade."

170 Mary Wroth

[MS 98]   [Print 92]

2   [fol. 48v]

Sweet Silvia[450] in a shadie wood
    w[th] her faire Nmphs[451] layde downe
sawe nott farr of[o] wher Cupid stood   off
    the Monarck of loves crowne;

All naked playing w[th] his wings
    w[th]in a mirtle[452] tree
w[ch] sight a soddaine laughter brings
    his godhead soe to see;

And fondly they beegan to jest
    w[th] scofing, and delight,   10
nott knowing hee did breed unrest,
    and that his will's his light;[453]

When hee perseaving of theyr scorne
    grew in such desp'rate rage
who butt for honor first was borne
    cowld nott his rage aswage;

Till shooting of his murdring dart
    w[ch] nott long lighting[o] was   alighting
knowing the next way to the hart
    did through a poore nimph pas;   20

This shott, the others made to bow
    beesids all those to blame
who scorners bee, or nott allow
    of powrfull Cupids name;

Take heede then, nor doe idly smyle
    nor loves commands despise
for soone will hee your strength beeguile
    although hee want his eyes; $

---

450. One of Diana's nymphs, who was sworn to chastity but in love with the shepherd Amyntas.

451. Wroth's three minims in "Nmphs" leave out the *i* or *y* after N required for 'Nimphs/Nymphs.'

452. An evergreen shrub, sacred to Venus. Myrtle garlands were used ceremonially as symbols of love, peace, honor, poetic glory, or immortality.

453. light] right 1621

Manuscript Text 171

[MS 99]   [Print 93]

                              3.   [fol. 49r]

Come merry spring delight us
for winter long did spite us
in pleasure still persever,
thy beauties ending never,
        spring, and growe
        lasting soe
W^th joyes increasing ever;

Lett colde from hence bee banistt[454]
till hopes from mee bee Vanisht,
butt bless thy dainties[455] growing   10
in fullnes freely flowing
        sweet birds sing
        for the spring
all mirthe is now beestowing;

Philomeale[456] in this arbour
makes now her loving harbour
yett of her state° complaining   condition,
her notes in mildnes straining   circumstances
        wch though sweet
        yett doe meete   20
her former luckles payning; $
                      $

---

454. Wroth at first wrote "baniste" and then converted the *e* to a final *t*.

455. Favors; affections; delights, pleasures.

456. In Ovid's *Metamorphoses,* the Athenian princess, Philomela, is transformed into a nightingale after being raped by her brother-in-law, Tereus; she turns her pains into sweet birdsong.

172 Mary Wroth

[MS 100][457]   [*Urania* 1:490]

O! that I might but now as senceles bee   [fol. 49v]
of my felt paines, as is that pleasant tree
of the sweet musique thou deere bird dost make,
who I im*m*agin doth my woes partake,
yett contrary wee doe owr passions move[458]
since in sweet notes thou doest thy sorrowes prove,
I, butt in teares, and sighs can show I grieve
and best spent too, soe some will them beeleeve;
butt yett (allas) thy pleasure makes mee finde
that hapines to mee, as love is blinde,   10
and thus thy wrongs in sweetnes to attire
throwse downe my hopes while lasting woes aspire,°   breathe forth
beesids of mee th'advantage thou hast gott
thy griefe thou utterest, mine I utter nott
Yett thus att last wee may agree in one
I mourne for what now is, thou what is gone; $
$

---

457. This poem has no number and no catchword, either before or after. Wroth treated it as a separate song when she moved it to *Urania*, but it continues the allusion to Philomela from the previous page and may have originally been conceived as part of MS 99. Wroth departs from her usual practice by beginning the following poem on the same page.

458. Yet we change, disturb, or stir up our passions in opposing ways.

[MS 101]   [Print 94]

                        4.

Lovers learne to speake butt truthe
        sweare nott, and your othes forgoe,[459]
give your age a constant youth
        Vowe noe more then what you'll doe

Thinke itt sacrilidg to breake
        what you promise shall in love,
and in teares what you may[460] speake
        forgett nott when the ends you prove;[461]

Doe nott think itt glory is
        to intisce,° and then deseave   10   entice
your chiefe honors ly in this
        by worth what wunn is, nott to leave,

T'is nott for your fames[462] to try   [fol. 50r]
        what wee weake nott oft refuse
in owr bownty° owr faults ly   goodness, worth
        when you to doe a fault will chuse;[463]

Fy, leave this, a greater gaine
        't'is to keepe when you have wunn
then what purchaced is wᵗ paine
        soone after in all scorne to shun;   20

For if worthles to bee priz'd
        why att first will you itt move,°   pursue
and if worthy, why dispis'd
        you can nott sweare, and ly, and love;

Love (allas) you can nott like
        't'is butt for a fashion mov'd
non can chuse, and then dislike
        unles itt bee by faulshood prov'd

459. Don't swear and then break your oaths.

460. may] doe 1621

461. When these earlier aims or promises are put to the test.

462. Reputations. fames] fame 1621

463. When you choose to do something blameworthy.

174 Mary Wroth

Butt your choice is, and yor love
    how most numbers[464] to deseave,   30
as if honors claime did move
    like Popish lawe, non safe to leave;

Fly this folly, and returne
    unto truth in love, and try.
none butt Martirs[465] hapy burne
    more shamefull ends they have that lye $
                    $

---

464. numbers] number 1621

465. The Sidneys' staunch Protestantism may explain the poem's attitude toward Roman Catholic martyrs.

[MS 102]   [Print 40]

1.

Faulçe hope wch feeds butt to destroy, and spill   [fol. 50v]
    what itt first breeds; unaturall to the birth
    of thine owne wombe; conceaving butt to kill,
    and plenty gives to make the greater dearth,

Soe Tirants doe who faulsly ruling earth
    outwardly grace them, and wth profitts fill
    advance those who appointed are to death
    to make the greater[466] falle to please theyr will.

Thus shadow they theyr wicked Vile intent
    coulering evill wth the mask[467] of good
    while in faire showes theyr malice soe is spent
    hope kills the hart, and tirants shed the blood

For hope deluding brings us to the pride
of our desires[468] the farder downe to slide; $
                            $

---

466. the greater] their greater 1621

467. the mask] a show 1621

468. The high expectation or the consciousness of what befits our desires.

176 MARY WROTH

[MS 103]   [Print 47]

2.   [fol. 51r]

You blessed starrs wch doe heavns glory show,
   and att your brightnes makes our eyes admire[469]
   yett envy nott if[470] I on earth beelow
   injoy a sight wch moves in mee more fire;

I doe confess such beauty breeds desire,
   you shine, and cleerest light on us beestow,
   yett doth a sight on earth more warmth inspire
   into my loving soule, his force[471] to knowe;[472]

Cleere, bright, and shining as you are, is this
   light of my joye, fixt stedfast nor will move
   his light from mee, nor, I chang from his love,
   butt still increase as th'eith°[473] of all my bliss   the height

His sight gives[474] lyfe unto my love=rulde eyes
my love content beecause in his, love lies;[475] $
$

---

469. Regard with wonder or pleasure.

470. if] though 1621

471. force] grace 1621

472. "Know," in the biblical sense, was a common circumlocution for sexual relations.

473. th'eith] th'earth 1621

474. gives] give 1621

475. Cf. "you can nott sweare, and ly, and love" [MS 101: 24].

Manuscript Text 177

[MS 104]   [Print 41]

3.

[fol. 51v]

How well poore hart thou wittnes canst I love,
    how oft my griefe hath made thee shed for[476] teares
    drops of thy deerest blood, and how oft feares
    borne testimony of the paines I prove,

What torments hast thou sufferd while above
    joy; thou tortur'd wert w^t racks[477] wch longing beares
    pinch'd[478] w^t desires wch yett but wishing reares°   raises up
    firme in my faith, in constancy to move,

Yett is itt sayd that sure° love can nott bee   certain, assured
    wher soe small showe of passion is descrid,°   discerned
    when thy chiefe paine is that I must itt hide
    from all save only one who showld itt see

For know more passion in my hart doth move
then in a millian that make show they[479] love $
$

---

476. for] forth 1621] for *author's correction*

477. Instruments of torture.

478. Tormented, tortured.

479. they] of 1621

178 Mary Wroth

[MS 105]   [Print 98]

4

[fol. 52r]

When I beeheld the Image of my deere
    wth greedy lookes mine eyes would that way bend,
    fear, and desire did inwardly contend
    feare to bee mark'd,° desire to drawe still neere,   noticed

And in my soule a speritt° wowld apeer,   spirit
    wch boldnes waranted,° and did pretend   protected from danger
    to bee my genius,[480] yett I durst° nott lend   dared
    my eyes in trust wher others seemd soe cleere,

Then did I search from whence this danger 'rose,
    if such unworthynes in mee did rest
              nott[481]
    as my sterv'd eyes must ∧ wth sight bee blest;
    when jealousie her poyson did disclose;

Yett in my hart unseene of jealous eye
the truer Image shall in triumph lye; $
              $

---

480. Laid claim to be my tutelary spirit.

481. ∧nott∧] not 1621

[MS 106]   [Print 99]

5.   [fol. 52v]

Like to huge clowds of smoke wch well may hide
    the face of fairest day though for awhile,
    soe wrongs[482] may shadow mee, till truth doe smile,
    and justice (sun like) hath those Vapors tride,[483]

O doting Time, canst thou for shame lett slide
    soe many minutes while ills° doe beguile,°   evils ... deceive
                thus[484]
    thy age, and worth, and faulshoods ^ defile
    thy ancient good, wher now butt crosses 'bide,[485]

Looke once butt[486] up, and leave thy toyling° pace,   struggling, laborious
      my[487]
    and on ^ myseries thy dim*m* eyes[488] place
    goe nott soe fast, butt give my care° some end,   suffering, worry

Turne nott thy glas° (alas) unto my ill   hour glass
    since thou wth sand itt can[489] nott soe farr fill
    butt to each one my sorrows will[490] extend, $
                $

482. wrongs] wrong 1621

483. tride] tyde 1621

484. ^thus^] thus 1621

485. Where now only misfortunes or impediments to my love persist.

486. once butt] but once 1621

487. ^my^] my 1621

488. eyes] eye 1621

489. can] canst 1621

490. Wroth wrote "will" over an original "doe."] will 1621

180 Mary Wroth

[MS 107]   [Print 100]

6.   [fol. 53r]

O! that noe day would ever more appeere,
    butt clowdy night to governe this sad place,
    nor light from heav'n thes haples° rooms° to grace   unfortunate ...
    since that light's shadow'd wch my love holds deere;   rooms/stanzas

Lett thickest mists in envy master heere,
    and sunn=borne day for malice showe noe face,[491]
    disdaining light wher[492] Cupid, and the race
    of Lovers are dispisde, and shame shines cleere,[493]

Lett mee bee darke, since bard° of my chiefe light;   barred
    and wounding jealousie commands by might;
    butt stage play like disguised pleasures give,[494]

To mee itt seems as ancient fictions make
    the starrs all fashions, and all shapes partake
    while in my thoughts true forme of love shall live
$

491. Provide no daylight for malicious or wrongful intentions.

492. In these rooms where ...

493. Where the painful consciousness of dishonor or disgrace is all too clear.

494. Disguise pleasures by acting a role, like an actor on stage.

Manuscript Text 181

[MS 108]   [Print 101]

7.   [fol. 53v]

No time, noe roome, noe thought, nor[495] writing can
    give rest, or quiett to my loving hart,
    nor[496] can my memory or phantsie scan[497]
    the measure of my still renuing smart,[498]

Yett would I nott (deere love) thou should'st' depart
    butt lett thy[499] passions as they first began
    rule, wounde, and please, itt is thy choysest art
    to give disquiett wch seemes ease to man;

When all alone, I thinke upon thy paine
    how thou doest traveile[500] owr best selves to gaine;°   to secure
    then[501] howerly° thy lessons doe I[502] learne,   hourly

Think on thy glory wch shall still assend
    untill the world come to a finall end,[503]
    and then shall wee thy lasting powre deserne $
           $

495. nor] or 1621

496. nor] Or 1621

497. Test or evaluate, with an allusion to scanning a line of poetry.

498. Her smart, or pain, continues to be a source of spiritual renewal.

499. thy] my 1621

500. Work; travel. "Traveil" was commonly used to designate the pains of childbirth.
 traveil] travell 1621

501. Wroth has written "then" over an original "an"] Then 1621

502. doe I] I doe 1621

503. Only on the final Judgement day will your eternal power be revealed.

182 Mary Wroth

[MS 109]   [Print 102]

8.

[fol. 54r]

How gloewoorme° like the sunn doth now apeere   lightning bug
    colde beames doe from his gloriouse face desend
    wch showes his days, and force draw to an end,
    or that to leave taking his time growes neere,

This[504] day his face did seeme butt pale, though cleere
    the reason is hee to the north must lend
    his light, and warmth must to that climate bend
    whose frozen parts cowld nott loves heat hold deere,

Alas if thou (bright sun*n*) to part from hence
    grieve soe, what must I haples? who from thence
    wher thou dost goe my blessing shall attend

Thou shalt injoye that sight for wch I dy,[505]
    and in my hart thy fortunes doe envy,
    Yett grieve,[506] I'le love thee, for this state may mend $
                        $

---

504. This] The 1621

505. A coded allusion to orgasm.

506. Even though I continue to mourn thy absence.

Manuscript Text 183

[MS 110]   [Print 103]

My muse now hapy, lay thy self to rest   [fol. 54v]
　　sleepe in the quiett of a faithfull love,
　　write you noe more, butt lett thes phant'sies[507] move
　　some other harts, wake nott to new unrest,

Butt if you study, bee those thoughts adrest°   addressed, directed
　　to truth, wch shall eternall goodnes prove;
　　injoying of true joye, the most, and best,
　　the endles gaine wch never will remove;

Leave the discource of Venus, and her sun*n*[508]
　　to young beeginers, and theyr brains inspire
　　wth storys of great love, and from that fire
　　gett heat to write the fortunes they have wun*n*,

And thus leave of,[509] what's past showes you can love,
Now lett your constancy your honor prove,° $ show by your actions

$
$ Pamphilia $
$

507. These fancies or fantasies; these poems.

508. sun*n*] sonne 1621

509. of] off 1621

184 Mary Wroth

[MS 111]   [*Urania* 1:460–61]

Sonett $.   [fol. 55r]

Unquiet griefe search farder, in my hart
    if place bee found wch thou hast nott possest
    or soe much space can build hopes smalest nest
    take itt from mee, I ame the lodg of smart,°   place of grief

Despaire, dispaire hath Us'd the skilfulst art
    to ruin hope, and murder easfull° rest,   comforting, soothing
    O mee, dispaire my Vine of hope hath prest
    ravisht° the grapes the leaves left for my part: ruined

Yett ruler griefe, nor thou dispaire deny
    this last request, proclaime t'was nott suspect°   suspicion
    grafted this bud of sorrow in my brest

Butt knowledg dayly doth my loss descry[510]
    colde love's now maskd w^t care;[511] chang w^t respect[512]   sorrow, grief
    When true flames liv'd thes faulse fires were supprest; $
                                 $

---

510. Proclaim; reveal; detect, perceive; denounce.

511. Love's true nature is disguised or hidden by her suffering, or by the role she is forced to play, or by the elusive ambiguity of her language.

512. These three words epitomize the poem's concealments, for the syntax is as ambiguous as the diction. *Change* could be either a noun or a verb, meaning among other things, exchange, alter, passing from life to death, giving or receiving reciprocally, while "respect" could mean notice, regard, appearance, or the act of looking back over what has occurred.

Manuscript Text 185

[MS 112]   [Print omitted]

Sonett $ [fol. 55v]

Can the lov'd Image of thy deerest face
 soe miroir like present thee to my sight
 yett Cristalls coldenes gaine loves sweetest place
 When warmth wth sight hath ever equall might

You say t'is butt the picture of true light
 wherof my hart is made the safest case
 faithfully keeping that rich pourtraits right
 from change or thought y^t relique[513] to displace,

My brest doth nourish itt, and wth itt lives
 as oyle to Lamps theyr lasting beeing gives
 each looke alures a wish of meeting joye;

Iff butt a picture, then restore wth ease
 the lyfe peece of my soule, and lett itt seaze
 this chillnes into heate, and barrs° destroy; $ impediments, barriers
$

---

513. Sacred artifact or ornament; memento or souvenir; precious, beloved person.

186 Mary Wroth

[MS 113]   [Print omitted]

Sonett $ [fol. 56r]

Oft did I wounder why the sweets of Love
    were counted paines, sharp wounds, and cruell smarts
    till one blow sent from heavnly face prov'd darts
    enough to make those deem'd°=sweets bitter prove,   seeming

One shaft° did force my best strength to remove,   arrow
    and armies brought of thoughts, wch thought imparts,
    one shaft soe spent may conquer courts of harts
    one shott butt dubly sent my sprite° did move,   spirit

Tow sparckling eyes were gainers of my loss [514]
    while love=begetting lips theyr gaine did cross,
    and chaleng'd haulf of my hart=master'd prise,

Itt humbly did confess they wan the field, [515]
    yett equall was theyr force, soe did itt yeeld
    equally still to serve those lips, and eyes; $
                    $

---

514. Her heart and spirit have left her body to take up residence in his eyes.

515. It, her heart, humbly did confess that his eyes and lips won the contest or battlefield.

Manuscript Text 187

[fol. 56v, blank]

188 MARY WROTH

[MS 114]   [*Urania* 1:614–23]

.I.

[fol. 57r]

A sheapherd who noe care did take
    of aught butt of his flock
whose thoughts noe pride cowld higher make
    then to maintaine his stock,
Whose sheepe his love was, and his care
    theyr good his best delight,
the lambs his joye, theyr sport his fare,
    his pleasure was theyr sight,

2.

Till love, an envier of mans blis
    did turne this merry lyfe   10
to cares, to wishes wch ne're° miss   never
    incombrances wth strife,
for wheras hee was best content
    wth looking on his sheepe
his time in woes must now bee spent,
    and broken is his sleepe;

3.

Thus first his woefull chang began
    a lambe hee chanc'd to miss
wch to find out about he ran
    yett finds nott wher itt is,   20
Butt as hee past° O! fate unkind   ran past
    his ill lead° him that way   led
wheras a willow tree[516] behind
    a faire° young mayden lay;   beautiful

Her=

---

516. Symbol of unrequited love.

fol. 57v]

4.

Her bed was on the humble ground
 her hed upon her hand
While sighs did show her hart was bound
 in lov's fast tying band,
clear tears her cleerest eyes lett fall
 upon her love borne face   30
wch heavnly drops did sorrow call
 prowd wittnes of disgrace;[517]
    5.
The sheapherd stayd, and fed his eyes
 nor furder might hee pas
but ther his freedome to sight ties
 his bondage his joye was,
His lambe hee deems nott haulf soe faire
 though itt were Very° white,   true, pure
and liberty hee thinks a care°   burden, sorrow
 nor breathes butt in her sight,   40
    6.
His former lyfe is alterd quite
 his sheep feed in her eyes
her face his field is of delight,
 and flocks hee doth dispise,°   deride, despise
The rule of them hee leaves to none
 his scrip° hee threw away,   shepherd's bag
and many hee forsakes for one
 One hee must now obay.

      Unhapy=

---

517. Ignominy; disfavor; misfortune.

190 Mary Wroth

7.

[fol. 58r]

Unhapy man whose loosing° found
  what better had bin lost   50
whose gaine doth spring from such a grownd°
  wherby hee must bee crost,
The worldly cares hee now neglects
  for Cupids service ties
care only to his fond respects°
  wher wavelike treasure lies,

     releasing

     ground

     doting love

8.

As this lost man still gazing stood
  amased att such light
immagining noe heavnly food
  to feed on butt her sight   60
wishing her bright beams to behold
  yett grievd hee for her griefe
when mournfully she did unfolde[518]
  her woes wth out reliefe

9.

His new sun rose, and rising sayd
  farwell faire willow tree
the triumph of my state decayd°
  the fruit for haples mee,
What though thy branch a signe be made
  of labor lost in love   70
thy beauty doth noe sooner Vade°
  then those best fortunes move;

     impaired, ruined

     fade

My=

---

518. Display, disclose; release sheep from a fold.

Manuscript Text 191

10.   [fol. 58v]

My songs shall end w^t willow still
    thy branches I will weare
thou wilt accompany my ill,
    and w^t mee sorrow beare,
true freind sayd she, then sigh'd, and turn'd
    leaving that restles place,
and sheapheard who in passion burn'd
    lamenting his sad case;   80
11.

The mayd thus gon, alone he left,
    still on her steps he gaz'd,
and hartles growne by love bereft
    of mirth in spiritt raysd,
to satisfy his toyling thought
    hee after her will hy,°   hasten
his ruin to bee surer bought,
    and sooner harme to try,
12.

Then thus his latest leave hee tooke
    my sheepe sayd hee farwell,   90
lett som new sheapherd to you looke
    whose care may mine excell,
I leave you to your freedome now
    loves lawes soe fast mee bind
as noe time I can you allow;
    Or goe poore flock, and find

The

192 Mary Wroth

13   [fol. 59r]

The mayd° whom I soe deerly love   maiden
    say itt was her deere sight
wch from your keepe° doth me remove,   sheepcote; care
    and kills my first delight,   100
goe you my dog who carefull were
    to guard my flock from harme,
looke to them still noe care forbear
    though love my sences charme;°   bewitch; control

14.

Butt you my pipe° y^t musique gave,   shepherd's flute
    and pleasd my silent rest
of you I company will crave
    our states now suteth best,
for if that faire° noe pitty give   that beautiful maiden
    my dying breath shall cry   110
through thee the paines wherin I live
    wherby I breathe to dy;

15.

Madly hee ran from ease to paine
    nott sick butt far from well
hart rob'd° by tow faire eyes, his gaine   robbed
    must prove his earthly hell,
After his hart hee fast doth hy,
    his hart to her did fly,
and for a byding° place did cry,   resting
    wthin her brest to ly;   120

She=

16.

[fol. 59v]

She that refus'd; When hee her spide°   spied
    her whom hee held most deere
ly weeping by a river side
    beholding papers neere
Her ruling eyes yett must bee dimd
    while pearlike° tears she shed   pearl-like
like shadowes on a picture limd,°   limned, painted
    att last thes words she read

17.

When I unconstant am to thee
    or faulse doe ever prove   130
lett hapines bee banisht mee
    nor have least taste of love;
Butt this too soone alas cride she
    is (ô) by thee forgott
my hopes, and joys now murderd bee,
    and faulshood is my lott;

18.

Too late I find what t'is to trust
    to words, or othes,° or tears,   oathes
since they that use them prove unjust,°   unfaithful
    and couler[519] butt owr fears   140
poore fooles ordain'd to bee deceav'd;
    and trust to bee betraide,
scornd when owr harts ar us bereav'd
    sought to, awhile delay'd;

Yett=

---

519. Put a favorable gloss on; misrepresent, falsify; embellish with poetic rhetoric.

194 MARY WROTH

19.

[fol. 60r]

Yett though that thou soe faulse have bin
    I still will faithfull bee,
and though thou think'st to chang, noe sin
    I'le make my loyalty
to shine soe cleere as thy foule fault
    to all men shalbee knowne   150
thy chang° to thy changd hart bee brought   inconstancy
    my faith abroad bee blowne°   trumpeted

20.

This having sayd againe she rose
    the papers putting by,
and once againe a new way chose
    striving from griefe to fly,
Butt as she going was along
    that pleasant runing streame
she saw the sallow° trees amonge   willow
    the sheapherd Aradeame,   160

2I.

For soe this woefull lad was call'de,
    but when she him beheld,
What wichcraft hath thee now inthralld,
    and brought thee to this field,
What can the cause or reason bee
    that thou art hether° come   hither
wher all must taste of misery,
    and mirth wth griefe intombe;

Iff=

Manuscript Text 195

[fol. 60v]

22.

Iff mirthe must heere intombed bee
    faire sheapherdes sayd hee   170
this place the fittest is for mee
    if you use crueltie,
For know I hether com to see
    thy self, wherin now lies
my lyfe, whose absence martirs mee
    whose sight my powre tyes[520]

23.

Give mee butt leave to live w^t you
    itt is the lyfe I crave
to you I bound am to bee true
    my self to you I gave,   180
When first I did behold you ly
    in shade of willow tree
that time, my soule did to you ty,
    those eyes did conquer mee,

24.

Is this the reason; ah cride she
    the more I waile thy cace
who thus partaker needs will bee
    in griefe, and in disgrace,
I pitty thee, butt can nott ayde
    thee, nor redress thy ill   190
since joy, and paine together payd
    scarce satisfies the will;

Iff=

520. Binds or controls all my abilities.

196 Mary Wroth

25.   [fol. 61r]

Iff I doe ty you I release
    the band wherin you are
your freedome shall nott finde decrease
    nor you accuse my care,
The paine I have is all mine owne
    non of itt can beare part°   be shared
sorrow my strength hath overthrowne
    disdaine hath kil'd my hart,   200

26.

And sheapherd if that thou dost love
    this counsell take of mee
this humour fond,° in time remove   doting mood
    wch can butt torture bee,
take itt from her who too too well
    can wittnes itt is soe,
whose hope seem'd heav'n, yett prov'd a hell,
    and comfort° chang'd to woe   pleasure, happiness

27.

For I was lov'd, or soe I thought,
    and for itt lov'd againe°   210   in return
but soone those thoughts my ruin brought,
    and nourisht all my paine,
they gave the milk that fed beliefe
    till wean'd they proved dry,
theyr latter nourishment was griefe
    soe famish'd I must dy;

Then=

28.

[fol. 61v]

Then see your chance; I can nott chang
    nor my affection turne
disdaine, wch others move to rang°   to play the field
    makes mee more constant burne;   220
My sighs I'me sure can nott you please
    my griefe noe musique prove
my flowing teares your passions ease
    nor woes delight your love,

29.

Iff my sight have your freedome wun*n*
    receave itt back againe
soe much I find my self undun
    by guifts wch prove noe gaine
as I lament wth them that love
    soe true in love I ame,   230
and liberty wish all to prove
    whose harts waste in this flame,

30.

Yett give mee leave (sigh'd hee w^t tears)
    to live butt wher you are
my woes shall waite upon your fears
    my sighs attend your care,
I'le weepe when you shall ever waile
    if you sigh I will cry
when you complaine,[521] I'le never faile
    to plaine° my misery,   240   lament

I will=

---

521. Lament your lost love.

198 MARY WROTH

31.

I will you guard, and safely keepe   [fol. 62r]
 from danger, and from feare,
still will I wach when you doe sleep,
 and for both° sorrows beare,   for both of us
make mee nott free I bondage crave
 nor seek els butt to serve,
this freedom will procure my grave,
 thes bands° my lyfe preserve   bonds

32.

For lyfe, and joye, and ease, and all
 alas lies in your hands   250
then doe nott cause my only fall,
 I tyde ame in such bands
part hence° I can nott, nor love leave   leave here
 butt heer must ever byde°   stay
then pitty lett my paine receave
 doe nott from mercy slide;°   pass easily away

33.

Iff that sayd she you constant are
 unto your coming ill
I'le leave this place yett lett all care
 accompany mee still;   260
And sheapherd live, and hapy bee
 lett judgment rule thy will,°   desire, intention
seeke one whose hart from love is free,
 and who thy joye may fill;

For

Manuscript Text 199

34.

[fol. 62v]

For I lov's bondslave ame, and tyde
    in fetters of disdaine
my hopes ar frozen, my spring dri'de
    my autume drownd w^t paine;
I lov'd, and wurse, I sayd I lov'd
    free truth[522] my ruin brought,   270
and soe your state the like hath mov'd,
    and loss for gaining bought,

35.

Wth that away she hasted fast
    left him his cares to hold
who now to sorrow makes all hast,
    woes drive his hopes to fold,°   overthrow
now hee can see, and weeping say
    his fortune blind hee finds
a hart to harbour his decay,
    a state wch mischief° binds   280   trouble, distress

36.

This now hee feels, and woefully
    his birth, and lyfe hee blames,
yett passion rules when reasons ly
    in dark, or quenched flames;
That place hee first beheld her in
    his biding hee doth make,
The tree his liberty did win
    hee calls his martir stake;[523]

And=

---

522. Open acknowledgement of my love.

523. Stake at which martyrs were tortured or burned.

37.

And pleasingly doth take his fall,
    his griefe accounts delight,   290
freedome, and joye his bitter thrall,
    his food her absent sight,
In contraries his pleasures bee
    while mourning gives him ease,
his tomb must bee that haples tree
    wher sorrows did him seaze

38.

And thus did live, though dayly dide°   died
    the sheapherd Aradeame
whose ceasles tears wch never drid
    were turn'd into a streame,   300
him self the hed, his eyes the springs
    wch fed that river cleere,
that[524] unto lovers this good brings
    when they aproach itt neere,

39.

And drinke of itt to banish quite
    all ficle thought of chang
butt still in one choyce to delight,
    and never think to rang;
Of this sweet water I did drink
    wch did such faith infuse   310
as since to change I can nott think
    Love will death sooner chuse; $

---

524. Wroth has written "that" over two initial letters, possibly "ra."

[MS 115]   [Print omitted]

                 Sonett $ [fol. 63v]

Fly traiter joye whose end brings butt dispaire
      soone high, and prowd, and att the heith downe cast
      like stately trees whose leavy crowns have past
      to brave the clowds, and wth theyr state compare,

When for theyr heds the grownd theyr pillows are
      and theyr dispised roots by one poore blast
      rais'd up in spite, theyr tops by earth imbrast°   embraced
      glad of decline, for from thence springeth care,°   grief, worry

Even soe fond joye, thou raisest up our heads,
      when coms dispaire, and on thy pleasure treads,
      then languishingly dost thou pine, and cry,

Haples joye that can nott act joys kind part
      butt must bee masterd by dispayrs sharp smart,
      Thus faine° thou wouldst bee kind, butt must deny;   gladly
                                            $

202 MARY WROTH

[MS 116]   [*Urania* 1:198]

Sonett $.   [fol. 64r]

How did I find my paines extreamest anguish
    wth restles care my soules eternall languish°   weakness; languor
    torments in lyfe increasing greatest anguish,
    unquiet sleep wch made my sences languish

Till hope apeer'd wch somwhat help'd my anguish
    and gave new lyfe wch ending was w^t languish,
    breath to desire, and help to forgon° anguish   former
    baulmes to cares wounds, and cures to bitter languish,

Butt O! I now doe find hope proves° my anguish   tests, demonstrates
    faulse in itt self to mee brings cruell languish
    had I nere° hop'd, I might have borne my anguish   never
    at least wth lesser torment felt my languish

Now rebell hope I see thy smiles are anguish,
Father, and children butt of endles languish; $

[MS 117]   [*Urania* 1:326–27]

I, who doe feele the highest part of griefe   [fol. 64v]
    shall I bee left wth out reliefe:
I, who for you my torments patient beare
    now doe nott leave mee in my feare;
O comfort never could more wellcom bee
    then in this needfull time to mee,
One drop of pitty[525] will bee higher priz'd
    then seas of joye, if once dispisd;
Turne nott the tortures wch for you I try°   experience
    upon my hart to make mee dy;   10
Have I offended? t'was att your desire
    when by your words, you felt lov's fire;
Iff I did ill, itt was to please your will,°   wish, sexual desire
    can you gett,° and the ofspring kill?   beget
The fault wch I in this committed have
    was, you did ask, I freely gave,
show yett som pitty, then lett torments hy,
    give butt one sigh, I blest shall dy:
Butt O you can nott, I have you displeasd,
    and change, from mee your hart hath seaz'd;° 20   settled upon
Now lett noe fauning° hope of fained skill   fawning
    seeke any joye, butt joyes to kill;
Lett all conspire to breed my wrack,° and end,   downfall, ruin
    yett nott enough my days to spend;
My state I see, and you your ends have gain'd
    I'me lost, since you have mee obtain'd,
Yett though I can nott please your first desire
    I yett may joye in scorners fire;
               As=

---

525. Compassion; tenderness; mercy.

As Salimanders[526] in the fire doe live   [fol. 65r]
    soe shall love flames my living give,   30
And though against yor minde I bee, and move
    forsaken creatures feede on love;
Doe you proceed, you one day may confess
    you wrong'd my care,[527] when I care less; /

---

526. Salamanders were believed to live in fire (cf. Pliny, *Natural History*, 10:86).

527. Grief; concern; affection.

PAMPHILIA *TO AMPHILANTHUS*: THE PRINTED TEXT

[Print 1]

MS 1]

1

[sig. 4A1r]

ᵂHen night's blacke Mantle could most darknesse prove,
And sleepe (deaths Image) did my senses hyre,
    From Knowledge of my selfe, then thoughts did move
    Swifter then those, most swiftnesse[1] neede require.

In sleepe, a Chariot drawne by wing'd Desire,
    I saw; where sate bright *Venus* Queene of Love,
    And at her feete her Sonne, still adding Fire
    To burning hearts, which she did hold above,

But one heart flaming more then all the rest,
    The Goddesse held, and put it to my breast,
    Deare Sonne now shut,° said she, thus must we winne;   shoot

He her obeyd, and martyr'd my poore heart.
    I waking hop'd as dreames it would depart,
    Yet since, O me, a Lover I have[2] beene.

[Print 2]

[MS 2]

2

ᴰEare eyes how well indeed, you doe adorne
    That blessed Sphere, which gazing soules[3] hold deare?
    The loved place of sought for[4] triumphs, neere
    The Court of Glory, where Loves[5] force was borne.

How may they terme you *Aprills* sweetest morne?
    When pleasing lookes, from those bright lights appeare
    A Sunne-shine day, from clowdes, and mists still cleare:
    Kinde nursing fires for wishes yet unborne.

---

1. switnesse 1621] swiftnes MS

2. I have] have I MS

3. soules] eyes MS

4. sought for] Cupids MS

5. Loves] his MS

205

206 MARY WROTH

Two Starres of Heaven sent downe to grace the Earth,
    Plac'd in that Throne which gives all joyes their birth,
    Shining, and burning; pleasing yet their Charmes:

Which wounding even[6] in hurts are deem'd delights;
    So pleasant is their force, so great their mights,
    As happy they can tryumph in their harmes.

[Print 3]   [MS 3]

3   [sig. 4A1v]

*Y*Et is there hope, then Love but play thy part,
Remember well thy selfe, and thinke on me;
    Shine in those eyes which conquer'd have my heart,
    And see if mine, be slacke to answer thee.

Lodge in that breast, and pitty mooving see,[7]
    For flames which in mine burne in truest smart,
    Exciling thoughts, that touch Inconstancy,
    Or those which waste not in the constant Art.

Watch but my sleepe, if I take any rest,
    For thought of you, my spirit so distrest,
    As pale and famish'd, I for mercy cry.

Will you your servant leave? thinke but on this,
    Who weares Love's Crowne, must not doe so amisse
    But seeke their good, who on thy force doe lye.[8]

[Print 4][9]   [*replaces* MS 4]

4

*F*Orbeare darke night, my joyes now budd againe,
    Lately growne dead, while cold aspects, did chill
    The roote at heart, and my chiefe hope quite kill,
    And thunders strooke me in my pleasures waine.° wane

Then I alas with bitter sobs, and paine,
    Privately groan'd, my Fortunes present ill;

---

6. even] yett MS

7. mooving see] move to bee; to *written over* for, *and the* b *in* bee *written over an original* m MS.

8. doe lye] rely MS

9. This poem occurs only in the printed version of the sequence.

Printed Text 207

All light of comfort dimb'd,° woes in prides fill,   dimmed
  With strange encrease of griefe, I griev'd in vaine.

And most, when as a memory to good
  Molested me, which still as witnes stood,
  Of those best dayes, in former time I knew:

Late gone as wonders past, like the great Snow,[10]
  Melted and wasted, with what, change must know:
  Now backe the life comes where as once it grew.

[Print 5]   [MS 5]

      5

CAn pleasing sight misfortune ever bring?
  Can firme desire a painefull torment[11] trye?
  Can winning eyes prove to the heart a sting?
  Or can sweet lips in Treason hidden lye?

The Sunne most pleasing, blindes the strongest eye,
  If two°[12] much look'd on, breaking the sights string; too
  Desires still[13] crost must unto mischiefe[14] hie,
  And as Despaire, a lucklesse chance may fling.

Eyes having none,[15] rejecting prooves a sting,   [sig. 4A2r]
  Killing the budd before the tree doth spring;
  Sweet lipps, not loving, do[16] as poyson prove:

Desire, sight, eyes, lipps; seeke, see, prove, and finde,
  You love may winn, but curses, if unkinde,
  Then shew you harmes dislike, and joy in love.

10. Sow 1621

11. a painefull torment] ever, torments MS

12. two] to MS

13. still] *omitted* MS

14. mischiefe] mischiefes MS

15. none] wunn MS

16. do] doth MS

208 Mary Wroth

[Print 6]   [MS 6]

6

O Strive not still to heape disdaine on me,
    Nor pleasure take, your cruelty to show
    On haplesse me, on whom all sorrowes flow,
    And byding make, as given, and lost by thee.

Alas, even griefe is growne to pitty me,
    Scorne cryes out 'gainst it selfe such ill to show,
    And would give place for joyes delights to flow;
    Yet wretched I, all torture[17] beare from thee.

Long have I suffer'd, and esteem'd it deare,
    Since such thy will,[18] yet grew my paine[19] more neere:
    Wish you my[20] ende, say so, you shall it have;

For all the deapth of my heart-held[21] despaire,
    Is that for you, I feele not Death for care,
    But now Ile° seeke it, since you will not save.   I'll

[Print 7]   [MS 7]

Song. I.

THe Spring now come at last
    To Trees, Fields, to Flowres,
And Meadowes makes to taste
    His pride, while sad showres
Which from mine[22] eyes doe flow
    Makes knowne with cruell paines,
    Cold Winter yet remaines,
No signe of Spring wee[23] knowe.

The Sunne which to the Earth
    Gives heate, light, and pleasure,   10

---

17. torture] torturs MS

18. such thy will] you soe wil<l>d MS

19. paine] paines MS

20. may 1621] my MS

21. hart-held] hart=kild MS

22. mine] my MS

23. wee] I MS

Joyes in Spring hateth Dearth,
  Plenty makes his Treasure.
His heate to me is colde,
  His light all darknesse is,
  Since I am barr'd²⁴ of blisse,
I heate, nor light behold

A Shepherdesse thus said,   [sig. 4A2v]
  Who was with griefe opprest,
For truest Love betrayd,
  Barrd her from quiet rest: 20
And weeping thus, said shee,
  My end approacheth neere,
  Now Willow must I weare,
My Fortune so will bee.

With Branches of this tree
  Ile° dresse my haplesse head,   I'll
Which shall my witnesse bee,
  My hopes in Love are dead:
My cloathes imbroder'd all,
  Shall be with Garlands round,   30
  Some scatter'd, others bound;
Some tyde, some like to fall.

The Barke my Booke shall bee,
  Where dayly I will write,
This tale of haples mee,
  True slave to Fortunes spite.
The roote shall be my bedd,
  Where nightly I will lye
  Wailing in constancy,
Since all true love is dead.   40

And these Lines I will leave,
  If some such Lover come,
Who may them right conceive,
  and place them on my Tombe:
She who still constant lov'd.
  Now dead with cruell care,
  Kill'd with unkind Dispaire,
And change, her end heere prov'd.

24. barr,d] bar'd MS

210 MARY WROTH

[Print 8]   [MS 8]

7

ʟOve leave to urge, thou knowest thou hast the hand
 'Tis Cowardize° to strive where none resist,   cowardice
 Pray thee leave off, I yeeld unto thy band,
 Doe not thus still in thine owne power persist.

Behold, I yeeld; let forces be dismist,
 I am thy[25] Subject conquer'd bound to[26] stand
 Never thy[27] foe, but did thy[28] claime assist,
 Seeking thy[29] due of those who did withstand.

But now it seemes thou would'st[30] I should thee[31] love, [sig. 4A3r]
 I doe confesse, 'twas thy will made mee[32] choose,
 And thy[33] faire shewes made me a Lover prove,
 When I my freedome did for paine refuse.

Yet this, Sir god, your Boy-ship I despise,
Your charmes I obey, but love not want of eyes.

[Print 9]   [MS 9]

8.

ʟEdd by the power of griefe to wailings brought,
 By false conceit of change fallen on my part;
 I seeke for some small ease by lines which bought,
 Increase the[34] paine; griefe is not cur'd by Art.

Ah! how unkindnesse moves within the heart,
 Which still is true and free from changing thought:

25. thy] your MS

26. to] doe MS

27. thy] your MS

28. thy] your MS

29. thy] your MS

30. thou would'st] you would MS

31. thee] you MS

32. thy will made mee] you made mee first MS

33. thy] yoͬ MS

34. Increase the] increaseth MS

Printed Text 211

What unknowne woe it breeds, what endlesse smart,
With ceaslesse teares which causelesly are wrought.[35]

It makes me now to shun all shining light,
And seeke for blackest clouds me light to give:
Which to all others onely darknesse drive;
They on me shine, for Sunne disdaines my sight.

Yet though I darke doe live, I triumph may,
Unkindnes, nor this wrong shall love allay.

[Print 10]   [MS 10]

9.

*B*Ee you all pleas'd, your pleasures grieve not me;
Doe you delight? I envy not your joy:
Have you content? contentment with you be;
Hope you for blisse? hope still, and still enjoy.

Let sad misfortune, haplesse me destroy,
Leave crosses to rule me, and still rule free:
While all delights their contraries imploy,
To keepe good backe, and I but torments see.

Joyes are bereav'd me, harmes[36] doe only tarry,
Despaire takes place, disdaine hath got the hand:
Yet firme love holds my senses in such band,
As (since despised) I with sorrow marry.

Then if with griefe I now must coupled bee,
Sorrow Ile° wed; Despaire thus governes mee.   I'll

[Print 11]   [MS 11]

10.   [sig. 4A3v]

*T*He weary Traveller, who tyred, sought
In places distant farre, yet found no end
Of paine or labour, nor his state to mend:
At last with joy is to his home backe brought.

35. are wrought] ar brought *written over* ai wrought MS

36. me, harmes] <and> harmes MS

212 Mary Wroth

Findes not more ease though he with joy be fraught,
　　When past his[37] feare content like soules ascend:
　　Then I, on whom new pleasures doe descend,
　　Which now as high as first-borne blisse is wrought.

He tyred with his paines, I with my minde;
　　He all content receives by ease of lymbs:
　　I, greatest happinesse that I doe finde,
　　Beliefe for faith, while hope in pleasure swimmes.

Truth saith[38] 'twas wrong conceit bred my despight,
Which once acknowledg'd, brings my hearts delight.

[Print 12]　　　　　　　　　　　　　　　　　　　　　　[MS 12]

11.

*Y*Ou endlesse torments that my rest oppresse,
　　How long will you delight in my sad paine?
　　Will never Love your favour more expresse?
　　Shall I still live, and ever feele disdaine?

Alasse now stay, and let my griefe optaine°　　　　　obtain
　　Some end; feede not my heart with sharpe distresse:
　　Let me once see my cruell fortunes gaine,
　　At least[39] release, and long-felt woes redresse.

Let not the blame of cruelty disgrace
　　The honour'd title of your god-head Love;
　　Give not just cause for me to say, a place
　　Is found for rage alone on me to move.

O quickly end, and doe not long debate
My needfull ayd, lest helpe doe come too late.

[Print 13]　　　　　　　　　　　　　　　　　　　　　　[MS 13]

12.

*C*Loy'd with the torments of a tedious night,
　　I wish for day; which come, I hope for joy:

---

37. his] is MS

38. saith] says MS

39. last] l<e>ast MS

When crosse I finde, new tortures to destroy,
My woe-kild heart, first hurt by mischiefes might.

Then crye for night, and once more day takes flight.
    And brightnesse gone, what rest should heere injoy
    Usurped is: Hate will her force imploy;
    Night cannot Griefe intombe though blacke as spite.

My thoughts are sad, her face as sad doth seeme;   [sig. 4A4r]
    My paines are long, her howers tedious are;
    My griefe is great, and endlesse is my care;
    Her face, her force, and all of woes esteeme.
Then welcome Night, and farewell flattering day,
Which all hopes breed, and yet our joyes delay.

[Print 14]   [MS 14]

Song. 2

ALl Night I weepe, all Day I cry, Ay me,
I still doe wish, though yet deny, ay me:
I sigh, I mourne, I[40] *say that still,*
I only am the store for ill, ay me.

In coldest hopes I freeze, yet burne, ay me,
From flames I strive to flye, yet turne, ay me:
From griefe I hast, but sorrowes hye,
And on my heart all woes doe lye, ay me.

From contraries I seeke to run, ay me,
But contraries I cannot shun, ay me: 10
For they delight their force to trye,
And to Despaire my thoughts doe tye, ay me.

Whither alasse then shall I goe, ay me,
When as Despaire all hopes outgoe, ay me:
If to the Forrest Cupid hies,
And my poore soule to his law tyes, ay me.

To the Court: O no, he cryes fye, ay me,
There no true love you shall espye, ay me:
Leave that place to falsest Lovers,
Your true love all truth discovers, ay me,   20

Then quiet rest, and no more prove, ay me,
All places are alike to Love, ay me:

40. I] and MS

214 MARY WROTH

And constant be in this begun,
Yet say, till Life with Love be done, Ay me.

[Print 15]   [MS 15]

13.

ƊEare famish not what you your selfe gave foode,
  Destroy not what your glory is to save:
  Kill not that soule to which you spirit gave,
  In pitty, not disdaine, your triumph stood.

An easie thing it is to shed the bloud
  Of one who at your will yeelds to the grave:
  But more you may true worth by mercy crave,
  When you preserve, not spoyle, but nourish good.

Your sight is all the food I doe desire,   [sig. 4A4v]
  Then sacrifice me not in hidden fire,
  Or stop the[41] breath which did your praises move.

Thinke but how easie 'tis a sight to give,
  Nay, even desert, since by it I doe live,
  I but Camelion-like, would live, and love.

[Print 16]   [MS 16]

14.

ᴬm I thus conquer'd? have I lost the powers,
  That to withstand which joyes to ruine me?
  Must I bee still, while it my strength devoures,
  And captive leads me prisoner bound, unfree?

Love first shall leave mens fant'sies to them free,
  Desire shall quench loves flames, Spring, hate sweet showres;
  Love shall loose all[42] his Darts, have sight, and see
  His shame and wishings,[43] hinder happy houres.

Why should we not Loves purblinde charmes resist?
  Must we be servile, doing what he list?
  No, seeke some host to harbour thee: I flye

41. the] that MS

42. Love shall loose all] Cupid shall loose MS

43. wishings] Venus MS

Printed Text 215

Thy Babish tricks, and freedome doe professe;
    But O, my hurt makes my lost heart confesse:
    I love, and must; so farewell liberty.

[Print 17]   [MS 67]

15.

*T*Ruely (poore night) thou welcome art to me,
    I love thee better in this sad attire
    Then that which rayseth some mens fant'sies higher,
    Like painted outsides, which foule inward be.

I love thy grave and saddest lookes to see,
    Which seemes my soule and dying heart entire,
    Like to the ashes of some happy fire,
    That flam'd in joy, but quench'd in misery.

I love thy count'nance, and thy sober pace,
    Which evenly goes, and as of loving grace
    To us, and mee, among the rest opprest,

Gives quiet peace to my poore selfe alone,
    And freely grants day leave; when thou art gone,
    To give cleare light, to see all ill redrest.

[Print 18]   [MS 71]

16.

[sig. 4B1r]

*S*Leepe fye possesse me not, nor doe not fright
    me with thy heavy, and thy deathlike might:
    For counterfetting's vilder° then death's sight;   more vile; more wild
    And such deluding more my thoughts doe spight.

Thou suffer'st falsest shapes my soule t'affright,
    Sometimes in likenesse of a hopefull spright;
    And oft times like my Love, as in despight;
    Joying, thou canst with malice kill delight.

When I (a poore foole made by thee) thinke joy
    Doth flow, when[44] thy fond shadowes doe destroy
    My that while sencelesse selfe, left free[45] to thee.

44. Doth flow, when] itt is while MS

45. left free] then left MS

216 MARY WROTH

But now doe well, let me for ever sleepe,
    And so for ever that deere Image keepe
    Or still wake that my senses may be free.

[Print 19]   [MS 73]

17.

*S*Weet shades, why doe you seeke to give delight
    To me, who deeme delight in this vilde° place: vile; wild
    But torment, sorrow, and mine owne disgrace,
    To taste of joy, or your vaine pleasing sight?

Shew them your pleasures who saw never night
    Of griefe, where joyings fawning smiling face
    Appeares as day, where[46] griefe found never space:
    Yet for a sigh, a groane, or envies spite.

But O: on me a world of woes doe lye,
    Or els on me all harmes strive to relye,
    And to attend like servants bound to me.

Heate in desire, while frosts of care[47] I prove,
    Wanting my love, yet surfet doe with[48] love,
    Burne and yet freeze, better in Hell to be.

[Print 20]   [MS 20]

18.

*W*Hich should I better like of, day or night?
    Since all the day, I live in bitter woe:
    Injoying light more cleere my wrongs to know,
    and yet most sad, feeling in it all spite.

In night when darknesse doth forbid all light;
    Yet see I griefe apparant to the show,
    Follow'd by jealousie, whose fond tricks flow,
    And on unconstant waves of doubt alight.

I can behold rage cowardly to feede   [sig. 4B1v]

---

46. where] ^wher^ MS

47. care] cares MS

48. with] ^with^ MS

Upon foule error, which these humors breede,
Shame doubt and feare, yet boldly will thinke ill.

All those[49] in both I feele, then which is best
Darke to joy by day, light in night opprest?
Leave both and end, these but each other spill.

[Print 21]   [MS 21]

Song. 3.

STay my thoughts doe not aspire,
To vaine hopes of high desire;
See you not all meanes bereft,
To injoy no joy[50] is left,
Yet still me thinkes my thoughts doe say,
Some hopes doe live amid dismay.

Hope then once more, Hope for joy,
Bury feare which joyes destroy,
Thought hath yet some comfort given,
Which despaire hath from us driven: 10
Therefore deerely my thoughts cherish,
Never let such thinking perish.

'Tis an idle thing to plaine,
Odder farre to dye for paine;
Thinke and see how thoughts doe rise,
Winning where there no hope lies;
Which alone is lovers treasure,
For by thoughts we love doe measure.

Then kinde thought my fant'sie[51] guide,
Let me never haplesse[52] slide;   20
Still maintaine thy force in me,
Let me[53] thinking still be free;
Nor leave thy might untill my death,
But let me thinking yeeld up breath.

49. those] thes MS

50. joy] hope *written over* joye MS

51. fant'sie] phant'sies MS

52. haplesse] hopeles MS

53. me] my MS

218 Mary Wroth

[Print 22]   [MS 22]

19.

COme darkest Night, becomming sorrow best,
    Light leave thy light, fit for a lightsome soule:[54]
    Darknesse doth truely sute with me opprest,
    Whom absence power doth from mirth controule.

The very trees with hanging heads condole
    Sweet Summers parting, and of leaves distrest,
    In dying colours make a grief-full role;
    So much (alas) to sorrow are they prest.

Thus of dead leaves, her farewell carpets made,   [sig. 4B2r]
    Their fall, their branches, all their mournings prove,
    With leavelesse naked bodies, whose hues vade°   fade
    From hopefull greene to wither in their love.

If trees, and leaves for absence mourners be,
No marvell that I grieve, who like want see.

[Print 23]   [MS 23]

20.

THe Sunne which glads the earth at his bright sight,
    When in the morne he showes his golden face,
    And takes the place from tedious drowsie Night.
    Making the world still happy in[55] his grace.

Shewes happinesse remaines not in one place,
    Nor may the Heavens alone to us give light,
    But hide that cheerefull face, though no long space,
    Yet long enough for tryall of their might.

But never Sun-set could be so obscure,
    No Desart ever had[56] a shade so sad:

---

54. In the left margin opposite this line, Wroth wrote in the Kohler copy of *Urania* "For absence." If she intended this as an alternate reading, "sorrow" in line 1 of this sonnet lamenting absence is perhaps the best candidate for interpolation. As Wroth did not indicate where, if at all, "absence" was to be substituted, we merely record her annotation.

55. in] by MS

56. had] have MS

Nor could black darknesse ever prove so bad,
As paines which absence makes me now indure.

The missing of the Sunne a while makes Night,
But absence of my joy sees never light.

[Print 24]   [MS 24]

21.

WHen last I[57] saw thee, I did not thee see,
       It was thine[58] Image which in my thoughts lay
       So lively figur'd, as no times delay
       Could suffer me in heart to parted be.

And sleepe so favourable is to me,
       As not to let thy lov'd remembrance stray:
       Lest that I waking might have cause to say,
       There was one minute found to forget thee.

Then, since my faith is such, so kinde my sleepe,
       That gladly thee presents into my thought,
       And still true Lover-like thy face doth keepe,
       So as some pleasure shadow-like is wrought.

Pitty my loving, nay of conscience give
Reward to me in whom thy[59] selfe doth[60] live.

[Print 25]   [MS 75]

22.   [sig. 4B2v]

LIke to the Indians scorched with the Sunne,
       The Sunne which they doe as their God adore:
       So am I us'd by Love, for evermore
       I worship him, lesse favours[61] have I wonne.

Better are they who thus to blacknesse run,
       And so can onely whitenesse want deplore:

57. last I] I last MS

58. thine] thy MS

59. my] thy *written over* my

60. doth] doth *written over* doe MS

61. favours] favor MS

220 Mary Wroth

Then I who pale and white am with griefes store,
Nor can have hope, but to see hopes undone.

Besides their sacrifice receiv'd[62] in sight,
Of their chose Saint, mine hid as worthlesse rite,
Grant me to see where I my offerings give.

Then let me weare the marke of *Cupids* might,
In heart, as they in skin of[63] *Phoebus* light,
Not ceasing offerings to Love while I live.

[Print 26]   [MS 26]

23.

*W*Hen every one to pleasing pastime hies,
Some hunt, some hauke, some play while some delight
In sweet discourse, and musicke shewes joyes might:
Yet I my thoughts doe[64] farre above these prize.

The joy which I take is, that free from eyes
I sit and wonder at this day-like night,
So to dispose themselves as void of right,
And leave true pleasure for poore vanities.

When others hunt, my thoughts I have in chase;
If hauke, my minde at wished end doth flye:
Discourse, I with my spirit talke and cry;
While others musicke choose as[65] greatest grace.

O God say I, can these fond pleasures move,
Or musicke bee but in sweet[66] thoughts of Love?

[Print 27]   [MS 27]

24.

*O*Nce did I heare an aged father say
Unto his sonne, who with attention heares

---

62. receiv'd] receavd's MS

63. of] doe MS

64. doe] doe *written over* did MS

65. choose as] is theyr MS

66. sweet] deere MS

Printed Text 221

What Age and wise experience ever cleares
From doubts of feare, or reason to betray.

My sonne (said hee) behold thy father gray,
I once had as thou hast, fresh tender yeares,
And like thee sported destitute of feares;
But my young faults made me too soone decay.

Love once I did, and like thee, fear'd my Love,   [sig. 4B3r]
Led by the hatefull threed of Jealousie,
Striving to keepe, I lost my liberty,
And gain'd my griefe, which still my sorrowes move.

In time shun this, to love is no offence,
But doubt in Youth, in Age, breeds penitence.

[Print 28]   [MS 28]

Song. 4.

SWeetest Love returne againe,
Make not too long stay;
Killing mirth and forcing paine;
Sorrow leading way:
Let us not thus parted be,
Love, and absence nere agree.

But since you must needs[67] depart,
And me haplesse leave;
In your journey take my heart,
Which will not deceive: 10
Yours it is, to you it flies,
Joying in those loved eyes.

So in part we shall not part,
Though we absent be,
Tyme, nor place, nor greatest smart,
Shall my bands make free:
Tyed I am, yet thinke it gaine,
In such knots I feele no paine.

But can I live, having lost
Chiefest part of me?   20
Heart is fled, and sight is crost,

67. needs] now MS

222 MARY WROTH

These my fortunes be:
Yet deare heart goe, soone returne,
As good there as heere to burne.

[Print 29]   [MS 29]

25.

*P*Oore eyes bee blinde, the light behold no more,
    Since that is gone which is your deare delight:
    Ravish'd from you by greater power and might,
    Making your losse a gaine to others store.

Oreflow and drowne, till sight to you restore
    That blessed Starre, and as in hatefull spight,
    Send forth your teares in flouds to kill all sight,
    And lookes, that lost wherein you joy'd before.

Bury these[68] beames which in some kindled fires,   [sig. 4B3v]
    And conquer'd have their love-burnt hearts desires,
    Losing, and yet no gaine by you esteem'd;

Till that bright Starre doe once againe appeare,
    Brighter then *Mars* when hee doth shine most cleare;
    See not then by his might be you redeem'd.

[Print 30]   [MS 68]

26.

*D*Eare cherish this, and with it my soules will,
    Nor for it ran away doe it abuse:
    Alas it left (poore me) your brest to choose,
    As the best[69] shrine, where it would harbour still.

Then favour shew, and not unkindly kill
    The heart which fled to you, but doe excuse
    That which for better did the worse refuse;
    And pleas'd Ile be, though heartlesse my life spill.

But if you will bee kinde and just indeed,
    Send me your heart, which in mine's place shall feede
    On faithfull love to your devotion bound,

---

68. these] those MS

69. best] blest MS

There shall it see the sacrifices made
　　Of pure and spotlesse Love, which shall not vade,
　　While soule and body are together found.

[Print 31]　　　　　　　　　　　　　　　　　　　[MS 31]

27.

*F*Ie tedious[70] Hope, why doe you still rebell?
　　Is it not yet enough you flatter'd me,
　　But cunningly you seeke to use a Spell
　　How to betray; must these your Trophees bee?

I look'd from you farre sweeter fruite to see,
　　But blasted were your blossomes when they fell:
　　And those delights expected from hands free,[71]
　　Wither'd and dead, and what seemd blisse proves hell.

No Towne was won by a more plotted slight,
　　Then I by you, who may my fortune write,
　　In embers of that fire which ruin'd me:

Thus Hope your falshood calls you to be tryde,
　　You'r loth, I see, the tryall to abide;
　　Prove true at last, and gaine your liberty.[72]

[Print 32]　　　　　　　　　　　　　　　　　　　[MS 32]

28.　　　　　　　　　　　　　　　[sig. 4B4r]

*G*Riefe, killing griefe, have not my torments beene
　　Already great and strong enough? but still
　　Thou dost increase, nay glory in mine[73] il,
　　And woes new past, afresh new woes begin?

Am I the onely purchase thou canst[74] win?
　　Was I ordain'd to give despaire her fill,
　　Or fittest I should mount misfortunes hill,
　　Who in the plaine of joy cannot live in?

70. tedious] treacherous MS

71. from hands free] late from thee MS

72. gaine your liberty] I will sett thee free MS

73. mine] my MS

74. thou canst] you can MS

224 Mary Wroth

If it be so, Griefe come as welcome guest,
    Since I must suffer for anothers rest;
    Yet this (good Griefe) let me intreat of thee,

Use still thy force, but not from those I love
    Let me all paines and lasting torments prove;
    So I misse these, lay all thy waights on me.

[Print 33]   [MS 33]

29.

*F*Lye hence, O Joy, no longer heere abide,
    Too great thy pleasures are for my despaire
    To looke on, losses now must prove my fare;
    Who not long since on better foode relide.

But foole, how oft had I Heav'ns changing spi'de
    Before of mine[75] owne fate I could have[76] care:
    Yet now past time I can too late[77] beware,
    When[78] nothings left but sorrowes faster ty'de.

While I enjoyd that Sunne, whose sight did lend
    Me joy, I thought that day could have no end:
    But soone[79] a night came cloath'd in absence darke;

Absence more sad, more bitter then is gall,
    Or death, when on true Lovers it doth fall;
    Whose fires of love, disdaine reasts poorer[80] sparke.

[Print 34]   [MS 34]

30.

*Y*Ou blessed shades, which give me silent rest,
    Witnes but this when death hath clos'd mine eyes,
    And separated me from earthly tyes;
    Being from hence to higher place adrest.

---

75. mine] my MS

76. have] take MS

77. I can too late] too late I can MS

78. When] now MS

79. soone] O! MS

80. disdaine reasts poorer] disdaineth rests poore MS

Printed Text 225

How oft in you I have laine heere opprest?
    And have my miseries in wofull cryes
    Deliver'd forth, mounting up to the Skyes?
Yet helplesse, backe return'd to wound my brest.

Which wounds did but strive how to breed more harm   [sig. 4B4v]
    To me, who can be cur'd by no one charme
    But that of Love, which yet may me releeve;

If not, let Death my former paines redeeme,
    My trusty freinds, my faith untouch'd, esteeme,[81]
    And witnesse I could[82] love, who so could grieve.

[Print 35]   [MS 35]

Song. 5.

TIme onely cause of my unrest,
By whom I hop'd once to be blest,
    How cruell art thou turn'd?
That first gav'st life unto my love,
And still a pleasure not to move,
    Or change, though ever burn'd.

Have I thee slack'd, or left undone
One loving rite, and so have wonne,
    Thy rage, or bitter changing?
That now no minutes[83] *I shall see,*   10
Wherein I may least happy be,
    Thy favours[84] *so estranging.*

Blame thy selfe and not my folly,
Time gave time but to be holy,
    True Love such ends best loveth:
Unworthy Love doth seeke for ends,
A worthy Love, but worth pretends;
    Nor other thoughts it proveth.

Then stay thy swiftnes cruell Time,
And let me once more blessed clime   20

---

81. My trusty friends, my faith untouch'd, esteeme] and you my, trusty friends, my faith esteeme MS

82. I could] I well could MS

83. minutes] minute MS

84. favours] favor MS

226 Mary Wroth

to joy, that I may praise thee:
Let me pleasure sweetly tasting,
Joy in Love, and faith not wasting,
and on Fames wings Ile raise thee.

Never shall thy glory dying,
Bee untill thine owne untying,
that Tyme no longer liveth,
'Tis a gaine such time to lend,
Since so thy fame shall never end,
But joy for what she giveth.   30

[Print 36]   [MS 36]

31.

*A*Fter long trouble in a tedious way,
Of Loves unrest, laid downe to ease my paine,
Hoping for rest, new torments I did gaine   [sig. 4C1r]
Possessing me, as if I ought t'obey.

When Fortune came, though blinded, yet did stay,
And in her blessed armes did me inchaine:
I, cold with griefe, thought no warmth to obtaine,
Or to dissolve that yce° of joyes decay.   ice

Till rise (said she) Reward[85] to thee doth send
By me the servant of true Lovers joy:
Bannish all clouds of doubt, all feares destroy;
And now on Fortune, and on Love depend.

I her obey'd, and rising felt that Love
Indeed was best, when I did least it move.

[Print 37]   [MS 37]

32.

*H*Ow fast thou fliest, O Time, on Loves swift wings,
To hopes of joy, that flatters our desire:
Which to a Lover still contentment brings;
Yet when we should injoy, thou dost retire.

---

85. Reward] Venus MS

Printed Text 227

Thou stay'st thy pace (false Time) from our desire
    When to our ill thou hast'st with Eagles wings:
    Slow only to make us see thy retire
    Was for Despaire, and harme, which sorrow brings.

O slake thy pace, and milder passe to Love,
    Be like the Bee, whose wings she doth but use
    To bring home profit; masters good to prove,
    Laden, and weary, yet againe pursues.

So lade thy selfe with hony of sweet[86] joy,
And do not me (the Hive of Love) destroy.

[Print 38]   [MS 38]

33.

*H*Ow many eyes (poore Love) hast thou[87] to guard
    Thee from thy most desired wish, and end?
    Is it because some say th'art blinde, that barr'd
    From sight, thou should'st no happinesse attend?

Who blame thee so, small Justice can pretend,
    Since 'twixt thee and the Sunne no question hard
    Can be; his sight but outward, thou can'st bend
    The heart, and guide it freely thus unbar'd.

Art thou, while we both blinde and bold, oft[88] dare
    Accuse thee of the harmes our selves should finde:
Who led with folly, and by rashnesse blinde   [sig. 4C1v]
    Thy sacred power doe with a child's compare.

Yet Love, this boldnesse pardon; for admire
Thee sure we must, or be borne without fire.

[Print 39]   [MS 39]

34.

*T*Ake heed mine eyes, how you your looks doe cast,
    Lest they betray my hearts most secret thought:

---

86. sweet] sought MS

87. (poore Love) hast thou] hast thou poore Love MS

88. oft] thus MS

228 MARY WROTH

Be true unto your selves; for nothing's bought
More deare then Doubt, which brings a Lovers fast.

Catch you alwatching eyes ere they be past,
    Or take yours fix't, where your best Love hath sought
    The pride of your desires; let them be taught
    Their faults for[89] shame they could no truer last.

Then looke, and looke with joy, for conquest won,
    Of those that search'd your hurt in double kinde:
    So you kept safe, let them themselves looke blinde,
    Watch, gaze, and marke till they to madnesse run.

While you mine[90] eyes enjoy full sight of Love,
Contented that such happinesses move.

[Print 40]   [MS 102]
35.

*F*Alse Hope which feeds but to destroy and spill
    What it first breeds, unnaturall to the birth
    Of thine owne wombe, conceiving but to kill
    And plenty gives to make the greater dearth.

So Tyrants doe, who falsly ruling Earth,
    Outwardly grace them, and with profits fill,
    Advance those who appointed are to death;
    To make their greater[91] fall to please their will.

Thus shadow they their wicked vile intent,
    Colouring evill with a show[92] of good:
    While in faire showes their malice so is spent;
    Hope kills the heart, and Tyrants shed the blood.

For Hope deluding brings us to the pride
Of our desires the farther downe to slide.

89. for] wth MS

90. mine] my MS

91. their greater] the greater MS

92. a show] the mask MS

Printed Text 229

[Print 41]   [MS 104]

36.

𝓗Ow well (poore heart) thou witnesse canst, I love,
    How oft my grief hath made thee shed for[93] teares,
    Drops of thy dearest blood; and how oft feares   [sig. 4C2r]
    Borne testimony of the paines I prove?

What torments hast thou suffer'd, while above
    Joy thou tortur'd wert with racks, which longing bears:
    Pinch'd with desires, which yet but wishing reares
    Firme in my faith, in constancie, to move.

Yet is it said, that sure love cannot be,
    Where so small shew of passion is descri'd;
    When thy chiefe paine is, that I must it hide
    From all, save onely one, who should it see.

For know, more passion in my heart doth move,
Then in a million that make shew of[94] love.

[Print 42]   [MS 42]

Song. 6.

𝓨Ou happy blessed eyes,
    Which in that ruling place,
    Have force both to delight, and to disgrace;
Whose light allures and tyes
    All hearts to your command;
    O looke on me who doe at mercy stand.

'Tis you that rule my life,
    'Tis you my comforts give,
    Then let not scorne to me my ending drive:
Nor let the frownes of strife   10
    Have might to hurt those lights;
Which while they shine they are true loves delights.

See but when Night appeares
    And Sunne hath lost his force,
    How his losse doth all joy from us divorce:

---

93. for *Wroth's correction*] forth 1621] for MS

94. of] they MS

230 Mary Wroth

And when he shines, and cleares
  The Heavens from clowdes of Night,
  How happy then is made our gazing sight?

But more then Sun's faire light
  Your beames doe seeme to me,   20
  Whose sweetest lookes doe tye, and yet make free:
Why should you then so spight
  Poore me? as to destroy
  The only pleasure that I taste of joy.

Shine then, O dearest lights
  With favour and with love
  And let no cause, your cause of frownings move:
But as the soules delights,   [sig. 4C2v]
  So blesse my then blest eyes,
  Which unto you their true affection tyes.   30

Then shall the Sunne give place,
  As to your greater might,
  Yeelding that you doe show more perfect light.
O then but grant this grace,
  Unto your Love-tide slave,
  To shine on me, who to you all faith gave.

And when you please to frowne,
  Use your most[95] *killing eyes*
  On them, who in untruth and falshood lies,
But (Deare) on me cast downe   40
  Sweet lookes, for true desire;
  That banish doe all thoughts of faigned fire.

[Print 43]   [MS 43]

37.

ᴺIght, welcome art thou to my minde distrest,
  Darke, heavy, sad, yet not more sad then I:
  Never could'st thou finde fitter company
  For thine owne humour, then I thus opprest.

If thou beest[96] darke, my wrongs still unredrest
  Saw never light, nor smallest blisse can spye:

95. Use your most] then use your MS

96. beest] bee MS

Printed Text 231

If heavy joy from mee too fast doth hie,
    And care out-goes my hope of quiet rest.

Then now in friendship joyne with haplesse me,
    Who am as sad and darke as thou canst be,
    Hating all pleasure or delight of[97] life,
    Silence and griefe, with thee I best doe love.

And from you three I know I cannot move,
    Then let us live companions without strife.

[Print 44]   [MS 44]

38.

ᴡHat pleasure can a banish'd creature have
    In all the pastimes that invented are
    By wit or learning? Absence making warre
    Against all peace that may a biding crave.

Can wee delight but in a welcome grave,
    Where we may bury paines? and so be farre
    From loathed company, who alwaies jarre
    Upon the string of mirth that pastime gave.

The knowing part of joy is deem'd the heart,   [sig. 4C3r]
    If that be gone what joy can joy impart
    When senslesse is the feeler of our mirth?

No, I am banish'd and no good shall finde,
    But all my fortunes must with mischiefe binde;
    Who but for misery did gaine a birth.

[Print 45]   [MS 45]

39.

ɪF I were given to mirth, 'twould be more crosse,
    Thus to be robbed of my chiefest joy:
    But silently I beare my greatest losse;
    Who's us'd to sorrow, griefe will not destroy.

Nor can I as those[98] pleasant wits injoy
    My owne fram'd wordes which I account the drosse

97. of] in MS

98. those] thes MS

232 Mary Wroth

Of purer thoughts, or reckon them as mosse;
    While they (wit-sick) themselves to breath imploy.

Alas, thinke I, your plenty shewes your want;
    For where most feeling is, wordes are more scant;
    Yet pardon me, live and your pleasure take.

Grudge not if I (neglected) envy show,
    'Tis not to you that I dislike doe owe;
    But (crost my selfe) wish some like me to make.

[Print 46]   [MS 46]

40.

*T*T is not Love which you poore fooles doe deeme,
    That doth appeare by fond and outward showes
    Of kissing, toying, or by swearings gloze:
    O no, these are farre off[99] from loves esteeme.

Alas, they are not such[100] that can redeeme
    Love lost, or winning keepe those chosen blowes:
    Though oft with face and lookes love overthrowes;
    Yet so slight conquest doth not him beseeme.

'Tis not a shew of sighes or teares can prove
    Who loves indeed, which blasts of faigned love,
    Increase or dye, as favours from them slide;

But in the soule true love in safety lies
    Guarded by faith, which to desert still hies:
    And yet kinde[101] lookes do many blessings[102] hide.

[Print 47]   [MS 103]

41.

                                                [sig. 4C3v]

*Y*Ou blessed Starres, which doe Heaven's glory show,
    And at your brightnesse makes our eyes admire:

---

99. are farre off] far are of MS

100. they ...such] thes ...them MS

101. kinde] true MS

102. blessings] blessing MS

Printed Text 233

Yet envy not, though[103] I on earth below,
    Injoy a sight which moves in me more fire.

I doe confesse such beauty breeds desire
    You shine, and clearest light on us bestow:
    Yet doth a sight on Earth more warmth inspire
    Into my loving soule his grace[104] to know.

Cleare, bright, and shining, as you are, is this
    Light of my joy: fix't, stedfast, nor will move
    His light from me, nor I change from his love;
    But still increase as th'earth[105] of all my blisse.

His sight gives[106] life unto my love-rould° eyes   ruled
My love content, because in his love lies.

[Print 48]   [MS 48]

42.

*I*F ever love had force in humane brest,
    If ever he could move in pensive heart:
    Or if that he such powre could but impart
    To breed those flames, whose heat brings joyes unrest.

Then looke on me; I am to these adrest,
    I am the soule that feeles the greatest smart:
    I am that heartlesse Trunck of hearts depart;[107]
    And I that One, by love, and griefe opprest.

None ever felt the truth of loves great misse
    Of eyes, till I deprived was of blisse;
    For had he seene, he must have pitty show'd;

I should not have beene made this[108] Stage of woe,
    Where sad Disasters have their open show:
    O no, more pitty he had sure bestow'd.

103. though] if MS

104. grace] force MS

105. th'earth] th'eith MS

106. give 1621] gives MS

107. heartlesse Trunck of hearts depart] ~~body lives deprived of hart~~ ^hartles trunk of harts depart^ MS

108. this] the MS

234 MARY WROTH

[Print 49]   [MS 49]

Song. 7.

SOrrow, I yeeld, and grieve that I did misse;
Will not thy rage be satisfied with this?
     As sad a Divell as thee,
     Made me unhappy be:
Wilt thou not yet[109] *consent to leave, but still*
Strive how to show thy cursed divelish skill?

I mourne, and dying am, what would you more?   [sig. 4C4r]
My soule attends, to leave this cursed[110] *shoare*
     Where harmes doe onely flow,
     Which teach me but to know   10
The saddest houres of my lifes unrest,
And tyred minutes with griefes hand opprest.

Yet all this will not pacifie thy spight,
No, nothing can bring ease but my last night,
     Then quickely let it be,
     While I unhappy see
That time so sparing, to grant Lovers blisse,
Will see for time lost, there shall no griefe misse.

Nor let me ever cease from lasting griefe,
But endlesse let it be without reliefe;   20
     To winn againe of Love,
     The favour I did prove,
And with my end please him, since dying,[111] *I*
Have him offended, yet unwillingly.

[Print 50]   [MS 50]

43.

O Dearest eyes, the lights, and guides of Love,
     The joyes of *Cupid,* who himselfe borne blinde,
     To your bright shining, doth his tryumphs binde;
     For, in your seeing doth his glory move.

How happy are those places where you proove

109. yet] ^yett^ MS

110. cursed] wreched MS

111. dying] living MS

Your heavenly beames, which makes the Sun to find
Envy and grudging, he so long hath shin'd
For your cleare lights, to match his beames above.[112]

But now alas, your sight is heere forbid,
And darkenes must these poore lost roomes possesse,
So be all blessed lights from henceforth hid,
That this blacke deede of[113] darknesse have excesse.

For why should[114] Heaven affoord least light to those,
Who for my misery such[115] darknesse chose.

[Print 51]   [MS 51]

44.

*H*Ow fast thou hast'st O Spring with sweetest[116] speed
To catch thy water[117] which before are runne,
And of the greater Rivers welcome woone,
Ere these thy new-borne streames these places feede.

Yet you doe[118] well, lest staying here might breede   [sig. 4C4v]
Dangerous flouds, your sweetest bankes t'orerunn,
And yet much better my distresse to shunn,
Which makes my tears your swiftest course[119] succeed.

But best you doe when with so hasty flight
You fly my ills, which now my selfe outgoe,
Whose broken heart can testifie such woe,
That[120] so orecharg'd, my life-bloud, wasteth quite.

Sweet Spring then keepe your way be never spent,
And my ill dayes, or griefes, assunder rent.

---

112. For your cleare lights, to match his beames above.] ~~now to bee match'd on earth wher you doe move~~ ^and your cleer light showld mach his beames above^ MS

113. of] in MS

114. should] ^should^ MS

115. such] this MS

116. sweetest] swiftest MS

117. water] waters MS

118. you doe] doe yow MS

119. your swiftest course] butt yo[r] course to MS

120. that] w[ch] MS

236 MARY WROTH

[Print 52]   [MS 52]

45.

GOod now be still, and doe not me torment,
        With multitude[121] of questions, be at rest,
        And onely let me quarrell with my breast,
        Which stil lets in new stormes my soule to rent.

Fye, will you still my mischiefes more augment?
        You say, I answere crosse, I that confest
        Long since, yet must I ever be opprest,
        With your tongue torture which wil ne're be spent?

Well then I see no way but this will fright,
        That Devill speech; alas, I am possest,
        And madd folkes senseles are of wisdomes right,

The hellish spirit, Absence, doth arrest.
        All my poore senses to his cruell might,
        Spare me then till I am my selfe, and blest

[Print 53]   [MS 53]

46.

LOve thou hast all, for now thou hast me made
        So thine, as if for thee I were ordain'd,
        Then take thy conquest, nor let me be pain'd
        More in thy Sunne, when I doe seeke thy shade.

No place for helpe have I left to invade,
        That shew'd a face where least ease might be gain'd;
        Yet found I paine increase, and but obtain'd,
        That this no way was to have love allay'd

When hott, and thirsty, to a Well I came,
        Trusting by that to quench part of my flame,[122]
        But there I was by Love afresh imbrac'd

Drinke I could not, but in it I did see   [sig. 4D1r]
        My selfe a living glasse as well as shee;
        For love to see himselfe in, truely plac'd.

121. multitude] multituds MS

122. paine] flame MS

Printed Text 237

[Print 54]   [MS 54]

47.

O Stay mine eyes, shed not these fruitlesse teares,
    Since hope is past to win you back againe,
    That treasure which being lost breeds all your paine;
    Cease from this poore betraying of your feares.

Thinke this too childish is, for where griefe reares
    So high a powre for such a wretched gaine:
    Sighes nor laments should thus be spent in vaine;
    True sorrow never outward wailing beares.

Be rul'd by me, keepe all the rest in store,
    Till no roome is that may containe one more;
    Then in that Sea of teares drowne haplesse me,

And Ile provide such store of sighes, as part
    Shall be enough to breake the strongest heart:
    This done, we shall from torments freed be.

[Print 55]   [MS 55]

48.

$\mathcal{H}$Ow like a fire doth Love increase in me?
    The longer that it lasts the stronger still;
    The greater, purer, brighter; and doth fill
    No eye with wonder more then hopes still bee.

Bred in my breast, when[123] fires of Love are free
    To use that part to their best pleasing will,
    And now unpossible[124] it is to kill
    The heate so great where Love his strength doth see.

Mine eyes can scarce sustaine the flames, my heart
    Doth trust in them my passions[125] to impart,
    And languishingly strive to shew my love.

123. when] wher MS

124. unpossible] impossible MS

125. passions] longings MS

238 MARY WROTH

My breath not able is to breath least part
　　Of that increasing fuell of my smart;
　　Yet love I will, till I but ashes prove.

Pamphilia.

[Print 56]　　　　　　　　　　　　　　　　　　　[MS 56]

Sonnet.

[sig. 4D1v]

LEt griefe as farre be from your dearest breast
　　As I doe wish, or in my hands to ease;
Then should it banish'd be, and sweetest rest
　　Be plac'd to give content by Love to please.

Let those disdaines which on your heart doe ceaze,°　　　　　seize
　　Doubly returne to bring her soules unrest:
Since true love will not that belov'd displease;
　　Or let least smart to their minds be addrest.

But oftentimes mistakings be in love.
　　Be they as farre from false accusing right,
And still truth governe with a constant might
　　So shall you only wished pleasures prove.

And as for me, she that shewes you least scorne,
With all despite and hate, be her heart torne.

[Print 57]　　　　　　　　　　　　　　　　　　　[MS 57]

Song.

O Me, the time is come to part,
　　And with it my life-killing smart:
Fond Hope leave me, my deare must goe,
　　To meete more joy, and I more woe.

Where still of mirth injoy thy fill,
　　One is enough to suffer ill:
My heart so well to sorrow us'd,
　　can better be by new griefes[126] bruis'd.

Thou whom the Heavens themselves like made,
　　should never sit in mourning shade:　　　　　　10

---

126. griefes] griefe MS

Printed Text 239

No, I alone must mourne and end,
  Who have a life in griefe to spend.

My swiftest pace to wailings[127] *bent,*
  Shewes joy had but a[128] *short time lent,*
To bide in me where woes must dwell,
  And charme me with their cruell spell.

And yet when they their witchcrafts trye,
  They only make me wish to dye:
But ere my faith in love they change,
  In horrid darknesse will I range.   20

[Print 58]   [MS 59]

Song.[129]   [sig. 4D2r]

SAy Venus *how long have I lov'd, and serv'd you heere?*
  Yet all my passions scorn'd or doubted, although cleere;
Alas thinke love deserveth love, and you have lov'd,
  Looke on my paines and see if you the like have prov'd:

Remember then you are the Goddesse of Desire,
  and that your sacred powre hath touch'd and felt this fire.
Perswade these flames in me to cease, or them redresse
  in me (poore me) who stormes of love have in excesse,

My restlesse nights may show for me, how much I love,
  My sighes unfaignd, can witnes what my heart doth prove: 10
My saddest lookes doe show the griefe my soule indures,
  Yet all these torments from your hands no helpe procures.

Command that wayward Childe your Son to grant your right,
  and that his Bow and shafts he yeeld to your faire sight,
To you who have the eyes of joy, the heart of love,
  And then new hopes may spring, that I may pitty move:

Let him not triumph that he can both hurt and save,
  And more, bragge that to you your[130] *selfe a wound he gave.*

127. wailings] wailing MS

128. a] some MS

129. In 1621 this "Song" is presented as three six-line stanzas and a final couplet. The division of the
poem into quatrains follows Wroth's notes to the Kohler copy of 1621 (K), where the lines are num-
bered as quatrains, 1–5.

130. you your *Wroth's correction*] your 1621] you yo[r] MS

240 MARY WROTH

Rule him, or what shall I expect of good to see?
  Since he that hurt you, he (alas) may murther mee.   20

[Print 59]   [MS 60]
       Song.

1 That am of all most crost,
Having, and that had have lost,
May with reason thus complaine,
Since love breeds love, and Loves paine.

That which I did most desire,
To allay my loving fire,
I may have, yet now must misse,
Since another Ruler is.

Would that I no Ruler had,
Or the service not so bad,   10
Then might I with blisse enjoy
That which now my hopes destroy.

And that wicked[131] *pleasure got,*
Brings with it the sweetest lot:
I that must not taste the best,
Fed, must starve, and restlesse rest.

[Print 60]   [MS 61]
       Song.   [sig. 4D2v]

1Ove as well can make abiding
  In a faithfull Shepheards brest
As in Princes: whose thoughts sliding
  Like swift Rivers never rest.

Change to their minds is best feeding,
  To a Shepheard all his care,
Who when his Love is exceeding,
  Thinks his faith his richest fare.

Beauty but a slight inviting,
  Cannot stirre his heart to change;   10

---

131. wished *Wroth's correction*] wicked 1621] wished MS

Printed Text 241

Constancye his chiefe delighting,
Strives to flee[132] from fant'sies strange,

Fairnesse to him is no pleasure,
If in other then his love;
Nor can esteeme that a treasure,
Which in her smiles doth not move.

This a Shepheard once confessed,
Who lov'd well, but was not lov'd:
Though with scorne & griefe oppressed
could not yet to change be moved.   20

But himselfe he thus[133] contented,
While in love he was accurst:
This hard hap he not repented,
Since best Lovers speed the worst.

[Print 61]   [MS 62]

                    Song.

DEarest if I by my deserving,
May maintaine in your thoughts my love,
Let me it still enjoy;
Nor faith destroy:
But pitty Love where it doth move.

Let no other new[134] Love invite you,
To leave me who so long have servd:
Nor let your power decline
But purely shine
On me, who have all truth preserv'd.   10

Or had you once found my heart straying,   [sig. 4D3r]
Then would not I accuse your change,
But being constant still
It needs must kill
One, whose soule knowes not how to range.

Yet may you Loves sweet smiles recover,
Since all love is not yet quite lost,

132. flee] fly MS
133. he thus] thus hee MS
134. new] ^new^ MS

242 MARY WROTH

> *But tempt not Love too long*
> *Lest so great wrong*
> *Make him thinke he is too much crost.* 20

[Print 62]   [MS 64]

Song.

FAirest and still truest eyes,
Can you the lights be, and the spies
　　Of my desires?
Can you shine cleare for Loves delight,
And yet the breeders be of spight,
　　And Jealous fires?

Marke what lookes doe you behold,
Such as by Jealousie are told
　　They want your Love.
See how they sparckle in distrust,   10
Which by a heate of thoughts unjust
　　In them doe moove.

Learne to guide your course by Art,
Change your eyes into your heart,
　　And patient be:
Till fruitlesse Jealousie give[135] *leave,*
By safest absence to receive
　　What you would see.

Then let Love his triumph have,
And Suspition such a grave,   20
　　As not to moove.
While wished freedome brings that blisse
That you enjoy what all[136] *joy is*
　　Happy to Love.

[Print 63]   [MS 66]

Sonnet. 1.

*I*N night yet may we see some kinde of light,
　　When as the Moone doth please to shew her face,

---

135. give] gives MS

136. all] ^all^ MS

And in the Sunns roome yeelds her light,[137] and grace,
    Which otherwise must suffer dullest night:

So are my fortunes barrd from true delight,   [sig. 4D3v]
    Cold, and uncertaine, like to this strange place,
    Decreasing, changing in an instant space,
    And even at full of joy turnd to despight.

Justly on Fortune was bestowd the Wheele,
    Whose favours fickle, and unconstant reele,
    Drunke with delight of change and sudden paine;

Where pleasure hath no setled place of stay,
    But turning still, for our best hopes decay,
    And this (alas) we lovers often gaine.

[Print 64]   [MS 17]

2.

*L*Ove like a Jugler comes to play his prize,
    And all mindes draw his wonders to admire,
    To see how cunningly he (wanting eyes)
    Can yet deceive the best sight of desire.

The wanton Childe, how he can faine his fire
    So prettily, as none sees his disguise,
    How finely doe his trickes; while we fooles hire
    The badge, and office[138] of his tyrannies.

For in the ende such Jugling he doth[139] make,
    As he our hearts instead of eyes doth take;
    For men can onely by their slights abuse,

The sight with nimble, and delightfull skill,
    But if he play, his gaine is our lost will,
    Yet Child-like we cannot his sports refuse.

---

137. light] light *changed to* sight MS

138. The badge, and office] marke and service MS

139. he doth] doth hee MS

244 Mary Wroth

[Print 65]   [MS 30]

3.

*M*Ost blessed night, the happy time for Love,
    The shade for Lovers, and their Loves delight,
    The raigne of Love for[140] servants free from spight,
    The hopefull seasons[141] for joyes sports to moove.

Now hast thou made thy glory higher proove,
    Then did the God, whose pleasant Reede did smite
    All *Argus* eyes into a death-like night,
    Till they were safe, that none could Love[142] reproove.

Now[143] thou hast cloasd° those eyes from prying sight   closed
    That nourish Jealousie, more then joyes right,
    While vaine Suspition fosters their mistrust,

Making sweet sleepe to master all suspect,   [sig. 4D4r]
    Which els their private feares would not neglect,
    But would embrace both blinded, and unjust.

[Print 66]   [MS 69]

4.

*C*Ruell Suspition, O! be now at rest,
    Let daily torments bring to thee some stay,
    Alas, make not my ill thy ease-full pray,
    Nor give loose raines to Rage, when Love's opprest.

I am by care sufficiently distrest,
    No Racke can stretch my heart more, nor a way
    Can I finde out, for least content to lay
    One happy foot of joy, one step that's blest.

But to my end thou fly'st with greedy eye,
    Seeking to bring griefe by base Jealousie;
    O, in how strange a Cage am I kept in?

---

140. Love for] Venus MS

141. seasons] season MS

142. none could Love] love could non MS

143. Now] Butt MS

No little signe of favour can I proove,
But must be way'd, and turn'd to wronging love,
And with each humour must my state begin.

[Print 67]   [MS 70]

5.

*H*Ow many nights have I with paine endurd?
Which as so many Ages I esteem'd,
Since my misfortune, yet no whit redeem'd
But rather faster ty'de, to griefe assur'd.

How many houres have my sad thoughts endur'd
Of killing paines? yet is it not esteem'd
By cruell Love, who might have these redeemd,
And all these yeeres of houres to joy assur'd.

But fond Childe, had he had a care to save,
As first to conquer, this my pleasures grave,
Had not beene now to testifie my woe.

I might have beene an Image of delight,
As now a Tombe for sad misfortunes spight,
Which Love unkindly, for reward doth show.

[Print 68]   [MS 18]

6.

*M*Y paine still smother'd in my grieved brest,
Seekes for some ease, yet cannot passage finde,
To be dischargd of this unwelcome guest,
When most I strive, more fast his burthens binde.

Like to a Ship on *Goodwins* cast by winde,   [sig. 4D4v]
The more shee strive,[144] more deepe in Sand is prest,
Till she be lost: so am I in this kind
Sunck, and devour'd, and swallow'd by unrest.

Lost, shipwrackt, spoyld, debar'd of smallest hope,
Nothing of pleasure left, save thoughts have scope
Which wander may; goe then my thoughts and cry:

144. strive] strives MS

246 Mary Wroth

Hope's perish'd, Love tempest-beaten, Joy lost,
   Killing Despaire hath all these blessings[145] crost;
   Yet Faith still cries, Love will not falsifie.

[Print 69]   [MS 72]

7.

*A*N end fond Jelousie, alas I know
   Thy hiddenest, and thy most secret Art,
   Thou canst no new invention frame but part,
   I have already seene, and felt with woe.

All thy dissemblings, which by faigned showe,
   Wonne my beliefe, while truth did rule my heart,
   I with glad minde embrac'd, and deemd my smart
   The spring of joy, whose streames with blisse should flow.

I thought excuses had beene reasons true,
   And that no falshood could of thee ensue,
   So soone beliefe in honest mindes is wrought;

But now I finde thy flattery, and skill,
   Which idely made me to observe thy will,
   Thus is my learning by my bondage bought.

[Print 70]   [MS 19]

8.

*P*Oore Love in chaines, and fetters like a thiefe
   I met ledd forth, as chast Diana's gaine
   Vowing the untaught Lad should no reliefe
   From her receive, who gloried in fond paine.

She call'd him thiefe, with vowes he did mainetaine
   He never stole, but some sadd slight[146] of griefe
   Had given to those who did his power disdaine,
   In which revenge his honour was the chiefe.

Shee said he murther'd and therefore must dye,
   He that he caus'd but Love, did harmes deny,
   But while she thus discoursing with him stood;

---

145. blessings] blessing MS

146. sadd slight] slight touch MS

The Nymphes unti'de him and his chaines tooke off,   [sig. 4E1r]
    Thinking him safe; but he (loose) made a scoffe,
    Smiling and scorning them, flew to the wood.

[Print 71]   [MS 74]

9.

*P*Ray doe not use these wordes, I must be gone;
    Alasse doe not foretell mine[147] ills to come:
    Let not my care be to my joyes a Tombe;
    But rather finde my losse with losse alone.

Cause me not thus a more distressed one,
    Not feeling blisse, because[148] of this sad doome
    Of present crosse; for thinking will orecome
    And loose all pleasure, since griefe breedeth none.

Let the misfortune come at once to me,
    Nor suffer me with griefe[149] to punish'd be;
    Let mee be[150] ignorant of mine owne ill:

Then now with the fore-knowledge quite to lose
    That which with so much care and paines Love chose
    For his reward, but joy now then mirth kill.

[Print 72]   [MS 25]

10.

*F*Olly[151] would needs make mee a Lover be,
    When I did little thinke of loving thought;
    Or ever to be tyde, while shee[152] told me
    That none can live, but to these[153] bands are brought.

I (ignorant) did grant, and so was bought,
    And sold againe to Lovers slavery:

147. mine] my MS

148. because] for feare MS

149. griefe] paine MS

150. be] ^bee^ MS

151. Folly] Cupid MS

152. while shee] till hee MS

153. these] his MS

248 Mary Wroth

The duty to that vanity[154] once taught,
    Such band is, as wee will not seeke to free.

Yet when I well did understand his might,
    How he inflam'd and forc'd one to[155] affect:
    I lovd and smarted, counting it delight
    So still to waste, which Reason did reject.

When Love came blind-fold, and did challenge me.
Indeed I lov'd, but wanton Boy not hee,

[Print 73]   [MS 76]

Song.

The Springing[156] time of my first loving,
    Finds yet no winter of removing;
Nor frosts[157] to make my hopes decrease:
    But with the Summer still increase.

The trees may teach us Love's remaining,   [sig. 4E1v]
    Who suffer change with little paining:
Though Winter make their leaves decrease,
    Yet with the Summer they increase.

As birds by silence shew their mourning
    in cold, yet sing at Springs returning: 10
So may Love nipt a while decrease,
    but as the Summer soone increase.

Those that doe love but for a season,
    Doe falsifie both Love and Reason:
For Reason wills, if Love decrease,
    It like the Summer should increase.

Though Love sometimes may be mistaken,
    the truth yet ought not to be shaken:
Or though the heate a while decrease,
    It with the Summer may increase.   20

---

154. that vanity] the god of love MS

155. forc'd one to] cuningly ^forc'd one to^ MS

156. Springing *Wroth's correction*] Spring 1621] springing MS

157. frosts] frost MS

And since the Spring time of my loving
Found never Winter of removing:
Nor frosts[158] *to make my hopes decrease,*
Shall as the Summer still increase.

[Print 74]   [MS 78]

Song.

LOve a childe is ever crying,
Please him, and he strait is flying;
Give him, he the more is craving,
Never satisfi'd with having.

His desires have no measure,
Endlesse folly is his treasure:
What he promiseth, he breaketh,
Trust not one word that he speaketh.

Hee vowes nothing but false matter,
And to cousen you hee'l flatter: 10
Let him gain the hand, hee'l leave you,
And still glory to deceive you.

Hee will triumph in your wailing,
And yet cause be of your failing:
These his vertues are, and slighter
Are his guifts; his favours lighter.

F[e]athers[159] *are as firme in staying,*   [sig. 4E2r]
Wolves no fiercer in their praying.
As a childe then leave him crying,
Nor seeke him so giv'n to flying.   20

[Print 75]   [MS 79]

BEing past the paines of Love,
Freedome gladly seekes to move:
Sayes that Loves delights were pretty;
But to dwell in them twere pitty.

And yet truly sayes, that Love
Must of force in all hearts move:

158. frosts] frost MS

159. Fathers 1621] Feathers MS

250 Mary Wroth

But though his delights are pretty,
To dwell on[160] *them were a pitty.*

Let Love slightly passe like Love,
Never let it too deepe move: 10
For though Loves delights are pretty,
To dwell in them were great pitty.

Love no pitty hath of Love,
Rather griefes then pleasures move?
So though his delights are pretty,
To dwell in them would be pitty.

Those that like the smart of Love,
In them let it freely move:
Els though his delights are pretty,
Doe not dwell in them for pitty.   20

[Print 76]   [MS 81]

O Pardon *Cupid*, I confesse my fault,
     Then mercy grant me in so just a kinde:
     For treason never lodged in my minde
     Against thy might, so much as in a thought.

And now my folly I have dearely bought,
     Nor could my soule least rest of[161] quiet finde;
     Since Rashnes did my thoughts to Error binde,
     Which now thy fury, and my harme hath wrought.

I curse that thought and hand which that first fram'd,
     For which by thee I am most justly blam'd:
     But now that hand shall guided be aright,

And give a Crowne unto thy endlesse praise,
     Which shall thy glory and thy greatnesse raise,
     More then these poore things could thy honor spight.

---

160. on] in MS

161. of] or MS

Printed Text 251

A Crowne of Sonnets dedicated to Love. [sig. 4E2v]

[Print 77]   [MS 82]

IN this strange Labyrinth how shall I turne,
    Wayes are on[162] all sides, while the way I misse:
    If to the right hand, there in love I burne,
    Let mee goe forward, therein danger is.

If to the left, suspition hinders blisse:
    Let mee turne backe, shame cryes I ought returne:
    Nor faint, though crosses which[163] my fortunes kisse,
    Stand still is harder, although sure to mourne.

Thus let mee take the right, or left hand way,
    Goe forward, or stand still, or back retire:
    I must these doubts indure without allay
    Or helpe, but travell[164] finde for my best hire.

Yet that which most my troubled sense doth move,
Is to leave all and take the threed° of Love.   thread

[Print 78]   [MS 83]
2.

𝘛S to leave all and take the threed of Love,
    Which line[165] straight leades unto the soules content,
    Where choice delights with[166] pleasures wings do move,
    And idle fant'sie never roome had lent.

When chaste thoughts guide us, then our minds are bent
    To take that good which ills from us remove:
    Light of true love brings fruite which none repent;
    But constant Lovers seeke and wish to prove.

Love is the shining Starre of blessings light,
    The fervent fire of zeale, the root of peace,

---

162. on] ^on^ MS

163. which 1621] wth MS

164. travel] traveile MS

165. line] ~~path~~ ^line ^ MS

166. with] on *written over* W^th MS

252 MARY WROTH

The[167] lasting Lampe, fed with the oyle of right,
Image of Faith, and wombe for joyes increase.

Love is true Vertue, and his ends delight,
His flames are joyes, his bands true Lovers might.

[Print 79]   [MS 84]

3.

*H*Is flames are joyes, his bandes true Lovers might,
No staine is there, but pure, as purest white,
Where no cloud can appeare to dimme his light,
Nor spot defile; but shame will soon requite.

Heere are[168] affections tryde by Loves just might   [sig. 4E3r]
As Gold by fire, and black discern'd by white;
Error by truth, and darknes knowne by light,
Where Faith is vallu'd, for Love to requite.

Please him, and serve him, glory in his might
And firme hee'le be, as Innocency white,
Cleere as th'ayre, warme as Sun's[169] beames, as day light
Just as Truth, constant as Fate, joyd to requite.

Then Love obey, strive to observe his might
And be in his brave Court a glorious light.

[Print 80]   [MS 85]

4.

*A*Nd be in his brave Court a glorious light
Shine in the eyes of Faith, and Constancy
Maintaine the fires of Love, still burning bright,
Not slightly sparkling, but light flaming be.

Never to slake till earth no Starres can see,
Till Sun, and Moone doe leave to us darke night,
And second *Chaos* once againe doe free
Us, and the World from all divisions spight.

---

167. The] the *written over* that MS

168. are affections tryde] ^are^ affections, tri'de ~~are~~

169. Sun's] sunn MS

Printed Text 253

Till then affections which his followers are,
    Governe our hearts, and proove his powers gaine,
    To taste this pleasing sting, seeke with all care
    For happy smarting is it with small paine.

Such as although it pierce your tender heart,
And burne, yet burning you will love the smart.

[Print 81]   [MS 86]

5.

*A*Nd burne, yet burning you will love the smart,
    When you shall feele the waight of true desire,
    So pleasing, as you would not wish your part
    Of burthen should be missing from that fire.

But faithfull and unfaigned heate aspire
    Which sinne abollisheth, and doth impart
    Salves to all feare,[170] with vertues which inspire
    Soules with divine love; which shewes his chast Art.

And guide he is to joyings, open eyes
    He hath to happinesse, and best can learne
    Us, meanes how to deserve this he descries,
    Who blinde, yet doth our hidn'st thoughts[171] diserne.

Thus we may[172] gaine since living in blest Love,   [sig. 4E3v]
He may our Prophet,[173] and our Tutor proove.

[Print 82]   [MS 87]

6.

*H*E may our Prophet,[174] and our Tutor proove,
    In whom alone we doe this power finde,
    To joyne two hearts as in one frame to moove
    Two bodies, but one soule to rule the minde

170. feare] feares MS

171. thoughts] thought MS

172. we may] may wee MS

173. Prophet] profitt MS

174. Prophet] profitt MS

254 MARY WROTH

Eyes which must[175] care to one deare Object binde,
    Eares to each others speach as if above
    All else, they sweete, and learned were; this kind
    Content of Lovers witnesseth true love.

It doth inrich the wits, and make[176] you see
    That in your selfe which you knew not before,
    Forcesing° you to admire such gifts should be   forcing
    Hid from your knowledge, yet in you the store.

Millions of these adorne the throne of Love,
How blest are[177] they then, who his favours prove?

[Print 83]   [MS 88]

7.

*H*Ow bless'd be they then, who his favors prove,
    A life whereof the birth is just desire?
    Breeding sweete flame,[178] which harts invite to move,
    In these[179] lov'd eyes, which kindle[180] *Cupids* fire,

And nurse his longings with his thoughts intire,
    Fix't on the heat of wishes form'd by Love,
    Yet whereas[181] fire destroyes, this doth aspire,[182]
    Increase, and foster all delights above.

Love will a Painter make you, such, as you
    Shall able be to draw, your onely deare,
    More lively, perfect, lasting, and more true
    Then rarest Workeman,[183] and to you more neere.

These be the least, then all must needs[184] confesse,
He that shuns Love, doth love himselfe the lesse.

175. which must] wᵗ much MS

176. make] makes MS

177. are] bee MS

178. flame] flames MS

179. these] those MS

180. kindle] kindles MS

181. whereas] as wher MS

182. aspire] respire MS

183. Workeman] woorkmen MS

184. all must needs] needs must all MS

Printed Text 255

[Print 84]   [MS 89]
                    8.

*H*E that shuns Love, doth love himselfe the lesse,
    And cursed he whose spirit, not admires
    The worth of Love, where endlesse blessednes
    Raignes, & commands, maintain'd by heav'nly fires.

Made of Vertue, joyn'd by Truth, blowne by Desires,   [sig. 4E4r]
    Strengthned by Worth, renew'd by carefulnesse,
    Flaming in never-changing thoughts: bryers°   briars
    Of Jealousie shall here misse welcomnesse.

Nor coldly passe in the pursutes of Love
    Like one long frozen in a Sea of yce:
    And yet but chastly let your passions moove,
    No thought from vertuous Love your minds intice.

Never to other ends your Phant'sies place,
But where they may returne with honor's grace.

[Print 85]   [MS 90]
                    9.

*B*Ut where they may returne with Honor's grace,
    Where *Venus* follies can no harbour winne,
    But chased are, as worthlesse of the face,
    Or stile of Love, who hath lascivious beene.

Our hearts are subject to her Sonne,[185] where sinne
    Never did dwell, or[186] rest one minutes space;
    What faults he hath in her did still beginne,
    And from her breast he suck'd his fleeting pace.

If Lust be counted Love, 'tis falsely nam'd,
    By wickednesse, a fairer glosse to set
    Upon that Vice, which else makes men asham'd,
    In the own Phrase to warrant, but beget

This Childe for Love, who ought like Monster borne,
Be from the Court of Love, and Reason torne.

185. subject… Sonne] subjects … sunn MS
186. or] nor 1621

256 MARY WROTH

[Print 86]   [MS 91]

10.

ℬEe from the Court of Love, and reason torne,
    For Love in Reason now doth put his trust,
    Desert and liking are together borne
    Children of Love, and Reason, Parents just.

Reason adviser is, Love ruler must
    Be of the State, which Crowne he long hath worne;
    Yet so, as neither will in least mistrust
    The government where no feare is of scorn.

Then reverence both their mights thus made of[187] one,
    But wantonnesse, and all those errors shun,
    Which wrongers be, Impostures, and alone
    Maintainers of all follies ill begunne.

Fruit of a sower, and unwholesome grownd   [sig. 4E4v]
Unprofitably pleasing, and unsound.

[Print 87]   [MS 92]

11.

𝒰Nprofitably pleasing, and unsound.
    When Heaven gave liberty to fraile dull earth,
    To bring foorth plenty that in ills abound,
    Which ripest, yet doe bring a certaine dearth.

A timelesse, and unseasonable birth,
    Planted in ill, in worse time springing found,
    Which Hemlocke like might feed a sicke-wits mirth
    Where unrul'd vapours swimme in endlesse round.

Then joy we not in what we ought to shunne,
    Where shady pleasures shew, but true borne fires
    Are quite quench'd out, or by poore ashes won,
    Awhile to keepe those coole, and wann desires.

O no, let Love his glory have, and might
Be giv'n to him, who triumphs in his right.

187. of] butt MS

Printed Text 257

[Print 88]   [MS 93]

12.

BE giv'n to him, who triumphs in his right;
  Nor fading[188] be, but like those blossomes faire,
  Which fall for good, and lose their colours bright,
  Yet dye not, but with fruit their losse repaire:

So may Love make you pale with loving care,
  When sweet enjoying shall restore that light,
  More cleere in beauty, then we can compare,
  If not to *Venus* in her chosen might.[189]

And who so give themselves in this deare kinde,
  These happinesses shall attend them still,
  To be supplide with joyes enrich'd in minde,
  With treasures of content,[190] and pleasures fill.

Thus love to be divine, doth here appeare,
Free from all foggs, but shining faire and cleare.

[Print 89]   [MS 94]

13.

FRee from all foggs, but shining faire, and cleare,
  Wise in all good, and innocent in ill,
  Where holy friendship is esteemed deare,
  With Truth in love, and Justice in our Will.

In Love these titles onely have their fill   [sig. 4F1r]
  Of happy life-maintainer, and the meere
  Defence of right, the punisher of skill,
  And fraude, from whence directions[191] doth appeare.

To thee then, Lord commander of all hearts,
  Ruler of our affections, kinde, and just,
  Great King of Love, my soule[192] from faigned smarts,
  Or thought of change, I offer to your trust,

188. fading] Vading MS

189. might] night MS

190. content] contents MS

191. directions] directnes MS

192. soule] soule *written over* sence MS

258 Mary Wroth

This Crowne, my selfe, and all that I have more,
Except my heart, which you bestow'd before.

[Print 90]   [MS 95]

14.

*E*Xcept my heart, which you bestowd before,
    And for a signe of Conquest gave away
    As worthlesse to be kept in your choice store;
    Yet one more spotlesse with you doth not stay.

The tribute which my heart doth truely pay,
    Is faith untouch'd,[193] pure thoughts discharge the score
    Of debts for me, where Constancy beares sway,
    And rules as Lord, unharmd by Envies sore.

Yet other mischeifes faile not to attend,
    As enemies to you, my foes must be,
    Curst Jealousie doth all her forces bend
    To my undoing, thus my harmes I see.

So though in Love I fervently doe burne,
In this strange Labyrinth how shall I turne?

[Print 91]   [MS 97]

Song. 1.

*S*Weet, let me enjoy thy sight
    More cleare, more bright then morning Sun,
Which in Spring-time gives delight
    And by which Summers pride is wun.
Present sight doth pleasures move
    Which in sad absence we must misse:
But when met againe in love,
    Then twice redoubled is our blisse.

Yet this comfort absence gives,
    And only[194] faithfull loving tries,   10
That though parted, Loves force lives
    As just in heart,[195] as in our eyes:

193. Is faith untouch'd] faith untouch'd is MS

194. only] butt MS

195. hearts] hart 1621

But such comfort banish quite,
 Farre sweeter is it, still to finde
Favour in thy loved sight,
 Which present smiles with joyes combind.

Eyes of gladnesse, lipps of Love,
 And hearts from passion not to turne,
But in sweet affections moove,
 In flames of Faith to live, and burne. 20
Dearest[196] *then, this kindnesse give,*
 And grant me life, which is your sight,
Wherein I more blessed live,
 Then graced with the Sunnes faire light.

[Print 92]   [MS 98]

2.

*S*Weet Silvia *in a shady wood,*
 With her faire Nimphs layd downe,
Saw not farre off where Cupid *stood*
 The Monarch of Loves Crowne,
All naked, playing with his wings,
 Within a Mirtle Tree,
Which sight a sudden laughter brings,
 His Godhead so to see.

An[d] fondly they began to jest,
 With scoffing, and delight, 10
Not knowing he did breed unrest,
 And that his will's his right:[197]
When he perceiving of their scorne,
 Grew in such desperate rage,
Who but for honour first was borne,
 Could not his rage asswage.

Till shooting of his murth'ring dart,
 Which not long lighting was,
Knowing the next way to the heart,
 Did through a poore Nymph passe: 20
This shot the others made to bow,

196. Dearest] Dearest *written over* Bade MS
197. right] light MS

260 Mary Wroth

Besides all those to blame,
Who scorners be, or not allow
*   Of powerfull* Cupids *name.*

Take heede then, nor doe idly smile,
*   Nor Loves commands despise,*
For soone will he your strength beguile,
*   Although he want his eyes.*

[Print 93]   [MS 99]

3   [sig. 4F2r]

CO*me merry Spring delight us,*
For Winter long did spight us,
In pleasure still persever,
Thy beauties ending never:
*   Spring, and grow*
*   Lasting so,*
With joyes increasing ever.

Let cold from hence be banish'd,
Till hopes from me be vanish'd,
But blesse thy daynties growing   10
In fulnesse freely flowing:
*   Sweet Birds sing*
*   For the Spring,*
All mirth is now bestowing.

Philomel *in this Arbour*
Makes now her loving Harbour,
Yet of her state complaining,
Her Notes in mildnesse strayning,
*   Which though sweet,*
*   Yet doe meet.*   20
Her former luckelesse paining.

[Print 94]   [MS 101]

4.

L*Overs learne to speake but truth,*
*   Sweare not, and your oathes forgoe,*
Give your age a constant youth,
*   Vow no more then what you'le doe.*

Printed Text 261

Thinke it sacriledge to breake
    What you promise, shall in love
And in teares what you doe[198] *speake*
    Forget not, when the ends you prove.

Doe not thinke it glory is
    To entice, and then deceive,   10
Your chiefe honors lye in this,
    By worth what wonne is, not to leave.

'Tis not for your fame[199] *to try,*
    What we weake, not oft refuse,
In our bounty our faults lye,
    When you to doe a fault will chuse.

Fye leave this, a greater gaine,   [sig. 4F2v]
    tis to keepe when you have won,
Then what purchas'd is with paine,
    Soone after in all scorne to shun.   20

For if worthlesse to be priz'd,
    Why at first will you it move?
And if worthy, why dispis'd?
    You cannot sweare, and lie, and love.

Love alasse you cannot like,
    Tis but for a fashion mov'd,
None can chuse, and then dislike,
    Unlesse it be by falshood prov'd.

But your choyce is, and your love.
    How most number[200] *to deceive,*   30
As if honors claime did move
    Like Popish Law, none safe to leave.

Flye this folly, and returne
    Unto truth in Love, and try,
None but Martir's happy burne,
    More shamefull ends they have that lye.

198. doe] may MS

199. fame] fames MS

200. number] numbers MS

262 MARY WROTH

[Print 95]   [MS 40]

1.

MY heart is lost, what can I now expect,
　　An evening faire after a drowsie day?
　　Alas, fond Phant'sie, this is not the way,
　　To cure a mourning[201] heart,[202] or salve neglect:

They who should helpe, doe me, and helpe reject,
　　Embracing loose desires, and wanton play,
　　While wanton[203] base delights, doe beare the sway,
　　And impudency raignes without respect.

O *Cupid* let thy Mother know her shame,
　　'Tis time for her to leave this youthfull flame,
　　Which doth dishonor her, is ages blame,
　　And takes away the greatnes of thy name.

Thou God of Love, she only Queene of lust,
Yet strives by weakning thee, to be unjust.

[Print 96]   [MS 47]

2.   [sig. 4F3r]

LAte in the Forrest I did *Cupid* see
　　Cold, wett, and crying, he had lost his way,
　　And being blinde was farther like to stray;
　　Which sight, a kind compassion bred in me.

I kindly tooke, and dry'd him, while that he,
　　(Poore Child) complain'd, he sterved° was with stay　　starved
　　And pin'd for want of his accustom'd prey,
　　For none in that wilde place his Host would be.

I glad was of his finding, thinking sure,
　　This service should my freedome still procure,
　　And in my armes I tooke him then unharm'd,

Carrying him safe[204] unto a Myrtle bowre,

201. mourning] morning MS
202. heart] hurt MS
203. wanton] Venus MS
204. safe] *omitted* MS

But in the way he made me, feele his powre,
Burning my heart, who had him kindly warm'd.

[Print 97]   [MS 41]

3.

JUno still jealous of her husband *Jove,*
    Descended from above, on earth to try,
    Whether she there could find his chosen Love,
    Which made him from the Heav'ns[205] so often flye.

Close by the place where I for shade did lye,
    She chafing came, but when she saw me move,
    Have you not seene this way (said she) to hye
    One, in whom vertue never grownde° did prove?   ground

Hee, in whom Love doth breed, to stirre more hate,
    Courting a wanton Nimph for his delight;
    His name is *Jupiter,* my Lord, by Fate
    Who for her, leaves Me, Heaven, his Throne, and light.

I saw him not (said I)[206] although heere are
Many, in whose hearts, Love hath made like warre,

[Print 98]   [MS 105]

4.

*W*Hen I beheld the Image of my deare,
    With greedy lookes mine eies would that way bend
    Feare, and Desire, did inwardly contend;
    Feare to be mark'd, Desire to draw still neere.

And in my soule a Spirit would appeare,   [sig. 4F3v]
    Which boldnes warranted, and did pretend
    To be my *Genius;* yet I durst not lend,
    My eyes in trust, where others seem'd so cleare.

Then did I search, from whence this danger rose,
    If such unworthynesse in me did rest,
    As my starv'd eyes must not[207] with sight be blest,
    When Jealousie her poyson did disclose.

205. Heav'ns] heaven MS

206. him not (said I)] nott him, sayed I, MS

207. not] ^nott^ MS

264 Mary Wroth

Yet in my heart unseene of Jealous eye,
The truer Image shall in tryumph lye.

[Print 99]   [MS 106]

5.

ⱠIke to huge Clowdes of smoake which well may hide
    The face of fairest day, though for a while:
    So wrong[208] may shaddow me, till truth doe smile,
    And Justice Sunne-like hath those vapours tyde.[209]

O doating Time, canst thou for shame let slid,°   slide
    So many minutes, while ills doe beguile
    Thy age, and worth, and falshoods thus[210] defile
    Thy auncient good, where now but crosses bide?

Looke but once[211] up, and leave thy toyling pace
    And on my[212] miseries thy dimme eye[213] place,
    Goe not so fast, but give my care some ende,

Turne not thy glasse (alas) unto my ill
    Since thou with sand it canst[214] not so farre fill,
    But to each one my sorrowes will[215] extend.

[Print 100]   [MS 107]

6.

O That no day would ever more appeare,
    But clowdy night to governe this sad place,
    Nor light from Heaven these haples roomes to grace
    Since that light's shadow'd which my Love holds deare.

Let thickest mists in envy master here,
    And Sunne-borne day for malice show no face,

208. wrong] wrongs 1621

209. tyde] tride MS

210. thus] ^thus^ MS

211. but once] once but MS

212. my] ^my^ MS

213. eye] eyes MS

214. canst] can MS

215. will] will *written over* doe MS

Disdaining light, where *Cupid,* and the race
  Of Lovers are despisd, and shame shines cleere.

Let me be darke, since barr'd of my chiefe light,
  And wounding Jealousie commands by might,
  But Stage-play-like disguised pleasures give:

To me it seemes, as ancient fictions make   [sig. 4F4r]
  The Starrs, all fashions, and all shapes partake,
  While in my thoughts true forme of Love shall live.

[Print 101]   [MS 108]

7.

*N*O time, no roome, no thought, or[216] writing can
  Give rest, or quiet to my loving heart,
  Or[217] can my memory, or Phant'sie scan,
  The measure of my still renewing smart.

Yet would I not (deare Love) thou should'st depart,
  But let my[218] passions as they first began,
  Rule, wound, and please, it is thy choysest Art,
  To give disquiet, which seemes ease to man.

When all alone, I thinke upon thy paine,
  How thou dost travell[219] our best selves to gaine,
  Then[220] houerly thy lessons I doe[221] learne;

Thinke on thy glory, which shall still ascend,
  Untill the world come to a finall end,
  And then shall we thy lasting powre discerne.

[Print 102]   [MS 109]

8.

*H*Ow Glowworme-like the Sun doth now appeare,
  Cold beames doe from his glorious face descend

216. or] nor MS

217. or] nor MS

218. my] thy MS

219. travell] traveile MS

220. then] then *written over* an MS

221. I doe] doe I MS

266 MARY WROTH

Which shewes his daies, and force draw to an ende,
Or that to leave taking, his time growes neere.

The[222] day his face did seeme but pale, though cleare,
The reason is, he to the North must lend
His light, and warmth must to that Climat bend,
Whose frozen parts could not loves heat hold deare

Alas, if thou bright Sunne to part from hence
Grieve so, what must I haplesse who from thence,
Where thou dost goe my blessings shall attend;

Thou shalt enjoy that sight for which I dye,
And in my heart thy fortunes doe envy,
Yet grieve, I'le love thee, for this state may'mend.

[Print 103]   [MS 110]

9.

*M*Y Muse now happy lay thy selfe to rest,
Sleepe in the quiet of a faithfull love,
Write you no more, but let these Phant'sies moove
Some other hearts, wake not to new unrest.

But if you Study be those thoughts adrest   [sig. 4F4v]
To truth, which shall eternall goodnes proove;
Enjoying of true joy the most, and best
The endles gaine which never will remove.

Leave the discourse of *Venus,* and her sonne[223]
To young beginners, and their braines inspire
With storyes of great Love, and from that fire,
Get heat to write the fortunes they have wonne.

And thus leave off;[224] what's past shewes you can love,
Now let your Constancy your Honor prove.

FINIS.

222. The] This MS

223. sonne] sun*n* MS

224. off] of MS

Appendix 1: Herbert's "Elegy" and Wroth's "Penshurst Mount"

Elegy[1]

William Herbert, 3rd Earl of Pembroke

Why with unkindest Swiftnes doest thou turne
from me[2] whose absence thou didst only[3] mourne
of which thou mad'st me such a seeminge showe[4]
as unbeleevers would have thought it true.
Wee have bynn private, and thou know'st of mine
(which is even all)[5] as much as I of thine.
Dost thou remember? let me call to accompt°[6]   account
thy pleasant garden and that Leavy° mount,   leafy
whose topp is with an open Arbor crownd
and spanned with greenest Palizades° round,[7] 10 hedges
whereon the powers of the night may oft have seene us,
and heard the contracts, that have binn° betweene us.[8] been
Dost thou remember (o securest[9] beautie)[10]
whereof thine owne free motion° more then duty[11]   will, volition

---

1. From Huntington Library MS HM 198, Part 2, f. 105r–v, as edited by Garth Bond in "Amphilanthus to Pamphilia: William Herbert, Mary Wroth, and Penshurst Mount," *Sidney Journal* 31 (2013): 75–77; i/j, u/v have been normalized, abbreviations expanded, and annotations added. Additional copies: Huntington Library, MS HM101, Part 2, fol. 101r; *Poems, written by the Right Honorable William Earl of Pembroke* (1660), 56–58.

Elegy. /] No title HM101, 1660

2. me] one HM101

3. only] truly 1660

4. showe] hue HM101, view 1660

5. (…)] no parentheses HM101

6. to accompt] t'account HM101, 1660

7. 1660 omits lines 10–12.

8. HM101 omits line 12.

9. Carefree; free from doubt or mistrust.

10. (…)] no parentheses HM101

11. more then duty] (more then duty) 1660

268 *Appendix 1*

and unrequired[12] thou solemly did'st sweare
(of which avenging heaven can witness beare).[13]
That from the time, thou gav'st the[14] spoiles[15] to me
thou woudst mainetaine a spotles chastity
and unprophain'd by any second hande[16]
from sport° and loves delight removed stand   20   amorous activity
Till I whose absence seemingely was mourn'd[17]
should from a forraine[18] kingdome[19] be return'd
of this thou mad'st religion, and an oath
But see the fraylty of a woman's troth[20]
Scarce had the sunne (to many roomes° assign'd)   places
Bin thris° within the changefull waves confin'd,   thrice
and I scarce three daies Journey from thine eyes
when thou new love, did'st in thy hart[21] devise
and gav'st the reliques of thy virgin head
upon the easiest prayers as[22] could be said   30
Tis true?[23] I left thee to a daungerous age
where vice in Angells shape does title wage
with Auncient vertue, both disguisinge soe
That hardly weaker eyes can either knowe.
Besides I left thee in the houre of feares
and in the covetous springe of all thy yeares
What time a beauty that hath well begun
askes other then the solace of a Nunn.
But since thy wanton soule so deare did prize
the gaine[24] that thou for it did[25] underprize.   40

12. unrequired] required HM101

13. (of] of HM101; beare).] no parentheses HM105, HM101; bear) 1660

14. the] thy HM101, 1660

15. Pillage, plunder, rapine; goods taken from a defeated enemy.

16. HM101 omits lines 19–76.

17. whose … mourned] (whose … mourned) 1660

18. Distant; situated outside an estate, district, or kingdom.

19. Kingly function, authority, or domain.

20. Solemn promise, specifically an engagement to marry.

21. did'st in thy hart] in thy heart didst 1660

22. prayers as] prayer that 1660

23. true?] true, 1660

24. gaine] game 1660

25. did] didst 1660

Appendix 1 269

Thy faith and all that to good fame belongs
couldst thou not cover it from comon tongues.
But cheapest eyes, must see thee tread[26] amisse
my Rimes that wonn thee, never taught thee this
Thou might'st have wandred in the paths of Love
and neither leaveles hill, nor shady grove
have bynn unpressed by thie wanton waight°   weight
yet thou thought honest, hadst thou used sleight.° cunning, artifice
Much care and busines hath the chastest dame
to guard herselfe from undeiserved Blame   50
What artefice, and Cunninge then must serve
To colour them that just reproofe Deserve.
Tis not a worke for every womans witt
and the lesse marvell thou neglectedst itt.
That which amazes me the most is this
that havinge never troden but amisse
and done me wrongs that doe as much deny
To Suffer measure as infinitie,
When I approch, thou turn'st thy head awry
as if soure[27] eyes, and scorne could satisfye   60
Can second wrongs, the former expiate
and worke them out of memory and date?
Or teach me, ill in humane precepts nurst[28]
that second mischeifs,° doe secure[29] the first.   harm, injury;
Thou art malitious as incontinent   evildoing
and mightst have mett with such a patient°   one who suffers
whose wronged virtue to just rage invited
would have reveng'd, and in thie dust delighted
But I that have no gall where[30] once I love
and whom no great things[31] under heaven can move 70
am well secur'd, from fortune's weake Alarmes
and free from apprehension, as from harmes.
Thus doe I leave thee to the multitudes[32]

26. tread] do 1660

27. soure] sore 1660 Expressing displeasure, peevish, cross.

28. nurst] durst 1660

29. mischeifs, doe secure] wrongs can expiate 1660

30. where] when 1660

31. things] thinge 1660

32. multitudes] multitude 1660

270 *Appendix 1*

that on my leavings hastily intrudes[33]
Injoy thou many or rejoice[34] in one
I was before them, and before me none /

Penshurst Mount. $.[35]

Lady Mary Sidney/Wroth

Sweete solitarines joy to those hartes
That feele the pleasure of brave Cupids[36] darts,
Grudge mee not though a Vassall to hys might
And a Poor subject to curst changings spite
To rest in you, or rather restles move
In your contents[37] to sorrow for my love.
A love though[38] living lives as dead to mee
As Jewells which in richest boxes[39] bee
Plac'd in a Chest that our'throwes my joye
Shutt up in chang, which mor then Plagues destroy, 10
Thys[40] (O you solitarines)[41] may both indur°   endure
And be a surgeon[42] to find mee a Cur°   cure
For thys Curst Corsive° (eating my best rest)[43]   caustic medicine
Memory sad Memory in itt[44] once blest
But now most miserable with the weight

33. leavings … intrudes] leaving … intrude 1660

34. Be made joyful by; take as a lover.

35. From British Library, MS Additional 23229, f. 91r-92r, as edited by Garth Bond for "Amphilanthus to Pamphilia: William Herbert, Mary Wroth, and Penshurst Mount," *Sidney Journal* 31 (2013): 78–80; i/j, u/v have been normalized, abbreviations expanded, and annotations added. Other Copy: 1621, *The Countess of Montgomeries Urania* (1621), 110–11.
Penhurst Mount. $.] No title 1621

36. brave Cupid's] Love's sporting 1621

37. Things contained in a piece of writing, i.e., his poem.

38. though] which 1621

39. Jewells which in richest boxes] holy reliques which in boxes 1621

40. Thys] These 1621

41. (O] No parenthesis 1621; solitarines)] no parenthesis BL, 1621

42. surgeon] Chirurgion 1621

43. (…)] no parentheses 1621

44. itt] you 1621

Of that which only shewes loves strange deceipt.°   deceit
You ar that Cruell wound which[45] inly wears
My soule, my body wasting into Tears
You keepe my[46] Eyes unclos'd, my hart untide
From letting thought of my best dayes to slide,   20
Froward° Remembrance with[47] delight have you   troublesome,
Over my Miseryes to take a viewe   ungovernable
Why doe you tell mee in thys very[48] Place
Of Earths best blessings, I have seene the face
But maskt from mee I only see the shade
Of that which once my brightest sunshine made.
You tell mee that I first did her° knowe[49] love[50]   here
And mayden Passions in thys roome did move[51]
Ô why is thys alone to bring distresse
Without a salve but torturs[52] in Excesse   30
A Cruell steward[53] you ar to enrole°   record
My once blest time[54] of Purpose to controle
With Eyes of Sorow, yett leave mee undone
By too much confidence my thrid° thus[55] spun[56]   thread
In Conscience move not such a spleene of scorne
Under whose swelling[57] my Dispairs ar borne.
Ar you offended (choysest Memory)
That of your perfect guift I did glory.
Yf I did so offend, now[58] Pardon mee,
Since t'was to sett forth your true excellencye   40

45. which] that 1621

46. my] mine 1621

47. with] what 1621

48. very] same-like 1621

49. Know, in the biblical sense, meaning, to have intercourse.

50. first did her know love] then was blest in Love 1621

51.] When equall passions did together move 1621

52. torturs] torments 1621

53. A servant who controls the domestic affairs of his master's household; possible reference to William Herbert's steward, Hugh Sanford.

54. once blest time] once-good dayes 1621

55. thus] so 1621

56. The gods and fates were thought to spin the thread of mortal life.

57. swelling] swellings 1621

58. now] yet 1621

272 *Appendix 1*

Suffitiently I thus doe punisht stand°   remain steadfast
When all which[59] curst is you bring to my hand.[60]
Or is itt that I noe way worthy[61] was
In so rich honor[62] my past[63] dayes to passe.
Alas if soe and such a Treasun[64] given
Must I for thys to hell-like gaine°[65] be driven   profit
Fully torment mee now in[66] what is best
Togeather take remembrance[67] with the rest,
Leave not that to mee, if not for mor[68] ill
Which punish may and millions of harts kill   50
Then may I lonely sitt downe with my losse
Without Vexation for my Losses crosse,°   trial, affliction,
                 misfortune
Forgetting pleasures late embracd with love
Linckt with[69] a fayth the world cold° nev'r move could
Chaind in[70] Affection I hopt shold[71] nott change
Not thincking Earth had left[72] a Place to range[73]
But staying° cruelly you sett my blisse   remaining home
With deepest mourning In my sight for misse.[74]
And so shall[75] I imagine my Curse mor
When you I lov'd, ad to my mischeiefs stor,° 60 supply

59. When all which] While all that 1621

60. You attribute or give to me; you contribute to bestowing my hand in marriage.

61. Pun on worth/Wroth.

62. Chastity; reputation; common circumlocution for female genitalia.

63. honor my past] treasure my few 1621

64. Treasun] treasure 1621

 "Treasun" could be a copyist's slip for *treasure* or an idiosyncratic spelling of *treason.*

65. gaine] paine 1621

66. in] and 1621

67. take remembrance] take, and mem'ry 1621

68. if not for mor] since but for my 1621

69. with] to 1621

70. in] with 1621

71. shold] could 1621

72. had left] could yeeld 1621

73. To roam, wander; change affections; be inconstant.

74. Wrong, offense, injury; disappointment caused by loss or absence.

75. so shall] thus must 1621

Appendix 1 273

Then may I live in Niobes[76] sad state,[77]
Who weeping long indur'd her losses fate,
Till to a Rocke transformd from her Tears
She lives to feele mor drops which on her wears
Heaven weepes on her then thys example take
And soe I'le ty myselfe at Patience stake,
Yf not then Memory continue still
And tortur[78] mee with your best prized°[79] skill,   most valued
Whyle you deer° solitarines accept   dear
Mee to your charge, whose many Passions kept   70
In your sweete dwellings have this Profitt gained
That in mor delicacye[80] none was paind
Your rarenes[81] now receave my rarer woe
Which[82] change,° and love appoints my soule to knowe. $ changefulness,
                                                                                                    inconstancy

76. In Greek myth, Niobe's children were killed to punish her for boasting about them. She was turned
to a stone, and her unremitting tears poured forth from the porous stone.

77. 1621 omits lines 61–66.

78. tortur] vex 1621

79. best prized] perfectest knowne 1621

80. Pleasure, delight.

81. Rarity or absence; rarified or refined intellect.

82. Which] With 1621

Appendix 2: Table of Numbers for Manuscript and Printed Poems

Consecutive MS numbers	Wroth's MS numbers	Folio numbers	Consecutive print numbers	Roberts's numbers for 1621 poems and *Urania* poems	Numbers in 1621 text
MS 1	.1.	fol. 1r	Print 1	P 1	1
MS 2	.2.	fol. 1v	Print 2	P 2	2
MS 3	.3.	fol. 2r	Print 3	P 3	3
MS 4	.4.	fol. 2v		F1	
			Print 4	P 4	4
MS 5	.5.	fol. 3r	Print 5	P 5	5
MS 6	:6.(sideways)	fol. 3v	Print 6	P 6	6
MS 7	Song 1.	fol. 4r	Print 7	P 7	*Song.* 1.
MS 8	.7.	fol. 5r	Print 8	P 8	7
MS 9	.8.	fol. 5v	Print 9	P 9	8.
MS 10	.9.	fol. 6r	Print 10	P 10	9.
MS 11	.10.	fol. 6v	Print 11	P 11	10.
MS 12	.11.	fol. 7r	Print 12	P 12	11.
MS 13	.12.	fol. 7v	Print 13	P 13	12.
MS 14	.Song 2.	fol. 8r	Print 14	P 14	*Song.* 2.
MS 15	.13.	fol. 8v	Print 15	P 15	13.
MS 16	.14.	fol. 9r	Print 16	P 16	14.
MS 17	.15.	fol. 9v	Print 64	P 64	15.
MS 18	.16.	fol. 10r	Print 68	P 68	6.
MS 19	.17.	fol. 10v	Print 70	P 70	8.
MS 20	.18.	fol. 11r	Print 20	P 20	18.
MS 21	Song 3.	fol. 11v	Print 21	P 21	*Song.* 3.
MS 22	.19.	fol. 12r	Print 22	P 22	19.
MS 23	20.	fol. 12v	Print 23	P 23	20.

. . . .

276 *Appendix 2*

Table of Numbers for Manuscript and Printed Poems (cont'd)

Consecutive MS numbers	Wroth's MS numbers	Folio numbers	Consecutive print numbers	Roberts's numbers for 1621 poems and *Urania* poems	Numbers in 1621 text
MS 24	21.	fol. 13r	Print 24	P 24	21.
MS 25	22.	fol. 13v	Print 72	P 72	10.
MS 26	23.	fol. 14r	Print 26	P 26	23.
MS 27	2.4	fol. 14v	Print 27	P 27	24.
MS 28	Song 4.	fol. 15r	Print 28	P 28	*Song.* 4.
MS 29	25.	fol. 15v	Print 29	P 29	25.
MS 30	26.	fol. 16r	Print 65	P 65	3.
MS 31	27.	fol. 16v	Print 31	P 31	27.
MS 32	28.	fol. 17r	Print 32	P 32	28.
MS 33	29.	fol. 17v	Print 33	P 33	29.
MS 34	30.	fol. 18r	Print 34	P 34	30.
MS 35	Song 5.	fol. 18v	Print 35	P 35	*Song.* 5.
MS 36	31,	fol. 19r	Print 36	P 36	31.
MS 37	32.	fol. 19v	Print 37	P 37	32.
MS 38	33.	fol. 20r	Print 38	P 38	33.
MS 39	34.	fol. 20v	Print 39	P 39	34.
MS 40	35.	fol. 21r	Print 95	P 95	1.
MS 41	36.	fol. 21v	Print 97	P 97	3.
MS 42	Song vj.	fol. 22r	Print 42	P 42	*Song.* 6.
MS 43	37.	fol. 23r	Print 43	P 43	37.
MS 44	38	fol. 23v	Print 44	P 44	38.
MS 45	39.	fol. 24r	Print 45	P 45	39.
MS 46	40.	fol. 24v	Print 46	P 46	40.
MS 47	41.	fol. 25r	Print 96	P 96	2.
MS 48	42.	fol. 25v	Print 48	P 48	42.
MS 49	Song vij.	fol. 26r	Print 49	P 49	*Song.* 7.
MS 50	43.	fol. 26v	Print 50	P 50	43.

· · · · · · ·

Appendix 2 277

Table of Numbers for Manuscript and Printed Poems (cont'd)

Consecutive MS numbers	Wroth's MS numbers	Folio numbers	Consecutive print numbers	Roberts's numbers for 1621 poems and *Urania* poems	Numbers in 1621 text
MS 51	44.	fol. 27r	Print 51	P 51	44.
MS 52	45.	fol. 27v	Print 52	P 52	45.
MS 53	46.	fol. 28r	Print 53	P 53	46.
MS 54	47.	fol. 28v	Print 54	P 54	47.
MS 55	48.	fol. 29r	Print 55	P 55	48.
MS 56	Sonett; $	fol. 30r	Print 56	P 56	*Sonnet.*
MS 57	Song $.	fol. 30v	Print 57	P 57	*Song.*
MS 58	Song $	fol. 31r	*Urania* 1:212	U18	
MS 59	Song $	fol. 31v	Print 58	P 58	*Song.*
MS 60	Song $	fol. 32r	Print 59	P 59	*Song.*
MS 61	.Song. $	fol. 32v	Print 60	P 60	*Song.*
MS 62	Song $	fol. 33r	Print 61	P 61	*Song.*
MS 63	Song $	fol. 33v	*Urania* 1:173–74	U14	
MS 64	Song $	fol. 34r	Print 62	P 62	*Song.*
MS 65	Dialogue $	fol. 34v	*Urania* 1:171–72	U12	
MS 66	Sonett $ I.	fol. 35r	Print 63	P 63	*Sonnet.* 1.
MS 67	2.	fol. 35v	Print 17	P 17	15.
MS 68	3.	fol. 36r	Print 30	P 30	26.
MS 69	4.	fol. 36v	Print 66	P 66	4.
MS 70	5.	fol. 37r	Print 67	P 67	5.
MS 71	6.	fol. 37v	Print 18	P 18	16.
MS 72	7.	fol. 38r	Print 69	P 69	7.
MS 73	8.	fol. 38v	Print 19	P 19	17.
MS 74	9.	fol. 39r	Print 71	P 71	9.
MS 75	10.	fol. 39v	Print 25	P 25	22.
MS 76	Song $.	fol. 40r	Print 73	P 73	*Song.*

278 *Appendix 2*

Table of Numbers for Manuscript and Printed Poems (cont'd)

Consecutive MS numbers	Wroth's MS numbers	Folio numbers	Consecutive print numbers	Roberts's numbers for 1621 poems and *Urania* poems	Numbers in 1621 text
MS 77	Song; $	fol. 40v		F2	
MS 78	Song: $	fol. 41r	Print 74	P 74	*Song.*
MS 79	Song.	fol. 41v	Print 75	P 75	[Song.]
MS 80	Song;	fol. 42r	*Urania* 1:172–73	U13	
MS 81		fol. 42v	Print 76	P 76	
MS 82	A crowne	fol. 43r	Print 77	P 77	*A Crowne*
MS 83	2.		Print 78	P 78	2.
MS 84	.3.	fol. 43v	Print 79	P 79	3.
MS 85	4.		Print 80	P 80	4.
MS 86	5.	fol. 44r	Print 81	P 81	5.
MS 87	6.		Print 82	P 82	6.
MS 88	7.	fol. 44v	Print 83	P 83	7.
MS 89	8.		Print 84	P 84	8.
MS 90	9.	fol. 45r	Print 85	P 85	9.
MS 91	10.		Print 86	P 86	10.
MS 92	11.	fol.45v	Print 87	P 87	11.
MS 93	12.	fol. 46r	Print 88	P 88	12.
MS 94	13		Print 89	P 89	13.
MS 95	i4.	fol. 46v	Print 90	P 90	14.
MS 96	Sonett $.	fol. 47v		F3	
MS 97	1.	fol. 48r	Print 91	P 91	*Song.* 1.
MS 98	2.	fol. 48v	Print 92	P 92	2.
MS 99	3.	fol. 49r	Print 93	P 93	3
MS 100		fol. 49v	*Urania* 1:490	U34	
MS 101	4.		Print 94	P 94	4.
MS 102	1.	fol. 50v	Print 40	P 40	35.

. . . . . .

Appendix 2 279

Table of Numbers for Manuscript and Printed Poems (cont'd)

Consecutive MS numbers	Wroth's MS numbers	Folio numbers	Consecutive print numbers	Roberts's numbers for 1621 poems and _Urania_ poems	Numbers in 1621 text
MS 103	2.	fol. 51r	Print 47	P 47	41.
MS 104	3.	fol. 51v	Print 41	P 41	36.
MS 105	4	fol. 52r	Print 98	P 98	4.
MS 106	5.	fol. 52v	Print 99	P 99	5.
MS 107	6.	fol. 53r	Print 100	P 100	6.
MS 108	7.	fol. 53v	Print 101	P 101	7.
MS 109	8.	fol. 54r	Print 102	P 102	8.
MS 110		fol. 54v	Print 103	P 103	9.
MS 111	Sonnet $.	fol. 55r	_Urania_ 1:460–61	U32	
MS 112	Sonnet $.	fol. 55v		F4	
MS 113	Sonnet $	fol. 56r		F5	
MS 114	1.–39.	fol. 57r–fol. 63r	_Urania_ 1:614–23	U52	1.—39.
MS 115	Sonett $	fol. 63v		F6	
MS 116	Sonett $.	fol. 64r	_Urania_ 1:198	U17	
MS 117		fol. 64v	_Urania_ 1:326–27	U24	

Appendix 3:
Copies of the 1621 Printed Text

These abbreviations and descriptions, adapted from Roberts, *Urania* I:663–64, have been updated to reflect current owners and locations.

AL University of Alberta; includes signature of George Maule, Earl of Panmure; acquired in the late 1950s.

AS Sold to Anne Shaver of Denison University in June 1994, and gifted to Amy E. Leonard of the Georgetown History Department in 2016 while this edition was in publication; previously owned by David Evans; includes signature, "Benjamin Holder his Booke Given to him by Mr. Joseph Persevall ye 11th of September 1673; contains some seventeenth-century annotations.

AT Alexander Turnbull Library, New Zealand; includes signature Alexander Horsburgh Turnbull, who bequeathed his collection to the library in 1918.

AU University of Auckland; previously owned by Margaret McLaren; a table of variants, comparing this copy with AT, CM, and F1, appears in McLaren's dissertation.

BL1 British Library, Copy 1. Pressmark 86.h.9; previously owned by King George III and cover stamped with Order of the Garter; a duplicate from the Bridgewater Library.

BL2 British Library, Copy 2. Pressmark 2422; previously owned by Rt. Hon. Thomas Grenville.

CA University of California, Los Angeles; contains signature of Mary Plumley, 1663, and some pen-and-ink corrections, including a handwritten conclusion not by Wroth on p. 558.

CH University of Chicago. Acquired in 1910; no information on prior ownership.

CM King's College, Cambridge; previously owned by John A. Murphy and John Maynard Keynes, who bought it in 1944 and bequeathed it to King's College in 1946; contains some marginal annotations and two copies of sig. 2Y–2Yv (missing sig. 2Y2v–2Y3).

CT Chetham's Library, Manchester; includes signature of Samuel Baker, 1792, and of Henry Bulstrode (undated); lacks title page, sigs. B2 and 2D4.

D Dartmouth College; acquired by Victor Skretkowicz in 1972; previously owned by the Paston family; includes two copies of the sheet 2P1–2P4.

DU Dulwich College; lacks title page.

282 *Appendix 3*

F1 Folger Shakespeare Library, Copy 1; Harmsworth copy: includes autographs of Ann Morris (1723), Roger Jones (1725), and R. Leicester Harmsworth. Reproduced by University Microfilms (STC 26051).

F2 Folger Shakespeare Library, Copy 2; Earl of Lonsdale copy; includes autograph of Ellis Morgan (1635).

HD Houghton Library, Harvard University; sold by Christie's, June 1840; given to Houghton in memory of Lionel De Jersey, March 30, 1918.

HN Henry E. Huntington Library; owned by Robert Southey (signature and date, March 25, 1808) and Robert Hoe.

K University of Pennsylvania; contains Wroth's handwritten corrections and revisions; previously owned by James F. Gaines, Josephine Roberts, Charlotte Kohler (hence "K"), Howard C. Howe, Hugh Mcdonald (1783–1784), Fitzedward Hall, and W. B. Chorley.

LC Library of Congress; contains a reader's concluding poem written in pencil (p. 558).

LE University of Leeds; contains a bookplate of the Bosville family.

LP Lambeth Palace Library. Previously at Sion College; donated by Eleanor James, widow of the London printer, Thomas James, 1711.

LSU Louisiana State University, inscribed three times, "Dorothy Long her book"; missing title page; acquired by G. Blakemore Evans in Salisbury, 1944, and donated to LSU in 1991.

N Newberry Library; belonged to Robert Dormer, Baron of Wynge, ward of Philip Herbert, Earl of Montgomery.

NY New York University; signature of John Chamberman, July 5, 1865; remounted title page; final "and" on p. 558 is erased, and period inserted in ink. "Pamphilia to Amphilanthus" missing.

O1 Bodleian Library, Oxford University, Copy 1; pressmark M.5.6.Art.; bound with William Slayter, *The History of Great Britanie* (1621).

O2 Bodleian Library, Oxford University, Copy 2. Pressmark JJ Sidney 55; previously owned by Dr. Bent Juel-Jensen; includes annotations by the seventeenth-century book collector William Davenporte.

PN Princeton University; contains bookplate of Sir Richard Bedingfeld, Bt.; purchased by Robert H. Tayor in 1968.

T University of Texas; includes several marginal annotations: "many distressed and at last blessed" (p. 1); "the tale of Perissus" (p. 4); "the end of the tale of Perissus" (p. 15).

WN Winchester College; belonged to Alexander Thistlethwayte, Hampshire M.P. and book collector (1767); contains marginal note "Pamphilia self" (p. 31).

Y Beinecke Library, Yale University; sig. 2Fv, 2F2v, and 2F3v incorrectly ordered.

Appendix 3 283

Errors and Corrections in the Twenty-Eight Extant Copies of the 1621 Printed Text

Continuous print no.	MS no.	Poem	Folger spelling	1621 error	1621 correction	Corrected copies of 1621
4:12	N/A	Forbeare darke night		Sow		
5:1	5:1	Can pleasing sight	misfor-tune	misfor-tue	misfortune	AS, AT, AU, CA, CH, CM, CT, F1, F2, HD, HN, LE, LP, N, O1, O2, PN, WN, Y
5:6	5:6		to	two		
5:12	5:12		and	aud		
6:11	6:11	O strive not	my	may		
7:15	7:15	The spring now	bar'd	barr,d		
12:5	12:5	You endlesse torments	obtaine	optaine		
12:11			to say	so say		
13:10	13:10	Cloy'd with the torments	houers taedious	howerst-edious	howers tedious	AS, AT, AU, CA, CH, CM, CT, F1, F2, HD, HN, LE, LP, N, O1, O2, PN, WN, Y
15:6	15:6	Deare famish not	your	you	your	AL, AS, AT, AU, CA, CH, CM, CT, HD, HN, F1, F2, LE, LP, N, O1, O2, PN, WN, Y
16:5	16:5	Am I thus conquer'd	leaue	leane		
18:6	71:6	Sleepe fye possesse	liknes of	like-nesse of of	likenesse of	CT, D, K, N, PN

.   .   .   .

284 *Appendix 3*

Errors and Corrections in the Twenty-Eight Extant Copies of the 1621 Printed Text (cont'd)

Continuous print no.	MS no.	Poem	Folger spelling	1621 error	1621 correction	Corrected copies of 1621
24:8	24:8	When last I saw thee	minute	mnute		
25:7	75:7	Like to the Indians	then	Theu		
32:9	32:9	Griefe, killing griefe	ghest	ghest	guest	AL, AT, AU, BL1, BL2, CA, CH, CM, CT, D, DU, F1, F2, HN, K, LC, LE, LP, LSU, N, O1, O2, PN, T, WN, Y
33:14	33:14	Flye hence, O Joy	rests	reasts		
37:6	37:6	How fast thou	hast'st	hast	hast'st	AL, AS, AT, BL1, BL2, CA, CH, CM, CT, D, DU, F1, F2, HD, HN, LC, LE, LSU, LP, N, O1, O2, PN, T, WN, Y
40:2	102:2	False Hope which	birth	blrth	birth	AS, BL1, BL2, CA, CM, CT, D, DU, F2, HD, K, LC, LP, LSU, N, O1, O2, PN, WN, Y
40:12	102:12		kills	kill's		
40:13	102:13		hope	Hode	Hope	AS, BL1, BL2, CL, CM, CT, DU, HD, F2, K, LC, LSU, N, O1, PN, SI, SK, WN, Y
45:1	45:1	If I were given	mirthe 't'wowld	mirth, , twould		
45:10	45:10		is, words	is wordes	is, wordes	CM, CT, D, DU, F2, LSU, O1, PN, T, Y

. . . .

Appendix 3 285

Errors and Corrections in the Twenty-Eight Extant Copies of the 1621 Printed Text (cont'd)

Continuous print no.	MS no.	Poem	Folger spelling	1621 error	1621 correction	Corrected copies of 1621
47:2	103:2	You blessed Starres,	makes	make	makes	AT, AU, CA, CH, CM, CT, D, DU, F2, HD, HN, K, LP, LSU, N, O1, O2, PN, T, Y
47:10	103:10		fixt	fix't	fix't,	AT, AU, CA, CH, CM, CT, D, DU, F2, HD, HN, K, LP, LSU, N, O1, O2, PN, T, Y
47:13	103:13		eyes	eye	eyes	AT, AU, CA, CH, CM, CT, D, DU, F2, HD, HN, K, LP, LSU, N, O1, O2, PN, T, Y
48:10	48:10	If ever love	eyes,	eyes	eyes,	AT, AU, CA, CH, CM, CT, D, DU, F2, HD, HN, K, LP, LSU, N, O1, O2, PN, T, Y
48:11	48:11		show'd	show'd.	show'd;	AT, AU, CA, CH, CM, CT, D, DU, F2, HD, HN, JJ, K, LP, LSU, N, O1, O2, PN, T, Y
49:22	49:22	Sorrow, I yeeld	proue	proone		
51:1	51:1	How fast thou	speed	speed)		
51:6	51:6		t 'o'rerunn	fore-runn,	t'orerunn	AL, AS, AT, BL1, BL2, CA, CH, CM, CT, DU, F1, F2, HD, HN, LC, LE, LSU, N, O1, O2, T, WN, Y
51:8	51:8		makes	maks		

. . . .

286 *Appendix 3*

Errors and Corrections in the Twenty-Eight Extant Copies of the 1621 Printed Text (cont'd)

Continuous print no.	MS no.	Poem	Folger spelling	1621 error	1621 correction	Corrected copies of 1621
51:12	51:12		lyfe blood	life, bloud	life-bloud	AL, AS, AT, BL1, BL2, CA, CH, CM, CT, DU, F1, F2, HD, HN, LC, LE, LSU, N, O1, O2, T, WN, Y
52:12	52:12	Good now be still	speritt absence	spirit Absence	spirit, Absence	AL, AS, AT, BL1, BL2, CA, CH, CM, CT, DU, F1, F2, HD, HN, LC, LE, LSU, N, O1, O2, T, WN, Y
53:8	53:8	Love thou hast	loue	lone	loue	AL, AS, AT, BL1, BL2, CH, CA, CM, CT, DU, F1, F2, HD, HN, LC, LE, LSU, N, O1, O2, T, WN, Y
53:14	53:14		truly	trurly	truely	AL, AS, AU, BL1, BL2, CA, CH, CM, DU, F1, F2, HN, LC, LE, LSU, O1, O2, T, WN, Y
58:9	59:9	Say Venus how long	loue	lone		
60:20	61:20	Love as well can make	mou'd	mowd		
61:10	62:10	Dearest if I	mee,	me	me,	AL, AS, AT, AU, BL1, BL2, CA, CH, CM, CT, DU, F1, F2, LC, LE, LP, LSU, O1, O2, PN, T, WN

.   .   .   .

Appendix 3 287

Errors and Corrections in the Twenty-Eight Extant Copies of the 1621 Printed Text (cont'd)

Continuous print no.	MS no.	Poem	Folger spelling	1621 error	1621 correction	Corrected copies of 1621
62:14	64:14	Fairest and still	your eyes	you eyes	your eyes	AL, AS, AT, AU, BL1, BL2, CA, CH, CM, CT, DU, F1, F2, LC, LE, LP, LSU, O1, O2, PN, T, WN
65:9	30:9	Most blessed night	clos'd	cloasd		
72:14	25:14	Folly would needs make	thee.	hee,		
75:11	79:11	Being past the paines of	though	thongh		
82:11	87:11	He may our Prophet	forcing	Forces-ing		
82:13	87:13		throne	throane		
84:11	89:11	He that shuns	moue	moone		
87:1	92:1	Unprofit-ably pleasing	unsound	unsownd	unsound	AL, AS, AT, AU, BL1, BL2, CA, CH, D, DU, HD, HN, F1, F2, K, LC, LE, LP, LSU, N, O1, O2, PN, T, WN, Y
89:3	94:3	Free from all foggs	freind-ship	frindship	friendship	AL, AS, AT, AU, BL1, BL2, CH, CA, DU, HN, HD, F1, F2, K, LC, LE, LP, LSU, N, O1, O2, PN, D, T, WN, Y

.   .   .   .   .   .

288 *Appendix 3*

Errors and Corrections in the Twenty-Eight Extant Copies of the 1621 Printed Text (cont'd)

Continuous print no.	MS no.	Poem	Folger spelling	1621 error	1621 correction	Corrected copies of 1621
90:10	95:10	Except my heart	enimies	euemies	enemies	AL, AS, AT, AU, BL1, BL2, CA, CH, CM, CT, D, F1, F2, HN, K, LC, LE, LP, LSU, N, O1, O2, T, WN, Y
90:13	95:13		burne	burue	burne	AL, AS, AT, AU, BL1, BL2, CA, CH, CM, CT, D, F1, F2, HN, K, LC, LE, LP, LSU, N, O1, O2, T, WN, Y
94:2	101:2	Lovers learne to	and	aud		
94:21	101:21		For	Eor	For	AL, AS, AT, AU, CH, CM, CT, D, DU, F1, F2, HD, HN, K, LP, N, O1, O2, PN, WN
94:28	101:28		faul-shood	fashood		
95:8	40:8	My heart is lost	and	Aud	And	AT, CH, CM, CT, D, DU, HD, HN, F2, K, N, O1, O2, WN, Y
95:9	40:9		thy mother	they Mother		
97:10	41:10	Juno still jealous	wanton	wauton	wanton	AL, AS, AT, AU, CH, CM, CT, D, DU, F1, F2, HD, HN, K, LP, N, O1, O2, PN, WN
100:13	107:13	O That no day	fashions	fashious		
101:5	108:5	No time, no roome	would	whould		

Errors and Corrections in the Twenty-Eight Extant Copies of the 1621 Printed Text (cont'd)

Continuous print no.	MS no.	Poem	Folger spelling	1621 error	1621 correction	Corrected copies of 1621
102:13	109:13	How Glow-worme-like	fortunes	fortuues		

Bibliography

Alexander, Gavin. "Constant Works: A Framework for Reading Mary Wroth." *Sidney Journal* 14 (1996–1997): 5–32.

———. *Writing after Sidney: The Literary Response to Sir Philip Sidney, 1586–1640.* Oxford: Oxford University Press, 2006.

Anderson, Judith H. *Biographical Truth: The Representation of Historical Persons in Tudor-Stuart Writing.* New Haven: Yale University Press, 1984.

Ballard, George. *Memoirs of Several Ladies of Great Britain.* Oxford, 1752.

Bauman, Richard, and Charles L. Briggs. "Poetics and Performance as Critical Perspectives on Language and Social Life." *Annual Review of Anthropology* 19 (1990): 59–88.

Beal, Peter. *In Praise of Scribes, Manuscripts and their Makers in Seventeenth-Century England.* Oxford: Clarendon Press, 1998.

Beilin, Elaine V. *Redeeming Eve: Women Writers of the English Renaissance.* Princeton: Princeton University Press, 1987.

Bell, Ilona. *Elizabeth I: The Voice of a Monarch.* Basingstoke, UK: Palgrave Macmillan, 2010.

———. *Elizabethan Women and the Poetry of Courtship.* Cambridge: Cambridge University Press, 1998.

———. "'Joy's Sports': The Unexpurgated Text of Mary Wroth's *Pamphilia to Amphilanthus.*" *Modern Philology* 111 (2013): 231–52.

———. "The Role of the Lady in Donne's *Songs and Sonets.*" *Studies in English Literature* 23 (1983): 113–29.

———. "'A too curious secrecie': Wroth's Pastoral Song and *Urania.*" *Sidney Journal* 31 (2013): 23–50.

Belsey, Catherine. "The Myth of Venus in Early Modern Culture." *English Literary Renaissance* 42 (2012): 179–202.

Black, Joseph L. "The Sidneys and Their Books." In Hannay, Lamb, and Brennan, 2:3–20.

Bland, Mark. *A Guide to Early Printed Books and Manuscripts.* Malden, MA: Wiley-Blackwell, 2010.

Bond, Garth. "Amphilanthus to Pamphilia: William Herbert, Mary Wroth, and Penshurst Mount." *Sidney Journal* 31 (2013): 51–80.

Brayman Hackel, Heidi. *Reading Material in Early Modern England: Print, Gender, and Literacy.* Cambridge: Cambridge University Press, 2005.

Brennan, Michael G. "'A SYDNEY though un-named': Ben Jonson's Influence in the Manuscript and Print Circulation of Mary Wroth's Writings." *Sidney Journal* 17 (1999): 31–52.

_____. "Creating Female Authorship in the Early Seventeenth Century: Ben Jonson and Lady Mary Wroth." In Justice and Tinker, 73–93.

_____. "Family Networks: The Sidneys, Dudleys, and Herberts." In Hannay, Lamb, and Brennan, 1:3–19.

_____. *Literary Patronage in the English Renaissance: The Pembroke Family.* London: Routledge, 1988.

Brennan, Michael G., and Noel J. Kinnamon. *A Sidney Chronology, 1554–1654.* Basingstoke, UK: Palgrave Macmillan, 2003.

Briley, John Richard. "A Biography of William Herbert, Third Earl of Pembroke, 1580–1650." PhD dissertation, University of Birmingham, 1961.

Bromley, James M. *Intimacy and Sexuality in the Age of Shakespeare.* Cambridge: Cambridge University Press, 2011.

Bullard, Angela. "Love Melancholy and Creative Inspiration in Mary Wroth's *Pamphilia to Amphilanthus.*" *Sidney Journal* 33 (2015): 81–102.

Carrell, Jennifer Lee. "A Pack of Lies in a Looking Glass: Lady Mary Wroth's *Urania* and the Magic Mirror of Romance." *Studies in English Literature* 34 (1994): 79–107. Reprinted in Kinney, *Ashgate Critical Essays,* 105–33.

Cerasano, S. P., and Marion Wynne-Davies, eds. *Renaissance Drama by Women.* London: Routledge, 1996.

Chamberlain, John. *The Letters of John Chamberlain.* Edited by Norman E. McClure. 2 vols. Philadelphia: American Philosophical Society, 1939.

Clark, Danielle. *The Politics of Early Modern Women's Writing.* Harlow, UK: Longman, 2001.

Cressy, David. *Literacy and the Social Order: Reading and Writing in Tudor and Stuart England.* Cambridge: Cambridge University Press, 1980.

Distiller, Natasha. *Desire and Gender in the Sonnet Tradition.* Basingstoke, UK: Palgrave Macmillan, 2008.

Dubrow, Heather. "'And Thus Leave Off': Reevaluating Mary Wroth's Folger Manuscript, V.a.104." *Tulsa Studies in Women's Literature* 22 (2003): 273–91. Reprinted in Kinney, *Ashgate Critical Essays,* 3–21.

_____. *Echoes of Desire: English Petrarchism and Its Counterdiscourses.* Ithaca: Cornell University Press, 1995.

Dulong-Sainteny, Claude. "Les Signes Cryptiques dans la Correspondance d'Anne d'Autriche avec Mazarin, Contribution à l'emblématique du XVIIe Siècle." *Bibliothèque de l'école des chartes* 140 (1982): 61–83.

Duncan-Jones, Katherine. Introduction to *Shakespeare's Sonnets.* Edited by Katherine Duncan-Jones. Nashville, TN: Thomas Nelson, 1997.

Dyce, Alexander. *Specimens of British Poetesses.* London, 1825.

Ezell, Margaret J. M. *Social Authorship and the Advent of Print.* Baltimore: Johns Hopkins University Press, 1999.

Fall, Rebecca L. "*Pamphilia* Unbound: Digital Re-Visions of Mary Wroth's Folger Manuscript, V.a.104." In Larson and Miller, 193–207.

Fienberg, Nona. "Mary Wroth and the Invention of Female Poetic Subjectivity." In Miller and Waller, 175–90.

Findlay, Alison. "Lady Mary Wroth: *Love's Victory.*" In Hannay, Lamb, and Brennan, 2:211–21.

_____. "*Love's Victory* in Production at Penshurst." *Sidney Journal* 34 (2016): 107–21.

Frontain, Raymond-Jean. "'Since that I may know': Donne and the Biblical Basis of Sexual Knowledge." *John Donne Journal* 30 (2011): 157–71.

Gibson, Jonathan. "Cherchez la femme: Mary Wroth and Shakespeare's *Sonnets.*" *Times Literary Supplement* (August 13, 2004): 12–13.

_____, ed. "Lady Mary Wroth: *Pamphilia to Amphilanthus,* Folger Shakespeare Library V.a.104." In Millman and Wright, 35–56.

Gil, Daniel Juan. "The Currency of the Beloved and the Authority of Lady Mary Wroth." *Modern Language Studies* 29 (1999): 73–92.

Greg, W. W., ed. *Shakespeare's Hand in the Play of Sir Thomas More.* 1923; Cambridge: Cambridge University Press, 1967.

Hackett, Helen. "Lady Mary Sidney Wroth: *The Countess of Montgomery's Urania.*" In Hannay, Lamb, and Brennan, 2:127–49.

Hannay, Margaret P. "The Countess of Pembroke's Agency in Print and Scribal Culture." In Justice and Tinker, 17–49.

_____. "The 'Ending End' of Lady Mary Wroth's Manuscript of Poems." *Sidney Journal* 31 (2013): 1–22.

_____. *Mary Sidney, Lady Wroth.* Burlington, VT: Ashgate, 2010.

_____. *Philip's Phoenix: Mary Sidney, Countess of Pembroke.* Oxford: Oxford University Press, 1990.

_____. "Sleuthing in the Archives: The Life of Lady Mary Wroth." In Larson and Miller, 19–33.

_____. "'Your Vertuous and learned Aunt': The Countess of Pembroke as a Mentor to Mary Wroth." In Miller and Waller, 15–34. Reprinted in Kinney, *Ashgate Critical Essays,* 389–408.

Hannay, Margaret P., Mary Ellen Lamb, and Michael G. Brennan, eds. *The Ashgate Research Companion to the Sidneys,* 1500–1700. 2 vols. Burlington, VT: Ashgate, 2015.

Hanson, Elizabeth. "Boredom and Whoredom: Reading Renaissance Women's Sonnet Sequences." *Yale Journal of Criticism* 10 (1997): 165–91. Reprinted in Kinney, *Ashgate Critical Essays,* 409–35.

Haselkorn, Anne M., and Betty S. Travitsky, eds. *The Renaissance Englishwoman in Print: Counterbalancing the Canon.* Amherst: University of Massachusetts Press, 1990.

Bibliography

Hay, Millicent V. *The Life of Robert Sidney, Earl of Leicester (1563–1626)*. Washington, DC: Folger Books, 1984.

Heale, Elizabeth. *Autobiography and Authorship in Renaissance Verse: Chronicles of the Self*. Basingstoke, UK: Palgrave Macmillan, 2003.

Hecht, Paul. "Distortion, Aggression, and Sex in Mary Wroth's Sonnets," *Studies in English Literature* 53 (2013): 92–107.

Herbert, William. "Elegy." Huntington Library, MS HM 198, Part 2. 105r–v.

―――. Huntington Library, MS HM101, Part 2, fol. 101r.

―――. *Poems Written by the Right Honorable William Earl of Pembroke*. London, 1660.

Heywood, Thomas. *Gynaikeion*. London, 1624.

Hodgson-Wright, Stephanie, ed. *Women's Writing of the Early Modern Period, 1588–1688: An Anthology*. New York: Columbia University Press, 2002.

Johns, Adrian. *The Nature of the Book: Print and Knowledge in the Making*. Chicago: University of Chicago Press, 1998.

Jones, Ann Rosalind. *The Currency of Eros: Women's Love Lyric in Europe, 1540–1620*. Bloomington: Indiana University Press, 1990.

Jonson, Ben. *Ben Jonson*. Edited by C. H. Herford, Percy Simpson, and E. M. Simpson. 14 vols. Oxford: Clarendon Press, 1925–63.

Justice, George L., and Nathan Tinker, eds. *Women's Writing and the Circulation of Ideas: Manuscript Publication in England, 1550–1800*. Cambridge: Cambridge University Press, 2002.

Kinney, Arthur. "The Sidneys and Public Entertainments." In Hannay, Lamb, and Brennan, 1:241–59.

Kinney, Clare R. "'Beleeve this butt a fiction': Female Authorship, Narrative Undoing, and the Limits of Romance in *The Second Part of the Countess of Montgomery's Urania*." *Spenser Studies* 17 (2003): 239–50. Reprinted in Kinney, *Ashgate Critical Essays*, 153–64.

―――. "Mary Wroth's Guilty 'Secrett Art': The Poetics of Jealousy in *Pamphilia to Amphilanthus*." In Smith and Appelt, 69–85.

―――. "Mary Wroth's Poetry: An Electronic Edition, ed. Paul Salzman." *Spenser Review* 44.1.9 (2014). http://www.english.cam.ac.uk /spenseronline/review/volume-44/441/digital-projects/mary-wroths -poetry-an-electronic-edition-ed-paul-salzman/.

―――. "Turn and Counterturn: Reappraising Mary Wroth's Poetic Labyrinths." In Larson and Miller, 85–102.

―――, ed. *Ashgate Critical Essays on Women Writers in England, 1550–1700*. Vol. 4, *Mary Wroth*. Burlington, VT: Ashgate, 2009.

Kondoleon, Christine. "Introduction." *Aphrodite and the Gods of Love*. Edited by Christine Kondoleon with Phoebe C. Segal. Boston: MFA Publications, 2011.

Lamb, Mary Ellen. "The Biopolitics of Romance in Mary Wroth's *The Countess of Montgomery's Urania*." *English Literary Renassance* 31 (2001): 107–30. Reprinted in Kinney, *Ashgate Critical Essays*, 165–95.

———. "'Can you suspect a change in me?': Poems by Mary Wroth and William Herbert, Third Earl of Pembroke." In Larson and Miller, 53–68.

———. "Introduction." *Countesse of Mountgomeries Urania (Abridged)*. Tempe: Arizona Center for Medieval and Renaissance Studies, 2011.

———. "The Poetry of William Herbert, Third Earl of Pembroke." In Hannay, Lamb, and Brennan, 2:269–79.

———. Wroth [*née* Sidney], Lady Mary (1587–1651). In Matthew and Harrison, 536–39.

Larson, Katherine R. "Voicing Lyric: The Songs of Mary Wroth." In Larson and Miller, 119–36.

Larson, Katherine R., and Naomi J. Miller, eds., with Andrew Strycharski. *Re-Reading Mary Wroth*. Basingstoke, UK: Palgrave Macmillan, 2015.

Lennam, T. N. S. "Sir Edward Dering's Collection of Playbooks, 1619–1624." *Shakespeare Quarterly* 16 (1965): 145–53.

Lewalski, Barbara Kiefer. *Writing Women in Jacobean England*. Cambridge: Harvard University Press, 1993.

Lodge, Edmund, ed. *Illustrations of British History, Biography, and Manners in the Reign of Henry VIII … James I*. 3 vols. London: John Chidley, 1838.

Marotti, Arthur F. *John Donne, Coterie Poet*. Madison: University of Wisconsin Press, 1986.

———. *Manuscript, Print, and the English Renaissance Lyric*. Ithaca: Cornell University Press, 1995.

Masten, Jeff. "'Shall I turne blabb?': Circulation, Gender, and Subjectivity in Mary Wroth's Sonnets." In Miller and Waller, 67–87. Reprinted in Kinney, *Ashgate Critical Essays*, 23–43.

Matthew, H. C. G., and Brian Harrison, eds. *Oxford Dictionary of National Biography: In Association with the British Academy: From the Earliest Times to the Year 2000*. Oxford: Oxford University Press, 2004. Online edition 2008–.

May, Steven W. *The Elizabethan Courtier Poets: The Poems and Their Contexts*. Columbia: University of Missouri Press, 1991.

McCarthy, Penny. "Autumn 1604: Documentation and Literary Coincidence." In Salzman and Wynne-Davies, 37–46.

Miller, Naomi J. "Re-Imagining Mary Wroth through Fiction." *Sidney Journal* 32 (2014): 40.

———. "Rewriting Lyric Fictions: The Role of the Lady in Lady Mary Wroth's *Pamphilia to Amphilanthus*." In Haselkorn and Travitsky, 295–310. Reprinted in Kinney, *Ashgate Critical Essays*, 45–60.

296 *Bibliography*

Miller, Naomi J., and Gary Waller, eds. *Reading Mary Wroth: Representing Alternatives in Early Modern England*. Knoxville: University of Tennessee Press, 1991.

Millman, Jill Seal, and Gillian Wright, eds. *Early Modern Women's Manuscript Poetry*. Manchester: Manchester University Press, 2005.

Moore, Mary B. "The Labyrinth as Style in *Pamphilia to Amphilanthus*." *Studies in English Literature* 38 (1998): 109–25. Reprinted in Kinney, *Ashgate Critical Essays*, 61–77.

O'Farrell, Brian. *Shakespeare's Patron: William Herbert, Third Earl of Pembroke, 1580-1630: Politics, Patronage, and Power*. London: Continuum, 2011.

O'Hara, Susan Lauffer. *The Theatricality of Mary Wroth's* Pamphilia to Amphilanthus: *Unmasking Conventions in Context*. Selinsgrove, PA: Susquehanna University Press, 2011.

Paulissen, May Nelson. *The Love Sonnets of Lady Mary Wroth: A Critical Introduction*. Salzburg Studies in English Literature, Elizabethan and Renaissance Studies, 104. Salzburg: Institut für Anglistik & Amerikanistik, University of Salzburg, 1982.

Peacham, Henry. *The Compleat Gentleman*. London, 1622.

Prescott, Anne Lake. "Mary Wroth, Louise Labé, and Cupid." *Sidney Journal* 15 (1997): 37–41.

Probert, Rebecca. *Marriage Law and Practice in the Long Eighteenth Century*. Cambridge: Cambridge University Press, 2009.

Rhodes, Neil, ed. *English Renaissance Prose: History, Language, and Politics*. Tempe, AZ: Medieval and Renaissance Texts and Studies, 1997.

Roberts, Josephine A. "The Biographical Problem of *Pamphilia to Amphilanthus*." *Tulsa Studies in Women's Literature* 1 (1982): 43–53.

_____. "Deciphering Women's Pastoral: Coded Language in Wroth's *Love's Victory*." In Pebworth and Summers, 163–74. Reprinted in Kinney, *Ashgate Critical Essays*, 305–16.

_____. "'The Knott Never to Bee Untide': The Controversy Regarding Marriage in Mary Wroth's *Urania*." Miller and Waller, 109–132.

Rowton, Frederic. *The Female Poets of Great Britain: Chronologically Arranged with Copious Selections and Critical Remarks*. Philadelphia, 1849.

Salzman, Paul. Critical Introduction. *Mary Wroth's Poetry: An Electronic Edition*. La Trobe University, 2012. http://wroth.latrobe.edu.au.

_____. "Lady Mary Wroth's Poetry." In Hannay, Lamb, and Brennan, 2:253–67.

_____. "*Love's Victory*, Pastoral, Gender, and *As You Like It*." In Salzman and Wynne-Davies, 125–36.

_____. "Me and My Shadow: Editing Wroth for the Digital Age." In Larson and Miller, 183–92.

_____. *Reading Early Modern Women's Writing.* Oxford: Oxford University Press, 2006.

_____. ed. *Early Modern Women's Writing: An Anthology, 1560–1700.* Oxford: World's Classics, 2008.

Salzman, Paul, and Marion Wynne-Davies, eds. *Mary Wroth and Shakespeare.* London: Routledge, 2015.

Sidney, Philip. *The Countesse of Pembrokes Arcadia.* London, 1593.

_____. *The Poems of Sir Philip Sidney.* Edited with an introduction by William A. Ringler, Jr. Oxford: Clarendon Press, 1962.

Sidney, Robert. *Domestic Politics and Family Absence: The Correspondence (1588–1621) of Robert Sidney, First Earl of Leicester, and Barbara Gamage Sidney, Countess of Leicester.* Edited with an introduction by Margaret P. Hannay, Noel J. Kinnamon, and Michael G. Brennan. Burlington, VT: Ashgate, 2005.

_____. *The Poems of Robert Sidney.* Edited with an introduction by P. J. Croft. Oxford: Oxford University Press, 1984.

Simpson, J. A., and E.S.C. Weiner, eds. *Oxford English Dictionary,* 2nd ed. Oxford: Oxford University Press, 1989. Online edition 2000–.

Skura, Meredith Anne. *Tudor Autobiography: Listening for Inwardness.* Chicago: University of Chicago Press, 2008.

Smith, Barbara, and Ursula Appelt, eds. *Write or Be Written: Early Modern Women Poets and Cultural Constraints.* Burlington, VT: Ashgate, 2001.

Smith, Rosalind. "Lady Mary Wroth's *Pamphilia to Amphilanthus:* The Politics of Withdrawal." *English Literary Renaissance* 30 (2000): 408–31. Reprinted in Kinney, *Ashgate Critical Essays,* 79–102.

Spufford, Margaret. *Small Books and Pleasant Histories: Popular Fiction and Its Readership in Seventeenth-Century England.* Athens: University of Georgia Press, 1982.

Stater, Victor. "Herbert, William, third earl of Pembroke." In Matthew and Harrison.

Straznicky, Marta. "Lady Mary Wroth's Patchwork Play: The Huntington Manuscript of *Love's Victory.*" *Sidney Journal* 34 (2016): 81–91.

_____, and Sara Mueller, eds. *Women's Household Drama: "Loves Victorie," "A Pastorall," and "The concealed Fansyes."* Toronto: Iter Press and Tempe, AZ: Arizona Center for Medieval and Renaissance Studies, in progress.

Summers, Claude J., and Ted-Larry Pebworth, eds. *Representing Women in Renaissance England.* Columbia: University of Missouri Press, 1997.

Wall, Wendy. *The Imprint of Gender: Authorship and Publication in the English Renaissance.* Ithaca: Cornell University Press, 1993.

Waller, Gary F. *The Sidney Family Romance: Mary Wroth, William Herbert, and the Early Modern Construction of Gender.* Detroit: Wayne State University Press, 1993.

Warkentin, Germaine. "Robert Sidney's 'Darcke Offerings': The Making of a Late Tudor Manuscript Canzoniere." *Spenser Studies* XII (1998): 37–74.

Warley, Christopher. *Sonnet Sequences and Social Distinction in Renaissance England.* Cambridge: Cambridge University Press, 2005.

Wheale, Nigel. *Writing and Society: Literacy, Print, and Politics in Britain, 1590–1660.* London: Routledge, 1999.

Whyte, Rowland. *The Letters (1595–1608) of Rowland Whyte.* Edited with an introduction by Michael G. Brennan, Noel J. Kinnamon, and Margaret P. Hannay. Philadelphia: American Philosophical Society, 2013.

Wilson, J. Dover. "Bibliographical Links Between the Three Pages and the Good Quartos." In Greg, 113–41.

Witten-Hannah [McLauren], Margaret A. "Lady Mary Wroth's *Urania:* The Work and the Tradition." PhD dissertation, University of Auckland, 1978.

Wordsworth, William. *Selected Poems and Prefaces.* Edited by Jack Stillinger. Boston: Riverside, Houghton Mifflin, 1965.

Woudhuysen, H. R. *Sir Philip Sidney and the Circulation of Manuscripts, 1558–1640.* Oxford: Clarendon Press, 1996.

Wroth, Mary. *The Countesse of Mountgomeries Urania.* London: 1621.

———. *The First Part of the Countess of Montgomery's Urania.* Edited with an introduction by Josephine A. Roberts. Medieval and Renaissance texts and studies, vol. 140. Binghamton, NY: Medieval and Early Renaissance Studies, 1995.

———. *The Second Part of the Countess of Montgomery's Urania.* Edited by Josephine Roberts, completed with an introduction by Suzanne Gossett and Janel Mueller. Tempe, AZ: Renaissance English Text Society in conjunction with Arizona Center for Medieval and Renaissance Studies, 1999.

———. *The Countess of Montgomery's Urania (Abridged).* Edited with an introduction by Mary Ellen Lamb. Tempe, AZ: ACMRS, 2011.

———. *Lady Mary Wroth Poems: A Modernized Edition.* Edited with an introduction by R. E. Pritchard. Keele, UK: Keele University Press, 1996.

———. *Lady Mary Wroth's Love's Victory: The Penshurst Manuscript.* Edited with an introduction by Michael G. Brennan. London: Roxburghe Club, 1988.

———. *Love's Victory.* Edited with an introduction by Paul Salzman. Early Modern Women's Research Network. http://hri.newcastle.edu.au/emwrn/index. php?content=wrothhistory.

———. *Mary Wroth.* [the Kohler copy] Selected and introduced by Josephine A. Roberts. *The Early Modern Englishwoman: A Facsimile Library of Essential Works, Part 1, Printed Writings, 1500–1640.* Vol. 10. Edited by Betty Travitsky, and Patrick Cullen. Burlington, VT: Ashgate, 1996. The original is available online at http://dla.library.upenn.edu/dla/print/pageturn. html?id=PRINT_3441687&rotation=0&size=2&currentpage=557.

_____. *Mary Wroth's Poetry: An Electronic Edition.* Edited with an introduction by Paul Salzman. http://wroth.latrobe.edu.au/.

_____. "Pamphilia to Amphilanthus." Folger Library. Manuscript V.a.104. http://luna.folger.edu/luna/servlet.

_____. *Pamphilia to Amphilanthus.* Edited by Gary F. Waller. Salzburg: Institut für Englische Sprache und Literatur, 1977.

_____. "Pamphilia to Amphilanthus." Benediction Classic, 2007.

_____. "Penshurst Mount." British Library, MS Additional 23229. 91r–92r.

_____. *The Poems of Lady Mary Wroth.* Edited with an introduction by Josephine A. Roberts. Baton Rouge: Louisiana State University Press, 1983; Pb. 1992.

Wynne-Davies, Marion. "'Here is a sport will well befit this time and place': Allusion and Delusion in Mary Wroth's *Love's Victory.*" *Women's Writing: The Elizabethan to Victorian Period* 6 (1999): 47–64. Reprinted in Kinney, *Ashgate Critical Essays,* 317–34.

_____. "'So Much Worth as Lives in You': Veiled Portraits of the Sidney Women." *Sidney Journal* 14 (1996): 45–56.

_____, ed. *Women Poets of the Renaissance.* 1998; London: Routledge, 1999. 183–228.

Yaeger, Sandra. "'She who still constant lov'd': *Pamphilia to Amphilanthus* as Lady Wroth's Indictment of Male Codes of Love." *Sidney Newsletter* 10 (1990): 88–89.

Yeats, William Butler. *The Collected Poems of W. B. Yeats.* New York: Macmillan, 1903, repr. 1968.

Index of First Lines

First lines are transcribed here from the manuscript texts with two exceptions: "Forbeare darke night, my joyes now budd againe," which replaces MS 4, "Venus unto the Gods a sute did move, " and "Folly would needs make mee a Lover be," which begins with the word "Cupid" in MS V.a.104, and thus appears twice in this index.

	Page Numbers	
	manuscript	print
A crowne of Sonetts dedicated to Love	157	251
A sheapherd who noe care did take	188	
After long trouble in a tædious way	109	226
All night I weepe, all day I cry, Ay mee;	87	213
Am I thus conquer'd? have I lost the powers	89	214
An end fond jealousie alas I know	147	246
And bee in his brave court a gloriouse light,	159	252
And burne, yett burning you will love the smart,	160	253
Bee from the court of Love, and reason torne	163	256
Bee given to him who triumphs in his right	164	257
Bee you all pleas'd? your pleasures grieve nott mee;	83	211
Beeing past the paines of love	154	249
Butt wher they may returne w^t honors grace	162	255
Can pleasing sight, misfortune ever bring?	77	207
Can the lov'd Image of thy deerest face	185	
Cloy'd wth the torments of a tedious night	86	212
Come darkest night, beecoming sorrow best;	95	218
Come merry spring delight us	171	260
Cruell suspition, O! bee now att rest	144	244
Cupid would needs make mee a lover bee	98	
Deare cherish this, and wth itt my soules will,	143	222
Deare eyes how well (indeed) you doe adorne	74	205
Deare fammish nott what you your self gave food,	88	214
Deerest if I by my deserving	137	241
Except my hart wch you beestow'd before,	165	258
Eyes, can you tell mee wher my hart remaines?	168	

302 *Index of First Lines*

Fairest, and still truest eyes	139	241
Faulçe hope wch feeds butt to destroy, and spill	175	228
Fly hence O! joy noe longer heere abide	106	224
Fly traiter joye whose end brings butt dispaire	201	
Folly would needs make mee a Lover be,		247
Forbeare darke night, my joyes now budd againe,		206
Free from all fogs butt shining faire, and cleere	165	257
Fy treacherous Hope, why doe you still rebell?	104	223
Gon is my joy while heere I burne	133	
Good now bee still, and doe nott mee torment	126	236
Griefe, killing griefe; have nott my torments binn	105	223
Hee may owr profitt, and our Tuter prove	160	253
Hee that shunns love doth love him self the less	162	255
His flames ar joyes, his bands true lovers might,	158	252
How blest bee they then, who his favors prove	161	254
How did I find my paines extreamest anguish	202	
How fast thou fliest, O Time, on loves swift wings	110	226
How fast thou hastst (o spring) w^t swiftest speed	125	235
How gloewoorme like the sunn doth now apeere	182	265
How like a fire doth love increase in mee,	129	237
How many eyes hast thou poore Love to guard	111	227
How many nights have I w^t paine indur'd	145	245
How well poore hart thou wittnes canst I love,	177	229
I, that ame of all most crost	135	240
I, who doe feele the highest part of griefe	203	
If ever love had force in humaine brest?	122	233
Iff I were giv'n to mirthe 't'wowld bee more cross	119	231
In night yett may wee see some kind of light	141	242
In this strang labourinth how shall I turne?	157	251
Is to leave all, and take the thread of love	158	251
Itt is nott love which you poore fooles do deeme	120	232
Juno still jealouse of her husband Jove	114	263
Late in the Forest I did Cupid see	121	262
Led by the powre of griefe, to waylings brought	82	210
Lett griefe as farr bee from your deerest brest	131	238
Like to huge clowds of smoke wch well may hide	179	264

Index of First Lines 303

Like to the Indians, scorched wth the sunne,	150	219
Love a child is ever criing,	153	249
Love as well can make abiding	136	240
Love leave to urge, thou know'st thou hast ye hand;	81	210
Love like a jugler, comes to play his prise,	90	243
Love, thou hast all, for now thou hast mee made	127	236
Love what art thou? A Vaine thought	155	
Lovers learne to speake butt truthe	173	260
Most blessed Night, the happy time for love,	103	244
My hart is lost, what can I now expect,	113	262
My muse now hapy, lay thy self to rest	183	266
My paine, still smother'd in my grieved brest,	91	245
Night, welcome art thou to my mind destrest	117	230
No time, noe roome, noe thought, nor writing can	181	265
O dearest eyes the lights, and guids of love,	124	234
O mee the time is come to part,	132	238
O pardon, Cupid I confess my fault	156	250
O stay mine eyes, shed nott thes fruitles teares	128	237
O, strive nott still to heape disdaine on mee	78	208
O! that I might but now as senceles bee	172	
O! that noe day would ever more appeere,	180	264
Oft did I wounder why the sweets of Love	186	
Once did I heere an aged father say	100	220
Poore eyes bee blind, the light behold noe more	102	222
Poore Love in chaines, and fetters like a thiefe	92	246
'Pray doe nott use thes words I must bee gone,	149	247
Say Venus how long have I lov'd, and serv'd you heere	134	239
She: Deare how doe thy wining eyes	140	
Sleepe fy possess mee nott, nor doe nott fright	146	215
Sorrow, I yeeld, and greive that I did miss:	123	234
Stay, my thoughts, do nott aspire	94	217
Sweet lett mee injoye thy sight	169	258
Sweet shades why doe you seeke to give delight	148	216
Sweet Silvia in a shadie wood	170	259
Sweete solitarines joy to those hartes	270	
Sweetest love returne againe	101	221

Take heed mine eyes, how you yor lookes doe cast	112	227
The birds doe sing, day doth apeere	152	
The spring now come att last	79	208
The springing time of my first loving	151	248
The Sunn wch glads, the earth att his bright sight	96	218
The weary traveller who tired sought	84	211
Time only cause of my unrest	108	225
Truly poore Night thou wellcome art to me:	142	215
Unprofitably pleasing, and unsound	164	256
Unquiet griefe search farder, in my hart	184	
Venus unto the Gods a sute did move,	76	
W^{ch} should I better like of, day, or night	93	216
What pleasure can a bannish'd creature have	118	231
When every one to pleasing pastime hies	99	220
When I beeheld the Image of my deere	178	263
When I last saw thee, I did nott thee see,	97	219
When nights black mantle could most darknes prove,	73	205
Who can blame mee if I love	138	
Why with unkindest Swiftnes doest thou turne	267	
Yett is ther hope: Then Love butt play thy part	75	206
You blessed shades, wch give mee silent rest,	107	224
You blessed starrs wch doe heavns glory show,	176	232
You endless torments that my rest oppress	85	212
You happy blessed eyes,	115	229

Index

Numbers in italics refer to pages on which illustrations are to be found.

Alexander, Gavin, 4n3, 21n34, 58n123, 67n157, 67n159
Anderson, Judith H., 13n15
Anne, Queen (consort of James I), 24–25, 34

Ballard, George, 64, 65n150
Bauman, Richard, 45n101
Baynard's Castle (London), 27, *29*, 32
Behn, Aphra, 65
Bell, Ilona, 15n22, 46n102, 49n104, 53n109
Beilin, Elaine V., 15, 15n24, 17
Belsey, Catherine, 44n98
Black, Joseph L., 22n38
Bland, Mark, 5n6
Bloom, Harold, 12n12
Bodleian Library (Oxford University), 25
Bond, Garth, 25n50, 39n91, 40n92, 42n96, 61n136, 267, 270
Boyle, Elizabeth, 13
Brayman Hackel, Heidi, 15n21
Brennan, Michael G., 17, 17n29, 23n43, 25n48, 26n51, 53, 53n110, 54n113
Briggs, Charles L., 45n101
Briley, John Richard, 33n72, 35n78, 35n79
Bromley, James M., 18, 18n31
Bullard, Angela, 17n28

Carrell, Jennifer Lee, 13n17
Cary, Elizabeth, 65
Cerasano, S. P., 53n110

Chamberlain, John, 31, 31n62
Chapman, George, 26
Clarendon, Earl of. *See* Hyde
Cressy, David, 19n32
Cupid, 22, 41, 44–46, 51, 62, 68, 74, 76, 76n20, 87, 89, 98, 113, 121, 124, 150, 156, 161, 170, 180, 190, 213, 220, 234, 250, 254, 259, 260, 262, 265, 270

Daniel, Samuel, 22
Davies of Hereford, John, 26
Denny, Edward, Baron Denny of Waltham, 61–62, 64
Dering, Edward, 55, 55n118, 56n120
de Vere, Henry, eighteenth Earl of Oxford, 32
Distiller, Natasha, 16
Donne, Anne (More), 14

Donne, John, 13–14, 44, 45, 49–51
"Extasie, The," 51
"Good Morrow, The," 50
"Songs and Sonnets," 13–14, 44, 45
"Sun Rising, The," 50
Drummond of Hawthornden, William, 26
Dubrow, Heather, 4n3, 16–17, 17n28, 67n157
Dudley, Robert, Earl of Leicester, 21
Duncan-Jones, Katherine, 25n49
Dulong-Sainteny, Claude, 58n122
Durance (Enfield), 24, 30
Dyce, Alexander, 65

305

306 *Index*

editorial principles and practices in this edition, 66–71
Edmondes, Thomas, 35
Elizabeth I, Queen of England, 13, 19, 21, 23, 24, 26, 27, 30, 31
elocutionary cues, 2, 45, 45n101
Elsings castle (Enfield), 24
Ezell, Margaret J. M., 15n21

Fall, Rebecca L., 8n8
Fienberg, Nona, 17, 17n29
Findlay, Alison, 13n14, 55, 55n117
Fitton, Mary, 23, 40n92
Fleet prison (London), 23
Flushing (Netherlands), 27
Folger Shakespeare Library, 8, *29*, *39*
    Folger MS V.a.104 (*see* Wroth, Mary, "Pamphilia to Amphilanthus")
Fox, Judith, 33
Frontain, Raymond-Jean, 41n94

Gaines, James, 14n20
Gamage, William, 26
Garnier, Robert, 22
Gheeraerts, Marcus, II, *28*
Gibson, Jonathan, 14n18, 65, 65n152
Gil, Daniel Juan, 17, 17n29
Greek art, 25
Greek manuscripts, 44n98

Hackett, Helen, 59, 59n131
Hannay, Margaret P., 4n3, 17, 24, 27, 32, 33, 34n73, 36, 37n86, 54n114, 60, 63, 65, 67n157, 67n159
Hanson, Elizabeth, 66n154
Hay, Millicent V., 23n41
Heale, Elizabeth, 13n16
Hecht, Paul, 18, 18n31
Herbert, Anne, 24

Herbert, Edward, Baron Herbert of Cherbury, 33
Herbert, Henry, second Earl of Pembroke, 23, 27, 59
Herbert, Katherine, 33
Herbert, Mary (Sidney), Countess of Pembroke, 10n11, 13, 19, 21–23, 25, 36, 54n114
    influence on Wroth's writing, 22–24
Herbert, Mary (Talbot), Countess of Pembroke, 32, 34–36, 42, 60, 63
Herbert, Philip, Baron Herbert of Shurland and Earl of Montgomery, 24, 35
Herbert, Susan (de Vere), Countess of Montgomery, 24, 43, 59
Herbert, Thomas, *Herbertorum Prosapia*, 33
Herbert, William, third Earl of Pembroke, 10, 10n11, 11, 12, 13–15, 19, 23–26, 31–38, 46, 50, 58–64
    affair with Mary Fitton, 23
    as Amphilanthus, 12, 34, 45, 50, 53, 58–64
    at Jacobean court, 22–25
    "Elegy," 38–44, 48, 50–51, 54, 56, 58, 60, 63, 64, 70, 267–70
    love affair with Mary Wroth, 11–13, 22–24, 26, 33–51, 53–55, 58, 60–64
    marriage, 32, 34–36, 38, 63
    patronage, 25
    poetry, 12n13, 16, 22, 25, 25nn48–50, 40–42, 45, 267n1
    portrait, *11*
Heywood, Thomas, 26, 26n53
Hodgson-Wright, Stephanie, 65, 65n152

Index 307

Hutchinson, Lucy, 65
Hyde, Edward, Earl of Clarendon, 32

Italian literature, 22, 23. *See also* Petrarchan literary tradition

Jacobean era, 19, 24–25, 66
James I, King of England, 24–25, 42, 42n96, 61
Johns, Adrian, 5n6
Jones, Ann Rosalind, 16, 16n27
Jonson, Ben, 24–26
    Masque of Beauty, 24
    Masque of Blackness, 24, 150n347
    "To Penshurst," 26
    "To Sir Robert Wroth," 26

Kinnamon, Noel J., 23n43
Kinney, Arthur, 22n40
Kinney, Clare R., 8n9, 16, 16n27, 50n106, 59n129
Kohler, Charlotte, copy of *Urania*, 5n5, 14n20, 66, 66n155, 69, 218n54, 239n129
Kondoleon, Christine, 44n98

Lamb, Mary Ellen, 12, 12n13, 25n50, 27n55, 30, 32n70, 38, 38n88, 41n93, 46n102, 58, 59n130, 63n143
Lanyer, Aemelia, 65
Larson, Katherine R., 8n8, 58n122, 63n143
La Trobe University, 8
Leicester, Countess of. *See* Sidney, Barbara
Leicester, Earl of. *See* Sidney, Robert
Lennam, T. N. S., 24n46
Lewalski, Barbara Kiefer, 16–17, 17n28, 65–66

London, 24, 27, 32
    map, *29*
Loughton Hall (Enfield), 30–33, *31*

Manners, George, seventh Earl of Rutland, 32, 61
Marriot and Grismand, 65
Marotti, Arthur F., 14n21
Masten, Jeff, 15–17, 16n25
May, Steven W., 14n21
McCarthy, Penny, 14n18
Miller, Naomi J., 8n8, 16, 16n26, 18, 18n31
Millman, Jill Seal, 65n152
Montgomery, Earl of. *See* Herbert, Philip
Moore, Mary B., 16, 16n26, 17, 18

Neoplatonism, 49, 65
Netherlands, 27
Newberry Library, 58, 62

O'Farrell, Brian, 25n48
O'Hara, Susan Lauffer, 18, 18n31
Ovid, 51
Oxford, Earl of. *See* de Vere
Oxford University, 25

Passe, Simon van de, *20*
pastoral, 14, 46, 46n102, 51, 54n111, 54n112, 55n117, 79n55
Paulissen, May Nelson, 65, 65n151
Peacham, Henry, 26, 26n53
Pebworth, Ted-Larry, 54n111
Pembroke, Countess of. *See* Herbert, Mary (Sidney), Mary (Talbot)
Pembroke, Earl of. *See* Herbert, Henry, William

308 *Index*

Penshurst Place, 23, 27, 32, 36, *39,*
  39n90, 41–42, 47, 53, 58, 61,
  63, 67
Petrarchan literary tradition, 1, 11,
  12, 12n12, 15–17, 22, 44, 47,
  49–53, 65, 137
Philips, Katherine, 65
Phillipps, Thomas, *3*
Prescott, Anne Lake, 1n1
Pritchard, R. E., 65
Protestantism, 17, 174n465

Renaissance literature, 1, 12, 14, 22,
  23, 27, 40, 44, 49, 66, 69, 143
Rich, Penelope, 13, 53
Roberts, Josephine A., 5, 5n5, 8,
  8n7, 10, 12, 12n13, 14–17,
  27n55, 35n76, 45, 50, 54–55,
  54n111, 54n114, 59, 59n125,
  62n140, 62n142, 65, 67n158,
  69, 71, 129n291, 150n347,
  275–79
Rowton, Frederic, 65
Rudyerd, Benjamin, 12n13
Rutland, Earl of. *See* Manners

Salzman, Paul, 8, 14n18, 17, 17n29,
  22n39, 26n52, 53n110,
  54n112, 55, 66, 66n154
Sanford, Hugh, 21, 35–38, 54, 59, 63,
  64, 271n53
Shakespeare, William, 16, 22, 24, 54,
  68n161
  As You Like It, 54, 54n112
  Sonnets 14, 25, 44, 49
    publication, 12, 14, 25, 44, 49
Shrewsbury, Earl of. *See* Talbot
Sidney, Barbara (Gamage), Coun-
  tess of Leicester, 27, 28, 30,
  34–38, 43, 55, 56, 59, 64

Sidney, Barbara (Mary Wroth's sis-
  ter), 55
Sidney, Henry, 27
Sidney, Mary. *See* Wroth, Mary
  (Sidney)
Sidney, Mary (Wroth's aunt). *See*
  Herbert, Mary (Sidney),
  Countess of Pembroke
Sidney, Philip, 12–14, 17, 19, 21–23,
  44–45, 53–54, 62, 64, 71,
  137
  "Astrophil and Stella," 11, 12, 13,
    21, 21n34, 22, 44–45, 53–54,
    71, 71n165
  Countess of Pembroke's Arcadia, 21,
    21n37, 24, 54, 55, 62, 64
  influence on Wroth's writing,
    22–24
Sidney, Philippa, 62
Sidney, Robert (Mary Wroth's broth-
  er), 23, 59, 137
Sidney, Robert, Earl of Leicester
  (Mary Wroth's father), 14,
  14n18, 19, 23–27, 30, 34, 43,
  47, 59, 71n165, 157n372
  arrangement of daughter Mary's
    marriage, 30, 34–38, 43, 46,
    56, 60, 64
Skura, Meredith Anne, 46n103
Smith, Rosalind, 17, 17n30
Spenser, Edmund, 13–14, 17, 44, 59,
  137, 157n372
  "Amoretti," 13–14, 44
  "Epithalamion," 13
Spenser, Elizabeth (Boyle), 13
Spufford, Margaret, 19n32
Straznicky, Marta, 53n110, 56,
  56n120
Summers, Claude J., 54n111
Sylvester, Joshua, 26

Talbot, Gilbert, seventh Earl of
    Shrewsbury, 35, 42, 56, 64

van de Passe, Simon, 58
Venus, 4, 22, 44–45, 44n98, 46,
    50–52, 55–56, 62, 68, 73, 74,
    76, 76n20, 89, 102n169, 103,
    109, 113, 121n253, 134, 162,
    162n420, 164, 183, 205, 239,
    255, 257, 266
Vorsterman, Lucas, *11*

Wall, Wendy, 16
Waller, Gary F., 5, 11n12, 12n13, 15,
    16, 65
Waltham, Baron of. *See* Denny
Warkentin, Germaine, 15n21
Warley, Christopher, 21n34
Wheale, Nigel, 19n32
Whyte, Rowland, 23, 23n44, 27, 30,
    32
Wilson, J. Dover, 68n161
Wilton House (Salisbury), 24, 27, 52
Wither, George, 26
Witten-Hannah [McLaren], Margaret
    A., 65
women, early modern, 1, 10, 16, 17,
    18, 19, 19n32, 36, 44, 49
    writers, 1, 5, 5n6, 18, 51, 65
Wordsworth, William, 49
Woudhuysen, H. R., 15n21
Wright, Gillian, 65n152
Wroth, James, 31, 32
Wroth, John, 32
Wroth, Mary (Sidney)
    birth, 27
    childhood, 26–27, 30
    children, 30, 32, 33
    death, 33
    education, 19, 23, 27, 30
    family background, 19–23, 27

handwriting, 2, 53, 62, 67–68,
    71–72
fermesse (slashed *s*), 4, 6, *7*, 56,
    58, 58n122, 71
homes. *See* Durance, Loughton
    Hall, and Penshurst
influence of Mary Herbert's and
    Philip Sidney's works,
    21–22, 21n34, 24, 64
literary reputation, 25–26
love affair with William Herbert,
    11, 13, 22–24, 26, 33–51,
    53–54, 58, 60–64
maiden name, 10n11
marriage, 12, 30–31, 33–38, 54, 60,
    63, 64
portrait, *28*
politics, 17, 17n30, 19–26
works
    *Countess of Montgomeries
        Urania, The*, 2, 2n2, 4, *7*, 8,
        8n7, 12, 13, 15, 17, 18, 19,
        20, 24, 26, 32, 33, 34, 39, 42,
        43, 45, 47, 50, 51, 55–56,
        58–64, 68n162; manuscript
        continuation (part 2), 12,
        34, 50, 56, 58–62; family
        and friends as counterparts
        of fictional characters, 34,
        59–63; literary criticism,
        14–18, 65–66
    Love's Victory, 12–13, 15, 18,
        43, 53–57, 61, 62, 63, 65,
        67; Penshurst manuscript,
        53–56, 58
    "Pamphilia to Amphilanthus,"
        MS V.a.104, 2, *3*, 4–5, *6*, 8,
        8n8, *9*, 10, 44, 65, 65n152,
        66–69, 72, 73–74

Pamphilia to Amphilanthus,
1621 printed text, 1, 2, *7,*
8, 10, 12, 45, *57,* 58, 66–69,
205–66
"Penshurst Mount," 10, 12,
38–39, 41–42, 44, 48, 49, 55,
56, 61, 63, 64, 70, 270–73;
stylistic features, 42, 47, 51,
55
Wroth, Robert, 26, 30–32, 43, 55,
59, 63

arrangement of marriage to Mary
Sidney, 12, 30, 36–38, 42,
54, 60, 63
Wynne-Davies, Marion, 14n18,
54n114, 55, 65

Yaeger, Sandra, 45n100
Yeats, William Butler, 21

Zutphen, Battle of, 19